A trial at the Old Bailey of grave international importance suddenly collapses when the chief defendant is revealed as a courageous undercover agent for MI6 – and dazzling cross-examination by his lawyer forces a Minister of the Crown to tell the truth.

Rarely has one trial caused such a sensation. For it was secret exports from firms like Matrix Churchill that meant British-machined shells, rockets and Scud missiles were fired at British troops in the Gulf War.

Greed or conspiracy? Arms for Iraq is the biggest scandal to engulf the Conservative administration in thirteen years of power. It will erupt explosively this year, when the Scott Judicial Inquiry holds its hearings.

This book documents the real story of the case; how weapons equipment was shipped to Iraq with government collusion; how two Coventry businessmen played an astonishing role as British intelligence agents in Iraq; how they were in effect framed by the government to protect its image; and how, in an unprecedented legal battle, top-secret Whitehall papers were released which implicated the Conservative administration in a trail of deceptions and cover-ups.

Geoffrey Robertson QC claimed his biggest scalp ever when he forced the then Trade Minister Alan Clark to tell the truth in the witness box. But the evidence in the trial – reported here fully for the first time – shows much bigger and more sinister forces at work than one maverick minister. It shows exactly how ministers tried to prevent the truth from being told: and put innocent men at risk of jail.

D1023593

BETRAYED

The Real Story of the
Matrix Churchill Trial

BETRAYED

The Real Story of the Matrix Churchill Trial

DAVID LEIGH
with Richard Norton-Taylor

BLOOMSBURY

First published 1993
Copyright © 1993 by David Leigh

The moral right of the author
has been asserted

Bloomsbury Publishing Ltd
2 Soho Square, London W1V 5DE

A CIP catalogue record for this book
is available from the British Library

ISBN 0 7475 1552 2

Typeset by Hewer Text Composition Services, Edinburgh
Printed in Great Britain by Clays Ltd, St Ives plc, Bungay, Suffolk

CONTENTS

ACKNOWLEDGEMENTS

Richard Norton-Taylor of the *Guardian* was one of the first reporters to appreciate the significance of the Matrix Churchill case. His trial-notes form the invaluable basis for this book. I should like to thank Peter Weatherby, from the Doughty Street defence team; Kevin Robinson from solicitors Irwin Mitchell; Bobby Lee Cook; Chris Sallon; Mark Gutteridge; and Paul Henderson, the principal defendant, who was so spectacularly acquitted. Paul Woolwich, editor of Thames Television's *This Week*, and producer Martyn Gregory made the TV film *The Spies Left Out in the Cold*, which I reported and which was the origin of this project. I owe a large debt to Jeannie Mackie.

PREFACE

Britain secretly helped to arm Saddam Hussein's Iraq. The facts about this were concealed until the Matrix Churchill trial took place. The trial began at the Old Bailey before a jury on 12 October 1992. The three defendants, accused of illegally exporting munitions machinery to Baghdad, had been charged twenty months earlier, in February 1991. But extraordinary delays had stopped their case from being heard in public until well after the general election of April 1992 which confirmed John Major—victor of the Gulf War against Iraq – in office. The eventual trial of the three men was scheduled to last until Christmas. But four weeks later, after a memorable cross-examination of Alan Clark, a former Minister of the Crown, it abruptly halted. The prosecutor of the charge brought by HM Customs had not even finished presenting his case: but the jury was discharged and the three defendants in the dock formally acquitted. That afternoon's splash front page in the London *Evening Standard* accurately conveyed a sense of the storm that was about to break: 'IRAQI ARMS DEAL TRIAL COLLAPSES. Three cleared as ex-Minister's evidence is called inconsistent.'

Alan Moses, QC for HM Customs, told the judge that the Crown could no longer continue with the case because Alan Clark's evidence under oath was 'inconsistent' with what he had originally told Customs investigators in a witness statement. Clark's testimony had been elicited by Geoffrey

Robertson QC, counsel for the main defendant, with the help of a stack of Whitehall documents of the type normally kept secret in Britain – briefings prepared by top officials for Ministers; records of meetings of those Ministers; and, most secret and unprecedented of all, records from Britain's two intelligence agencies, MI5 and MI6. John Major's Cabinet Ministers had signed orders concealing all this information from the court—Ministerial orders eventually overturned by the judge. Intelligence officers, as well as senior civil servants and government Ministers, were forced to come to the Old Bailey to testify.

The outcome of the case caused a political crisis. Quite how big that crisis is has so far been concealed, because the Prime Minister felt he had no alternative but to bow immediately to opposition demands for a judicial inquiry into the biggest scandal of the Conservative administration. Lord Justice Scott, a senior High Court judge, has been authorised to conduct an inquiry which begins this year. His terms of reference enable him to sit in private to investigate the circumstances in which Britain secretly armed Iraq.

It was the extraordinary history of the Matrix Churchill trial which brought to light what happened. The conduct of the case was a legal *tour de force*. Government Ministers have been since all too anxious to muddy the waters—claiming the outcome of the case had nothing to do with the secret Whitehall files. They also said that Ministers never tried to suppress the truth. This book simply documents what happened and what facts really have emerged. They make startling, and sometimes bizarre, reading.

There has never before been such authentic and detailed material available about the operations of the British secret services and their influence on Whitehall—right down to verbatim copies of their own agents' reports and their internal memoranda. Was the chief defendant betrayed by MI6? Was the Foreign Secretary betrayed by his colleagues? And were the victims of Saddam Hussein betrayed by the British government? HM Customs' determination to investigate and prosecute the defendants did not succeed in convicting them. But it did surgically slice open the underbelly of government, to reveal corruption within. Had the trial occurred earlier, it would have been much more difficult for John Major and the Conservative Party to win the last general election. It remains to be seen how much effect it will have on the next one.

D.L.   London, January 1993

NOTE

The Arms Machinery Sent to Iraq

The Matrix Churchill trial, in the nature of all trials, was complicated to follow at the time. Crown witnesses come up in an order that is often not very comprehensible. To make life easier for the reader, this narrative has moved around the order in which witnesses testified. For the same reason, events occur, seen through the different eyes of intelligence men, civil servants and Ministers.

The story centres on the three times government Ministers personally decided to grant export licences to the firm of Matrix Churchill, allowing machine-tools to be shipped to Iraq to make arms. These three times were:

1. December 1987

2. February 1989

3. November 1989

The machines were ultimately used to manufactures shells, mortars, artillery rockets, fuses for howitzers, Scud missile parts, and gas centrifuge components for the development of nuclear weapons. Their purpose was usually described on forms as 'general engineering'.

The quotations in the book come from the following sources:

1. The secret British intelligence and government documents disclosed and read in court.
2. Records of courtroom oral testimony.
3. Statements made by Paul Henderson and Mark Gutteridge.

Glossary of terms

ABA project: Secret Iraqi contract to build the Supergun's rocket-shells.
Babylon: Secret Iraqi project to build the Supergun.
Box 500: Whitehall address code for MI5.
Box 850: Whitehall address code for MI6.
Cardoen: Chilean arms manufacturing firm.
DTI: Department of Trade and Industry.
ECGD: Export Credits Guarantee Department.
ELU: Export Licensing Unit.
FCO: Foreign and Commonwealth Office. (Sometimes: FO)
IDC: Inter-Departmental Committee (for export licensing).
Iraq Gun Group: Secret Cabinet Committee set up by Margaret Thatcher.
MI5: Domestic security service.
MI6: Secret intelligence service (SIS).
MOD: Ministry of Defence.
MODWG: Ministry of Defence Working Group.
MTTA: Machine Tools Technologies Association.
PII: Public Interest Immunity.
PPS: Principal Private Secretary.
Project K1000: Iraqi contract to build parts for nuclear centrifuges.

PSIS: Permanent Under-Secretary's Committee on the Intelligence Services.

PUSD: Permanent Under-Secretary's Department at Foreign Office.

REU: Restricted Enforcement Unit (secret Whitehall committee studying the embargo on arms to Iran and Iraq).

Source 528: MI5 code-name for Mark Gutteridge.

Supergun: The gigantic Iraqi gun that was to be assembled from tubes engineered in Britain and intercepted by HM Customs.

CHRONOLOGY

1979		Mrs Thatcher becomes PM
1980		Iran-Iraq war begins
1985		Howe 'Guidelines' ban military sales
1986		MI5 re-employ Mark Gutteridge as agent

FIRST SHIPMENTS

1987	October	Iraq takes control of Matrix Churchill
	Nov/December	DTI issues export licences
	30 November	MI6 reports Iraq contracts are for arms
1988	8 January	DTI freezes export licences
	20 January	Clark meets manufacturers
	8 February	Ministers release shipments

SECOND SHIPMENTS

	August	Iran-Iraq ceasefire
	November	Clark seeks to relax military sales ban
	December	MI6 report Iraq seeking nuclear material
1989	February	Ministers release ABA/Cardoen shipments

THIRD SHIPMENTS

	April	PM agrees action on Iraqi nuclear plans
		MI6 recruit Paul Henderson as agent
	September	Waldegrave and FO oppose new shipments
	November	MI6 tell Ministers of Supergun
	1 November	Ministers release ABA/Cardoen shipments

EXPOSURE

1990	March	Farzad Bazoft hanged by Iraq
	April	Customs move against Supergun
	June	Customs inspect Matrix Churchill
	19 July	Ministers plan to relax Iraq arms bans
	2 August	Iraq invades Kuwait
	October	Customs raid Matrix Churchill
	November	Mrs Thatcher replaced by John Major
1991	January	British forces fight in Iraq
	17 February	Paul Henderson and colleagues charged
1992	April	Major wins election
	October	Matrix Churchill trial begins

1

INSPECTED

HM Customs visits Matrix Churchill, June 1990

As I had been tipped off, I knew in advance.
MI6 telegram, 2 July 1990

When Customs investigator Peter Wiltshire decided to have
a look inside a factory in the Midlands, panic ran at once
through all the secret parts of Whitehall. Before he had had
time to do as much as peer through the iron railings round the
Matrix Churchill engineering works, Number 10 had been
alerted by an alarmed Cabinet Minister. Important people
wanted the Customs man called off: within a month, Cabinet
Ministers were to meet, chaired by the Foreign Secretary
himself, Douglas Hurd. The activities of Wiltshire and his
Customs team were on the agenda, as part of a problem.

The essence of the problem was Iraq. In 1990, at the time
of Wiltshire's unwelcome intervention, the Middle Eastern
state was run – as it still is today – by a murderous despot: a
regime that was gassing babies, hanging journalists, seeking
to procure nuclear weapons, and secretly about to invade its
neighbour, Kuwait. The attitude of the British government
to this dictatorship was – officially – chilly. On the quiet,

however, for several political reasons, the relationship was warmer, even encouraging.

HM Customs and Excise does not see its role as being muddied by politics. Theoretically an arm of the Treasury, the 'duty men' hunt down VAT fraudsters, drug smugglers and embargo busters with equal zeal. They are armed with formidable powers of search and arrest. So Wiltshire's men had, on the face of it, their usual freedom of action in June 1990, when they received a tip from their German colleagues in the port of Bremen that something illegal might be going on.

Like others, German Customs had been on the alert that spring for Iraqi smuggling, ever since gigantic steel parts for a planned 'Supergun' had started to turn up all over Europe, illegally bound for Baghdad and causing an international uproar. Now, the Germans reported through a secure telex, crates of English heavy machinery were accumulating on the Bremen dockside. They allegedly belonged to a weapons firm from Chile called Cardoen. But they were going to Iraq. And the machines were clearly intended to equip a large munitions factory, making hundreds of thousands of fuses for artillery shells.

The machine-tools in the crates – big, squat automated lathes, driven by electric motors and programmable by computer – came from the firm of Matrix Churchill, based in their factory in Coventry. Did the company have permission to export such military machinery to Iraq? Apparently not. British Customs may have been – in principle – as independent in action as it pleased. In practice, it behaved cautiously at the news from Bremen of an apparent crime. There were two reasons.

First, Customs was well aware that Matrix Churchill exported machinery to Iraq. It was a subject of intense – if subterranean – Whitehall controversy. A Customs representative had attended, nearly every fortnight since 1987, a highly secret Whitehall committee, alongside officers from

MI5, the domestic security service, and MI6, the secret intelligence service. Their minutes carried Whitehall's third-tightest security classification: SECRET – UK EYES ONLY. The Restricted Enforcement Unit (REU) was chaired by a high-ranking civil servant from the Department of Trade and Industry. In the REU they swapped notes about the arms embargo which Britain supposedly enforced on exports to both Iraq and Iran, opponents in a bloody eight-year war, only recently suspended.

Britain was occupying the moral high ground, in theory at least, by pledging that it would not sell arms to either side. Geoffrey Howe, then Foreign Secretary, promised in 1985 that the government was doing everything possible to stop 'this tragic conflict'. Parliament was told – and told repeatedly – that Howe's published Ministerial guidelines ensured that nothing went to Iraq which would 'significantly enhance' its military strength. REU members knew that the secret history of Matrix Churchill and its repeated acquisition of export licences would, if ever published, tell a different story.

There was a second reason for caution by HM Customs. It had already provoked one political row over arms for Iraq and was wary of plunging into another one so soon. For it was Customs officers who had confiscated eight huge steel pipes, each three feet in diameter, on the dock at Teesport, claiming that they were illegal parts for Iraq's 'Supergun'. The previous month they had charged the managing director of the steel firm concerned with the criminal offence of illegal exporting, amid controversy over the role of the Department of Trade and Industry.

The 'Department for Enterprise', as the Thatcherites had dubbed it, had proved astonishingly – some said suspiciously – easy to bamboozle over export licences. The uproar over the Supergun had been so great that, three months earlier, Mrs Thatcher had been forced to set up a secret Cabinet committee with a supporting team of officials, dedicated to containing the political damage. It was called the Iraq Gun

Group. The skeletons in the cupboard at Matrix Churchill had already appeared on officials' agendas there.

In what Whitehall spoke of as 'this highly charged atmosphere', the Customs men moved carefully. There was no surprise raid on Matrix Churchill. Instead, they privately approached the Department of Trade and Industry, saying that they would like to visit the firm in one week's time to obtain evidence. Did the DTI, headed by the arch-Thatcherite Nicholas Ridley, agree that they could do this?

Michael Coolican, the new head of the DTI's export control division, had been in the job for only three months. But he had read the back files, and knew what Customs would discover. That Thursday, at his Kingsgate House office, he dictated an urgent two-page memo to Trade Secretary Nicholas Ridley. And he, too, classified it: SECRET.

The dirty washing liable to emerge from the action proposed by Customs and Excise will add to the problems posed by the gun. For DTI the timing is extraordinarily embarrassing.

Ministers in the Iraq Gun Group would need urgent advice. For the dirty washing in question had been piling up for years:

1 Are Ministers willing to have the 1987 and subsequent decisions exposed, and made the subject of courtroom argument?

2 Are Ministers willing to face a worsening in our relations with Iraq?

What was constitutionally intriguing about Coolican's secret memo was his implication that the government, if it liked, could answer 'No' to these two questions. Could Ministers block a Customs prosecution for reasons of their own? It seemed so.

Inside the 'Department for Enterprise' that June, after receipt of this shocking news from Customs, the rest of the week and the weekend went by in anxious conferences: a decision was taken that officials would approach the Foreign Office for support. According to the secret FO minute, Coolican assured the Foreign Office that he had heard the news from Customs only that Monday – and Customs were about to swoop, probably within two days . . .

Coolican's Monday afternoon meeting gave the impression that the DTI was furious, and determined, even threatening to take the issue to Cabinet level. And officials complained that the 'current wave of investigations' was ruining trade with Iraq. These objections to Customs behaviour elicited some sympathy from the Foreign Office head of Middle East desk, Rob Young. The next day, Tuesday, he warned of the danger of a further trade freeze by the truculent Iraqis. Customs, he warned, ominously perhaps, were 'raking over old history' by 'questioning the validity of past export licences'. These notes were for the eyes of Ministers.

Margaret Thatcher, for all her protestations about meritocracy and the virtues of small businessmen, was surprisingly susceptible to obscure aristocrats. Some of the favourites to whom she gave jobs quickly acquired reputations for arrogance. Appointed as her Trade Secretary, the Honourable Nicholas Ridley was the younger son of a North of England peer. His enthusiasms, both for Mrs Thatcher and for trade with Iraq, were shared by the then junior Minister for defence procurement, the Honourable Alan Clark. He was the son of the distinguished – and very rich – art historian, Lord Clark. The third member of this team of Iraq enthusiasts was Ridley's junior Minister at Trade, David, the second Baron Trefgarne, who had inherited a seat in the House of Lords.

Over at the Foreign Office, there were aristocrats too, of course. But their political attitudes did not always coincide with those of the abrasively 'dry' Thatcherites. Most gilded of all was the junior Minister, William Waldegrave (pronounced – as outsiders had to be reminded – 'war-grave'). He was currently Minister of State to old Etonian Douglas Hurd, having previously served under John Major (briefly) and Geoffrey Howe, who in his stint as Foreign Secretary had clashed irrevocably with Thatcher and was soon to resign from the government. The 44-year-old Waldegrave was son of the 12th Earl Waldegrave; Eton and Oxford; Fellow of All Souls; impeccably connected, but on the 'wet' wing of the party. To Waldegrave, the name Matrix Churchill was a reminder of secret Whitehall battles he had long fought – and frequently lost. 'Disingenuous', 'special pleading' and 'astonishing' were the words used by his officials in the written record about the tactics of the DTI.

At the very moment when news of the planned Customs raid arrived, Waldegrave was engaged in these battles again. The DTI wanted to award Matrix Churchill yet more export licences to ship machine-tools to Iraq. Waldegrave and the Foreign Office were well aware from intelligence reports that the Iraqi government secretly controlled the company's management; and that many of the shipments were going to equip munitions factories for an increasingly menacing regime.

The day after the Foreign Office heard about the proposed raid, Waldegrave signed a letter to Lord Trefgarne, his DTI counterpart, (classification: SECRET). He repeated that he did not want to approve any more Matrix Churchill licences, because the 'overall intelligence picture' suggested that the machines were being used for arms:

If, as seems likely, there are further revelations about indigenous Iraqi arms manufacture and Matrix Churchill are again implicated, we would – entirely justifiably in my view – be sharply criticised for approving such licences. We could not argue that we had not been adequately warned.

The following day, Waldegrave placed on record his unwillingness to join in a cover-up. His head of department, David Gore-Booth, accepted that an 'increase in Iraqi paranoia' would certainly be likely following the Customs raid. But, he said: 'We are bound to be suspicious. Why else would the Iraqis have bought the company?' He concluded: 'I cannot see any grounds for trying to prevent the Customs & Excise going in.' Waldegrave scrawled across the top of the memo: 'I agree.'

That afternoon, Martin Stanley, Principal Private Secretary to Nicholas Ridley, picked up the secure phone on the Ministerial floor of the DTI block in Victoria Street. 'Simon? . . .' he said.

A government Minister runs his department through his 'private office': and a Minister's Private Secretary, in the Whitehall hierarchy, is a senior official. He is, in effect, the Minister's chief of staff. There was certainly little support feeding in from the Foreign Office that Wednesday. But Ridley's private office were moving with frantic speed to lobby on their own high-level network. The man Ridley's PPS was telephoning was Simon Woodside, Private Secretary to Brian Unwin. Unwin was a top Whitehall official and chairman of the Commissioners of Excise – the head man at HM Customs.

Ridley's message, as conveyed by his Private Secretary, was this: a major disturbance was in store if Unwin allowed the planned Customs inspection of Matrix Churchill to go ahead. Ridley was going to write to Mrs Thatcher herself, Stanley warned, and demand an urgent, Cabinet-level meeting on the issue. It was, of course, made clear that it was for Customs to decide whether or not to go ahead with the proposed action.

Simon Woodside fielded the ball. The raid would be only a 'routine' visit to the factory, he said: it was now due for Thursday, the following day. Did DTI Ministers want to register an official objection, having been given just this opportunity by Customs?

The conversation must have been delicate. It ended with Ridley's man saying that he did not want to object formally. He promptly recorded the promise he had extracted in writing and sent it round to Customs. It was a striking agreement for a supposedly independent prosecuting authority to make: 'You assured me that the visit would be used for fact finding only, and no action would be taken as a result without consulting Ministers.'

That letter – again classified: SECRET – was copied on the Private Secretaries' network to the offices of the Cabinet Ministers serving in the Iraq Gun Group. They were Mrs Thatcher herself (through her chief adviser, Charles Powell), Douglas Hurd, the Foreign Secretary; Tom King, the Defence Secretary; and a certain party who later said that he took no notice at all of what was occurring – John Major, then Chancellor, subsequently to become Prime Minister.

When the Matrix Churchill affair threatened to engulf the new Prime Minister in 1992, John Major was faced with the classic questions: what did he know and when did he know it? Major's defence was that he perhaps had not been on top of the job. During those nights of 1990, he had apparently not been memorising the contents of his Ministerial red box. For of this letter from Ridley's private office, he said, on 30 November 1992: 'Papers in connection with Matrix Churchill were copied to my office at the Treasury in June . . . Treasury records do not indicate whether I saw those documents, but I have no recollection of doing so.'

Peter Wiltshire's plan to head a Customs inspection of the Matrix Churchill factory had already embroiled his chairman, set off detonations in several government departments and brought him to the notice of Number 10. But that was just the start of it. The next ring on the Customs officer's phone came from British intelligence.

The man who called himself 'Balsam' wrote up his own report of that call a fortnight later. It went in a secret telegram to the outworn tower block which houses the head office of the Secret Intelligence Service – popularly known as MI6. 'As I had been tipped off,' he recorded, 'before the visit I knew in advance, and managed to speak to Peter Wiltshire.' Wiltshire was prepared to be 'very helpful'. The Customs man was willing to keep 'Balsam' informed on 'the general thrust of the investigation and detailed points about it'. Following his orders, the MI6 man arranged for the two men to meet for a private talk after the Customs inspection at Coventry.

What 'Balsam' needed to know was how much trouble and embarrassment were likely to come MI6's way. For one thing, he was in possession of a pile of Matrix Churchill blueprints which Customs might well be looking for. As Wiltshire already suspected, MI6 were running a high-level agent inside Matrix Churchill. They had a 'mole', and 'Balsam' was his handler.

No one knew at the time of this call that a fuse was being lit which would lead to disaster – to the arrest of MI6's agent; to the destruction of his company; to the discrediting of a Minister in a sensational trial; and against a backcloth of British troops sent to war, to a potentially devastating judicial inquiry into the conduct of the whole Conservative government. Peter Wiltshire, perhaps, was the one with least suspicion of the size of the explosion his visit would bring about.

While Wiltshire and his Customs team went to the Coventry factory as planned, Nicholas Ridley on the Ministerial floor at Victoria Street was dictating an angry letter about them. It was addressed to the Prime Minister herself. And it went on for four A4 pages:

Customs are today making an ostensibly routine visit to that company . . . Any action following that visit is likely to worsen relations with Iraq.

. . . Further Customs investigations could strengthen Iraqi accusations that we are interfering with civil trade.

. . . I can see no prospect of any improvement in the position while investigations into possible breaches of export controls continue. On the contrary . . . only our competitors can benefit.

. . . A Customs investigation is likely to be reported to Baghdad . . . This could provoke further reprisals against our exports . . .

The Secretary of State for Trade and Industry did not mention anywhere in this lengthy letter the secret briefing his civil servants had given him – that if Customs were allowed to persist in their investigation, what would be exposed would in fact be his own department's 'dirty washing'. Instead, he gave a statistic likely to make the PM's flesh creep. Encouraged by his department, Britain provided no less than £1 billion to Iraq in trade finance, through the government's Export Credits Guarantee Department. If Customs made Iraq really angry, a default on such a scale 'would have implications for the Public Sector Borrowing Requirement'.

Ridley's letter was self-evidently an attempt to persuade the Prime Minister to block a criminal investigation. Ridley, perhaps demonstrating that the best form of defence is attack, also made an urgent counter-proposal. Why not scrap the arms embargo altogether? This was not a completely new idea: DTI Ministers had chafed under the widely-drawn military trade ban since the Iran-Iraq ceasefire two years before. If the war was over, why keep the embargo? Furthermore, with the end of the Cold War, many machine-tools were about to be dropped from the banned list of high-tech exports to Eastern Europe. This was bound to have a knock-on effect. In the crisis over Peter Wiltshire's Customs inspection, there were two positive consequences of his proposal. It would please Iraq. It would also destroy the Customs investigation. There would be no point in prosecuting the managers of Matrix Churchill for export crimes which had subsequently become perfectly legal. Customs would certainly take that view. No prosecution: no 'dirty washing'. This letter, too, was copied to not only the Cabinet Secretary, Sir Robin Butler, but to the Foreign and Defence Secretaries. It was also copied to the fourth member of the Overseas and Defence Committee of the Cabinet – the then Chancellor of the Exchequer, John Major. As before, John Major's position is that his mind was elsewhere. Did he read the letter? 'I have no recollection of doing so.'

At the Matrix Churchill factory, Peter Wiltshire from Customs, having phoned for an appointment four days in advance, poked around on Thursday 21 June and interviewed one or two managers. Wiltshire cautioned a sales manager before questioning him. But he did not interview the managing director himself, a Mr Paul Henderson. He pursued some rather questionable statements that seemed to have been made to get permission from Tokyo to send a Japanese machine to Iraq as part of the contract. He did not find very much relevant paperwork about. And the remaining machines for the Cardoen contract were off the premises, being worked on at a sub-contractors in Leicester. There would have to be another inspection there to trawl for evidence.

At the Foreign Office, there were signs of fuming at the inconclusive results. 'The DTI chooses to interpret this as evidence that Matrix Churchill has not been involved in any wrongdoing,' minuted the Middle East desk. 'In fact this merely proves that the paperwork which was found is in order. An investigative journalist . . . informed the FCO several weeks before the Customs visit that Matrix Churchill had removed all incriminating papers from their headquarters.'

Within MI6, the atmosphere was more one of relief. On

Wiltshire's return to London, he went to see 'Balsam'. He told him the Matrix Churchill case was 'sensitive and political'. The company seemed to have supplied masses of documentation and component drawings to the DTI when successfully applying for the original Cardoen licences. 'Balsam's' MI6 memo records: 'Therefore any prosecution would risk a large amount of potentially damaging Government documentation being produced in court.'

After the weekend, 'Balsam' went to Euston station and boarded a train for Coventry. At the other end, a dark grey Daimler was waiting for him. Its driver was the slim, silver-haired managing director of Matrix Churchill, Paul Henderson. It was Henderson himself who was MI6's secret agent – in place for more than a year. And before that, Matrix Churchill's export manager, Mark Gutteridge, had been doing the same job. They were spies, unpaid, on Iraq and the Iraqis. These days Henderson is self-deprecating about the label: 'I don't think of myself so much as a spy. I was an informer.'

Back in his office at the factory, with 600 workers employed in the machine-sheds, Henderson seemed to 'Balsam' surprisingly untroubled by the Customs visit: 'He seemed slightly more concerned by the company's financial problems than by the threat of prosecution.'

Naturally, recorded Balsam, he was somewhat concerned for himself and his staff, as they had been warned to get legal advice. But Customs had seemed 'low-key'. Matrix Churchill had indeed supplied to the DTI many drawings of components of the Cardoen contract, and kept copies.

The MI6 officer found himself giving advice to the businessman, telling him not to alarm Matrix Churchill's Iraqi chairman and shareholders about the risk of prosecution. 'Balsam' didn't want to frighten off the true intelligence targets. 'I think he enjoyed a chance to speak frankly to someone,' 'Balsam' testified later.

I honestly think we got on well, as I am a Middle East expert. I could see he was in a problem where his company might lose hundreds and hundreds of jobs. It would be a catastrophe for his company if the Iraqis suddenly walked away, destroying it at a blow. We all agreed that after the initial investigation by Customs, things might be alright [sic].

Henderson himself remembers his MI6 case officer's reassurances: 'He said, "You've got an export licence for it: you've got nothing to worry about." He stressed we shouldn't worry about Customs as it wasn't going to be a problem.' Privately, 'Balsam' was almost as sanguine as he appeared to his agent. 'Speaking to both Henderson and Wiltshire, I got the feeling prosecutions are less likely,' he minuted to his MI6 superiors. He did not think the company had completely clean hands: its project office in Baghdad might have engaged in trickery over the Japanese machine. They might have done more work on the mysterious and possibly nuclear-related components for 'Project K1000' than Henderson had told him: 'Matrix Churchill undoubtedly have some skeletons in their cupboard.' But on the question of prosecution:

Any contraventions of the law might be described as 'technical', as DTI have large amounts of information; the companies concerned believed they were being encouraged to expand their trade in Iraq by the Government; also nearly all the equipment concerned will not be licenseable after 1 July [because of the planned Cold War rule abolitions]; and retrospective prosecutions are less likely.

So MI6 relaxed. Back in Whitehall, too, it looked as if Nicholas Ridley's campaign to get rid of the entire arms embargo was going well. Questions about the 'dirty washing' of the past were being swept aside, and a major Ministerial

meeting was planned for 19 July. It would be chaired by
Foreign Secretary Douglas Hurd; Mrs Thatcher would be
notified of the outcome; and with any luck it would be
presented to a formal Cabinet committee about a week later,
and ratified finally by the full Cabinet a little after that – at
the beginning of August, perhaps . . .

The Ministry of Defence was a reliable supporter of the
embargo abolition project. Alan Clark, the Minister of
Defence Procurement, was a former trade Minister, and
a loud advocate of what he saw as 'British interests'. He
had always been one of the most committed backers of
machine-tool sales to Iraq. The MOD stood right behind
British Aerospace, which stood to make a lot of money from
selling Hawk jet trainers to Iraq – there was a long-standing
project afoot for a factory in Iraq which would represent
contracts worth hundreds of millions of pounds. It was only
popular complaints about Iraq's human rights abuses that
stood in the way – that and the wording of the 'Ministerial
guidelines' which spelled out how the arms embargo was to
operate.

By 12 July, a full report had been commissioned by the
Cabinet Office from the Joint Intelligence Committee, giving
the latest assessment of Iraq's attempts to procure nuclear
weapons and missiles. Since the seizure of the 'Supergun',
and the seizure at the same time by United States and
British Customs of alleged electronic nuclear 'triggers', the
report might have been optimistic that the underground
procurement network – the source of professed Foreign
Office anxiety – was now in poor shape.

By 13 July, the Cabinet Office Gun Group had circulated
a background paper. One sentence in it brought a sharp
correction from MI6:

Ministers have allowed the supply of some Matrix Churchill
machine tools [in the past] for ad hoc reasons of an
intelligence nature.

The Secret Intelligence Service did not intend to be blamed by Ministers for any 'dirty washing'. MI6 quickly sought to change the record:

> The implication is that 'intelligence' considerations influenced Ministers to allow exports . . . our understanding of the situation is somewhat different.

The Cabinet Office paper suggested, in the traditional way, three options. Keep the 'guidelines'; scrap the guidelines; or compromise. The result of defining the problem in such a way was predictable. The option defined as compromise was the one chosen. Ridley and the DTI wanted to scrap the embargo. The Foreign Office wanted to keep it. The MOD briefed Clark – and he agreed – that he should argue to scrap the guidelines. They were irrelevant; penalised British exports; and enabled Britain's competitors to 'cash in'. The MOD's compromise option – the one that won – was further to relax the guidelines to the point where the only items banned were directly 'lethal'. Machine-tools, whatever they made, were certainly not lethal. All exports would be allowed. Indeed, any item might be allowed under this definition that did not actually explode with a bang: tank spares, for example, military radar, ships, or planes.

This was the decision taken in secret at the Foreign Office on 19 July 1990: 'To revise policy, but not to permit the export of lethal equipment' was how Michael Heseltine later couched the Ministers' recommendation. Exposed after the scandal broke, he sought to justify it to the House of Commons by saying: 'Equipment from all over the world was being sold to Iraq. British companies were at risk of losing orders.'

This decision was taken with the full knowledge of Margaret Thatcher, who had by then been in power, unchallenged, for eleven years, as Conservative Prime Minister. She was aware of Ridley's attempts to block a criminal investigation, and she was party to the decision to further re-arm Saddam Hussein's Iraq.

But once again, like Macavity the Mystery Cat in T.S. Eliot's poem, there is a figure in the story who simply isn't there. The Chancellor of the Exchequer's department had been invited to the Ministerial meeting. Whitehall papers show that the Treasury brief was to argue against the relaxation on the narrow financial grounds that a near-bankrupt Iraq should not be encouraged into 'large military sales'. They might default on payments.

We shall never know what John Major could have gone on to argue at that meeting: he might have electrified his audience with a denunciation of the immorality of helping a dictator; he might have uttered a ringing warning that one day British troops could find themselves facing the military monster his colleagues proposed to help create; he might have said that short-sighted greed and naïveté were not the weapons with which to deal with men like Saddam Hussein. But he did not give himself the chance to say any of those things. John Major stayed away. He sent his junior colleague Richard Ryder instead, explaining it thus: 'The public expenditure Cabinet was held on the same day and would have been my principal preoccupation at the time.'*

Had this commercially-minded proposal been confirmed at a future full Cabinet meeting as intended, the possibility of a prosecution of Matrix Churchill, and indeed other erring machine-tool companies, would have quietly disappeared. As it was, the last of the Cardoen machines were earmarked for release. The DTI rang up Paul Henderson at Matrix Churchill and told him the licences were coming through. On 1 August, the licences, it was promised, were finally on their way.

Twenty-four hours later, to Margaret Thatcher's and the British government's apparent astonishment, Saddam Hussein invaded Kuwait. Iraq became the enemy. All trade

* House of Commons written answer 30 November 1992.

was frozen, and within weeks war commenced. No member of the British government was now likely to admit how close they had come to legitimising large military exports to Baghdad. Instead of being snuffed out, Customs' legal fuse remained lit. What was to become the calamitous prosecution of Paul Henderson began to smoulder slowly forwards.

2

RAIDED

**HM Customs arrests three company executives,
October 1990**

I will play it very cool.
MI6 telegram, 31 October 1990

Paul Henderson's life as Matrix Churchill's managing director
became difficult after Saddam Hussein invaded the pro-
Western oil state of Kuwait. For a man who had reached a
pinnacle after leaving school at fifteen to start as an apprentice
at the Coventry factory, the downward trajectory was now
painful. Thirty redundancies on the sanctions-frozen Iraq
contracts were declared straightaway, to be followed in
the end by the sacking of most of Matrix Churchill's 600
workers. Henderson's £200,000 personal stake in the firm
was to become worthless.

Saddam looted, tortured, held Britons hostage and defied
the West. The United States and Britain, formerly so friendly
to Saddam, now denounced the dictator and all his works.
He was the personification of evil in the popular press: the
moustachioed demon in Western children's nightmares. Television programmes such as *Panorama* indignantly repeated

charges that Matrix Churchill and the other machine-tool companies had been selling equipment to Iraq to make munitions. The *Independent* highlighted Cardoen's Chilean fuse factory outside Baghdad with its Matrix Churchill machines. The Labour opposition called for action.

In September, the United States government seized Matrix Churchill's subsidiary in the US. The Iraqi controlling shareholders were deported from Britain by the Home Office. In October, while Paul Henderson was trying to organise a British management buy-out, a Customs team which had been checking out paperwork discovered at his sub-contractors descended on the factory, arrested him and two of his managers and imprisoned him overnight at Wormwood Scrubs.

Henderson was surprised. 'When I was first arrested and put into the cell, I felt "Nothing will ever come of this". Obviously I was going to have to answer questions. But I believed that eventually, it would go away.'

Up until then, he had been in fairly constant telephone contact with 'Balsam', his MI6 handler: 'He was extremely interested in how the Iraqis were reacting.' 'Balsam' assents on that point. He later testified: 'That was a natural item of interest. We were essentially on a war footing. These people would be taking the lead in trying to evade UN sanctions.'

Henderson says, angrily: 'When I told him a Customs officer called Christopher Constantine was coming to interview me, he said, "Hang on" – he'd speak to his friend, who was above Constantine. He phoned me back and repeated there was nothing to worry about. This turned out to be far from the truth as fifteen Customs officers attended and I was arrested.'

'Balsam' more or less confirms events happened that way: 'There seemed to be no worry . . . I merely passed on to him the information I had, that it was a reprise of Customs' June visit.'

After the shock of his arrest, Paul Henderson felt – like the fall guy in many an espionage novel – that he'd been left out in the cold by 'Balsam' and MI6. 'I tried to contact him after that . . . he was always unavailable and never returned any of my messages to call. I felt I'd been badly used – more than a little hurt by the way I'd been abandoned.'

In Coventry, a second MI6 officer was solemmly warning Mark Gutteridge to keep his mouth shut.

Gutteridge – tense, hunched, heavy-browed – had been export manager for Matrix Churchill for many years, and a lifelong friend of Paul Henderson. Now an international sales rep for several companies, he knew more than most about machine-tools for Iraq. That was why he was such a valuable secret agent. Gutteridge had made many sales to Eastern Europe and he'd spent years working for K3(a) – a section of the counter-espionage branch of the security service, MI5. They were Britain's nearest equivalent to the secret police – although its officers would have preferred any comparison to be made with the FBI in the United States, with whom they were normally in close liaison.

As 'Source 528' – his MI5 internal code-number – Gutteridge had reported on Matrix Churchill and the other companies in the early days of the Iraq shipments for a case officer, 'Michael Ford'. Now Gutteridge had been transferred to MI6 – a more appropriate department – and his new handler was 'Ian Eacott'. Gutteridge knew exactly what the 'dirty washing' in the machine-tools affair consisted of. And he was uneasy. Gutteridge told 'Eacott', on 23 October, that since the Customs raid on Matrix Churchill, Paul Henderson's state of mind had been troubling him – Henderson had been shocked at the 'unsanitary conditions' in his prison cell. Gutteridge's own signature was on some of the questionable arms contracts, and Customs might question him too.

'Eacott's' response – according to his memo of the conversation – was to play matters strictly by the book. If Gutteridge was interviewed, 'He should say nothing of his dealings with myself or previous case officers.' Any illegalities were Gutteridge's own problem: 'I pointed out . . . we could not, nor would we, help him out.'

MI6 seems to have taken the view that Gutteridge had been successfully put on ice, and contact with him could be safely suspended for the duration of the affair. '528 presented a responsible, if grave outlook and we believe will abide by this undertaking.' They passed on any gossip picked up from their other agents which might prove helpful in Henderson's prosecution:

> On 21 November, Henderson had spoken of but not named a British company which had sold a complete transfer line to Iraq. The company had not yet been investigated. But Henderson had every intention of revealing this and other information 'which would prove extremely embarrassing', if charges were pressed against him . . . Hope the above is of some assistance. We will, of course, pass on any other snippets we might glean.

A few days after the raid, in an MI6 office in London, two men met to go over exactly what Paul Henderson himself might have let slip about the 'dirty washing' during his Customs interrogation. They were the senior Customs investigator concerned, and Henderson's own MI6 'agent-runner'. Balsam was again getting a report from the helpful Peter Wiltshire: 'He does not resent my inquiries at all.'

Henderson and his colleagues had been released without charge after their interview. But it now seemed at least possible that there might be a prosecution and trial for falsifying export licences. Balsam told his superiors: 'Obviously I will have no further contact with Henderson, and if he telephones me, I will play it very cool.' Balsam's concern was whether Henderson, too, could be relied on to keep his mouth shut about his work for MI6. He and Peter Wiltshire had quickly grasped that some of the 'dirty washing' might come out in a trial. The MI6 telegram records his realisation:

> The Matrix Churchill case is likely to rest on the fact that HMG, especially the DTI and its Ministers, should have been aware that the huge growth in machine exports to Iraq must have been in part connected with the arms industry.

Henderson had already talked at length to his interrogators about a meeting with a government Minister. This was Alan Clark (then Trade Minister) and the meeting took place at the DTI's Victoria Street headquarters in January 1988. He and the other firms from the Machine Tools Technologies Association claimed to have been given a green light from the Minister to go ahead with military exports.

Would Henderson be tempted to reveal his MI6 role – particularly as his handler used to sign in at the factory gate as 'Mr Balsam of the DTI'? Fortunately, Henderson had kept quiet so far. 'Balsam' reported: 'We do not expect there to be any adverse implications from the forthcoming trial . . . I am sure he will concentrate on emphasising his contacts with the DTI and even the FCO, if he uses the "HMG knew" defence.' He added, primly perhaps for an officer of a secret intelligence agency: 'This case shows again the dangers of us concentrating our [nuclear] anti-proliferation efforts on British businessmen who end up getting into trouble.'

That autumn, Allied forces gathered in the Gulf, ready to face Saddam Hussein's artillery and rockets. Britain's centre stage was temporarily occupied, however, by a more domestic drama. An unintended tear glistening in her eye, Margaret Thatcher bent to enter the government Jaguar and leave Downing Street for the last time. The Prime Minister who had done more than anyone else to set the tone of British government behaviour had been ousted by her own party.

RAIDED

Ostensibly, her removal was caused by her extreme and hostile attitude towards Europe; and by the fiasco of her pet scheme, the Poll Tax.

However, the way that she stepped down, with her personal reputation untarnished as the Gulf War loomed, was, for the Prime Minister, a great stroke of luck. Had large numbers of British troops been killed – killed with weapons made by British machinery – and had the full story emerged of how those machines were allowed to be sold in the first place – then Mrs Thatcher would have faced a great crisis. It might have been a crisis she could have postponed: but when it eventually came, it would not have been one that she would have found easy to survive.

HOW MINISTER HELPED ARM SADDAM'S SOLDIERS
Behind two huge ornamental gates, past the fortified guardhouse, thousands of production workers are feeding Saddam's burgeoning war machine . . . The *Sunday Times* Insight Team has investigated . . . and discovered that a government Minister allowed firms to break the spirit of the government's arms embargo.

The article opened in characteristic style: the cinematic tone was easy to parody. But there was no doubt that someone had given the newspaper a pretty good story. This was the way the true nature of part of the government's 'dirty washing' peeked into the open on 2 December that year – on the very eve of a long-awaited assault on Saddam's forces by American and British troops.

The *Sunday Times* clearly had had access to the impressions of the three legally-endangered Matrix managers – Paul Henderson, Trevor Abraham, his commercial manager, and Peter Allen, for a period the sales manager. There was a graphic description of Henderson's recollection of Shed C at the Nassr factory in Iraq, where many of the first batch of Matrix Churchill machines had been installed: '. . . row upon row of computer-controlled lathes programmed to make the casings, fins and nose-cones of mortar shells'.

The article quoted from a set of MTTA (Machine Tools Technologies Association) minutes that had been supplied to the authors, and alleged that the January 1988 meeting with the Minister, Alan Clark, had effectively cleared the machines for export: 'According to one managing director present . . . "The Minister was giving us a nod and a wink." ' There was a threat in the article. It was not a thinly-veiled one: 'If they are charged [the Matrix Churchill executives] plan to testify in court that they had the government's backing for their Iraq contracts, and that Clark advised them.'

That the government would have been deterred by such a threat would have been a perfectly reasonable assumption for Paul Henderson and his colleagues to make. Only a fortnight earlier, Customs prosecutions in the notorious Supergun affair had been suddenly dropped. Two men had actually been formally charged, six months earlier, with involvement in illegal exports. Both Peter Mitchell, director of the steel firm which had helped make the gun-barrels, and Christopher Cowley, head of the British team which had procured the parts and assembled the guns in the mountains of Iraq, were to be allowed to walk away from the law.

A local MP, Hal Miller, claimed that he contacted the DTI and the intelligence services on behalf of the firm at an early stage in the contract, warning that the deal seemed to involve a missile of some kind. But the DTI had shown no interest in blocking export licences. Cowley admitted that a fairly flimsy cover had been prepared for public consumption: officially, the pipes were for a petrochemical plant. But everyone at the factory knew the truth.

Cowley worked for the notorious Space Research Corporation of Brussels – the corporate vehicle for one man, the visionary artillery designer Gerald Bull, Iraq's employee and architect of the Supergun. In the world of murder and intrigue which surrounded Saddam Hussein, Bull had become a spectacular victim – one of a trio of brutal deaths, while a big gun, successfully smuggled out of Britain and assembled, was being test-fired in the mountains.

That March, precisely one week after Saddam Hussein hanged *Observer* journalist Farzad Bazoft in Baghdad for 'spying', a hit-man with a silenced pistol fired two shots into the back of Bull's neck, killing him at the door of his Brussels flat. Exactly a week later, a young British defence journalist with a military background – Jonathan Moyle – was found hanged in a hotel cupboard in Chile. He had been asking questions about Cardoen and the company's arms shipments to Iraq. Those suspected of working either for Iraq or for its enemies seemed liable to meet bloody ends.

Cowley, a middle-aged engineer from Bristol, has a simple explanation for why the Customs prosecution against him was dropped: the DTI was embarrassed by its incompetent failure to spot the Supergun transactions, and by its general hypocrisy: 'You have a declared policy where you will have nothing to do with Iraq in terms of weapons sales, and in the background you're doing the exact opposite.' Not just the Supergun pipes were involved, said Cowley:

> We would have cited numerous other cases where weapons had been exported and the DTI knew – battlefield radar, for example; ejector seats for fighter aircraft that the DTI said were safety equipment; and tank engines we were supplying as a 'non-lethal' component. What the British government was saying was not necessarily the policy they were following.*

The witnesses Cowley and his lawyer were threatening to demand to call to prove this were Trade Secretary Nicholas Ridley; and the former Minister for Trade, Alan Clark.

The Supergun case could be dropped and hushed up: why

* Interview with author.

couldn't Matrix Churchill? If the *Sunday Times* article about Matrix Churchill contained a threat made in the hope of heading off Customs prosecution, it did not work. If anything, it backfired. Nonetheless, there was certainly uproar in Whitehall and at Westminster. The head of the Middle East desk at the Foreign Office, Rob Young, was on the phone as soon as the paper hit the newsstands, calling for a confidential memo. David Hope, staffing the Gulf emergency unit, spent his Sunday penning some surprising words.

There had been a long history of battles over this issue between the Foreign Office and the DTI, he said. The DTI 'line' had always been that there was no evidence to prove machine-tools exported to Iraq were being put to military use: 'This line was, to say the least, disingenuous.'

The Foreign Office seemed to have got off relatively lightly, in comparison to the allegation about Alan Clark:

The article makes it clear that we had grave misgivings . . . and were the main opposition within Whitehall to the granting of licences. Our case is not helped however by the fact that my predecessor, Mark Higson, is quoted as saying that: 'Everybody knew the equipment could be used for making shells.'

On the Monday morning, Alan Clark's period in the limelight continued. He was sent for by John Major, the Prime Minister. Were these allegations true? According to Major (much later), Clark strongly denied the whole story. He made a public statement that the *Sunday Times* article was 'highly defamatory' and drawled to reporters; 'I have never given a nod and a wink to anyone in my life.' With Clark sitting beside him on the government benches, the current Trade Minister, Tim Sainsbury, issued to Parliament an official statement. It did put the onus on Clark: 'Mr Clark strongly denies the interpretation put on the remarks alleged to have been made by him.'

But on behalf of the government, Sainsbury went on to give two dangerous hostages to fortune. First, he refused to disclose the contents of the DTI's official minute of the disputed meeting, saying that the government customarily kept secret such 'working papers'. It was a piece of Whitehall paper that was eventually, in the hands of Paul Henderson's QC, to prove devastating. And second, Sainsbury was to utter a claim about the government Iran-Iraq export guidelines – presumably on departmental advice – that was false. He said that the guidelines, banning defence sales which 'significantly enhanced' either side's aggressive capacity, had been publicly set out in October 1985: 'The guidelines are clear . . . and since then, they have been scrupulously and carefully followed.'

On the same day that a Minister of the Crown was telling Parliament what was to prove to be a ludicrous untruth, a second incriminating piece of paper was being shuffled away deep in Whitehall. It was a report summarising a military intelligence survey, completed back in 1989. It had been presented to the Ministry of Defence working group advising on arms sales to Iraq.

On 3 December, the day after the newspaper exposure, and the Monday that Sainsbury was assuring Parliament of the integrity of the guidelines, the security branch of MOD, 'Land Services Operations [Requirements] 10 c', had the summary withdrawn and given a British security classification, 'UK RESTRICTED', meaning its disclosure was 'undesirable in the national interest'.

However embarrassing Whitehall found its home truths, this must have been a difficult thing to do while keeping a straight face. For the report's authors had written, pointedly, in one of their opening paragraphs: 'This paper . . . is unclassified because the information it contains is in the public domain already. All it needs is someone like an investigative journalist to pull together the threads.'

What the report had to say was disturbing. Intelligence

showed that Iraq was operating a plan to set up its own arms industry, using a deliberately confusing variety of foreign contractors. The situation was building up because of 'the amount of assistance that "UK Ltd", and in particular our machinery manufacturers, are giving to Iraq, towards the setting up of a major arms research and development, and production industry.'

The report listed examples – a long catalogue of export licences for particularly sensitive goods granted by the DTl: and they probably represented less than 10 per cent of the overall flow of unlicensed arms industry material going to Iraq, said the report's authors. Their ambition – a vain one – was 'to draw the attention of the Minister to the way in which "UK Ltd" is helping Iraq, often unwillingly, but sometimes not, to set up a major indigenous arms industry.'

One export licence for apparently innocuous electronic components was part of an enormous project by the Saad organisation to construct no fewer than seventy-six weapons research and development laboratories, mostly built by the Germans. A 'vacuum precision furnace' from Britain could make jet engine parts. Moulds for steel ingots were going to a factory making gun-barrels and tank parts (partly equipped by the Swiss).

The report pinpointed plans to set up complete new production lines in Iraq. The electronics firm Racal had applied to expand a national electronics manufacturing complex, turning out military radios. MSA (Britain) Ltd had applied to build a plant for thermal batteries, used in missiles and shells. Magnum Industrial Projects wanted to set up a parachute factory. And prominent on the list was an application granted in February 1989 to Matrix Churchill for machine-tools destined for the Nassr complex – sufficient, said the report, 'to equip a factory designed to produce 500,000 155-millimetre shells per annum'.

The MOD working group had their eyes fixed backward. Their concerns were that Iraq might restart the war with

Iran, or that it might pass on valuable technical know-how to the Soviet Union. A third fear was that Iraq might be able to steal some of Britain's own lucrative worldwide arms trade. But their factual conclusion was nonetheless chilling. Taken together, the Iraq sales represented 'a very significant enhancement to the ability of Iraq to manufacture its own arms'.

Sir Geoffrey Howe, the Foreign Secretary, had promised in 1985 just the opposite – that everything possible was going to be done to prevent 'significant enhancement' of the Iraqi war machine. The MOD report, by using Howe's phrase, rubbed in the fact that his policy had proved a failure. 'UK Ltd' and his own Ministerial colleagues had seen to that.

Yet, although there was so much Whitehall 'dirty washing' around, the prosecution of Paul Henderson and his colleagues at Matrix Churchill did not stop. It could have been halted, Supergun style, at this point. Indeed, the Matrix Churchill case was much easier to stop than the Cowley and Mitchell prosecution. In that case, the men were already facing specific charges and the legal machine had gathered momentum. Henderson and co had been released on 'police bail' six weeks earlier, and had not yet been charged with anything.

There were three reasons why the threat of publicity turned out to be so counter-productive. First of all, Alan Clark, like anyone faced with a public accusation in those circumstances, came under pressure to deny it. This he did. The evidence against the Matrix Churchill three looked as a consequence stronger after the publicity, not weaker. And so any counsel engaged by Customs would probably have advised.

Secondly, the enforced dropping of the Supergun prosecutions had embarrassed and angered the Customs teams concerned. Senior Treasury counsel had advised abandoning the case. Customs had been unhappy, and had consulted the Attorney-General. He had told them to take counsel's advice. The Christmas card sent out that year by Customs investigators became famous – to the discomfort of its designers. It showed a murdered figure lying face-down in a pool of blood. The legend was: 'Stabbed in the Back'. This atmosphere did not make it easier for Customs to abandon a second Iraq prosecution. It made it, if anything, harder.

And thirdly, there were profound political advantages to the Major government in a prosecution taking place. There is a traditional British way of putting the lid on a can of worms, and it is called the *sub judice* rule. While a prosecution is pending, Parliament will not debate an issue; a Parliamentary committee will not take evidence about it; Ministers and their Departments can simply refuse to answer questions; and the media remain virtually gagged. Prosecutions can remain pending for a very long time.

The trade committee's all-party inquiry into the Supergun and exports to Iraq had been strangled on the day of its birth by the charging with criminal offences of Christopher Cowley. That committee was now showing signs of wanting to return to life. John Major's inexperienced premiership faced, in the new year, what Saddam was promising would be the 'mother of all battles'. British troops might be killed in numbers by British-made artillery shells. And at some time in the next fifteen or sixteen months, Major would also have to fight a general election.

Magaret Thatcher and Nicholas Ridley (who had also resigned) were now figures from the political past. Clark, a Thatcher admirer, was politically finished. (And was eventually and suddenly to leave the Commons.) If mud stuck to those three in the end, it was of little concern to Major. Yet whatever happened in the long run, in the medium term the prospect of a lengthy period of *sub judice* on the government's 'dirty washing' could only be attractive.

Paul Henderson up in Coventry could have watched this political process at work in the immediate wake of the *Sunday Times* story, if he had travelled down to sit in the public gallery of the House of Commons. Henderson was not even near to being charged, let alone tried before a jury, but already Ministers were seeking to trundle on the protective screen of *sub judice*. Sainsbury, in his Ministerial statement, refused to say whether the MTTA minutes of the infamous Clark meeting were correct or not. The justification he offered for this attitude was merely: 'I am advised that to do so might prejudice possible proceedings.'

Clark himself, on the Sunday the story came out, success-fully ducked questions, saying that because an investigation was being conducted into Matrix Churchill by Customs, he 'could not comment'. And in the immediate run-up to the crucial general election, Conservative Ministers were able to use the Matrix Churchill prosecution to sabotage the resumed investigation by MPs into the Supergun scandal.

They exploited the *sub judice* rule to prevent the appearance before the Trade committee of the two senior officials at the DTI responsible for handling export licences for both the Supergun manufacturers and the machine-tools that went to Iraq. The two high-ranking civil servants were the head of the DTI's whole export control machine at the time of the crime – Eric Beston; and the man who ran the 60-strong unit actually handing out the licences, Tony Steadman.

These two men knew the buried location of more skeletons than the MPs on the committee realised. The published report – which found very little out – mournfully recorded: 'Two civil servants responsible for export control in 1988 did not give oral evidence on Ministerial instruction, because they were due to be key prosecution witnesses in a criminal case at the same time.'

Despite the fact that the central issue in the report was the way Steadman and Beston had handled licence applications from the steel manufacturers, the MPs consoled themselves with the thought that their absence did not really make a difference. And they may have been right. Civil servants generally find it easy to run rings around a committee of badly-briefed MPs with few legal powers.

The most dramatic example of this had been the recent downfall of Sir Robert Armstrong, the Cabinet Secretary, who effortlessly dodged the efforts at interrogation of a Commons committee who called him before them to testify over the Westland affair, (in which civil servants stood accused of a variety of improprieties and cover-ups when briefing journalists on Mrs Thatcher's behalf). Awed articles ensued about Sir Robert's 'Rolls-Royce mind'. A brisk cross-examination by a genuine criminal lawyer soon put paid to that. Sir Robert went to Sydney to testify for the British government during its futile attempts to ban the MI5 book *Spycatcher*. He was rattled by Australian solicitor Malcolm Turnbull and cajoled into admitting he had been 'economical with the truth'.

It was a phrase that instantly became famous. And it was to become famous again in the Matrix Churchill case. The two civil servants from the DTI may have been spared questioning from politicians. When they and Ministers were eventually to be cross-examined in court by a skilled QC like Geoffrey Robertson, it became very clear why their secret knowledge was dangerous enough to keep under wraps for as long as possible.

The situation after the Customs raid in Coventry and the trial balloon floated in the *Sunday Times* was this: Customs wanted to carry on prosecuting more than ever; the new Major government's Ministers had no incentive to try to prevent them; and the available evidence looked stronger than before. The fuse of the Matrix Churchill prosecution continued to smoulder.

3

CHARGED

**Henderson, Abraham and Allen in court,
February 1991**

It could not be said where all this would lead.
MI6 minute, 8 May 1991

It was a raw winter day in England. In Iraq the climate was more like hell, as painted by Hieronymus Bosch. During Operation 'Desert Storm', a charred and grinning skull appeared among the heroic news photographs, its cremated hands gripping the wheel of a burned-out lorry like Death himself at work. The fleeting television pictures of those burned bodies of conscripted Iraqi soldiers in their lines of strafed vehicles on the Basra road revealed the violence of the American attack which finally drove Saddam Hussein out of Kuwait. British troops and pilots had been sent to fight – and sometimes die – alongside the US forces. In this climate, support for Saddam was tantamount to treachery.

Paul Henderson, Trevor Abraham and Peter Allen were charged by HM Customs on 17 February with: 'Being knowingly concerned in the attempted exportation of goods with attempt to evade the prohibition thereon . . . imposed by the Export of Goods (Control) Orders 1987 and 1989'. Their alleged crimes began only after July 1988 and there were two contracts eventually named in the charges: machines and tools for Industrias Cardoen, Chile, and a second contract with machines for 'The ABA Project, NASSR Enterprise for Mechanical Industries, Iraq'. The Cardoen machines went to equip the April 7 Factory near Baghdad with fuses to go in shells and mortar-bombs. The ABA shipment was to make artillery rockets.

The charges were extremely simple. Henderson and his colleagues were accused of deceiving the Department of Trade and Industry. The deception was that they had pretended on their licence applications that their machines were for civilian use, claiming they were for 'general engineering' or 'metal components' when all the time they knew perfectly well that they were going to make munitions. The DTI, its officials and Ministers, in their simplicity had allowed themselves to be misled. Had they known the machines were for munitions, said those concerned, then they would never have permitted any of them to have been exported. Henderson and his fellow-defendants, if they insisted on fighting the case, faced jail sentences of up to seven years.

The basic Customs case was founded on a set of obliging witness statements from government officials. These witness statements carry a warning at the top:

> This statement . . . is true to the best of my knowledge and belief and I make it knowing that, if it is tendered in evidence, I shall be liable to prosecution if I have wilfully stated in it anything which I know to be false or do not believe to be true.

The top civil servant who ran the export control system at the time – Eric Beston – made just such a witness statement a fortnight before charges were formally laid.

He testified that:

• All export applications were considered in the light of Sir Geoffrey Howe's published 1985 guidelines, banning any defence exports which would 'significantly enhance' either side's fighting capability.

• He personally had never had any idea that any of Matrix Churchill's licence applications 'were for equipment specially designed for the production of controlled military goods'.

• If there had been any applications for machines to make munitions, they would have been refused.

Each of these three statements would transpire later to be far from correct. Beston's position was backed in statements from his subordinate who issued the licences, Tony Steadman; from the Trade Minister for the second half of the period concerned, Lord Trefgarne; and from the Trade Minister in 1988, Alan Clark.

Clark's statement was headed: 'The Rt Hon Alan Kenneth McKenzie Clark MP'. His age, he said, was over twenty-one; and his occupation was 'Minister of State'. Customs lawyer Cedric Andrew took the statement on 12 July 1991, five months after Paul Henderson had been charged. In it, Alan Clark denied outright the truth of the MTTA minutes of his meeting with the machine-tool manufacturers, when, so the *Sunday Times* alleged, he had given them a 'nod and a wink' to go ahead with military exports. It was a denial that was to assume extraordinary significance sixteen months later.

The confidential minutes made peculiar reading. They showed Clark congratulating the manufacturers and offering them his full backing up to Cabinet level: 'The inference was that deliveries under current export licences should be made as quickly as possible, in case some bureaucratic interference occurred at any time during any interdepartmental and Ministerial discussions.'

He then went on to give them advice about how to submit

future export licences 'so that they had a good chance of being granted.' He advised as follows:

- THE INTENDED USE OF THE MACHINES SHOULD BE COUCHED IN SUCH A MANNER AS TO EMPHASISE THE PEACEFUL ASPECT TO WHICH THEY WILL BE PUT . . .
- APPLICATIONS SHOULD STRESS THE RECORD OF 'GENERAL ENGINEERING' USAGE OF MACHINE TOOLS SUPPLIED IN THE PAST, GIVING AS MUCH DETAIL AS POSSIBLE, E.G. FOR RAILWAYS: AND STATE THAT THE NEW ORDERS HAVE COME AS PART OF A PLAN TO REPLACE AND REFURBISH THE AGEING STOCK OF MACHINE TOOLS CURRENTLY IN IRAQ.

Alan Clark rounded off this counselling session, according to the minute, with a very odd piece of advice indeed:

THE MINISTER ADVISED THAT THE ADVICE GIVEN DURING THE DISCUSSION WAS BASED ON THE CUR-RENT STATE OF PLAY. IF THE POLITICAL OVERTONES OF THE IRAN/IRAQ CONFLICT CHANGE, E.G. IF THE UNITED STATES BECOMES MORE SUPPORTIVE OF ONE SIDE THAN AT PRESENT, THEN THE CURRENT ORDER MAY CHANGE.

Clark wound up by telling the machine-tool companies to keep quiet and not talk to the press.

To an outsider, it was not at all obvious what the Minister was up to at this meeting. Strangely, the words 'military' or 'munitions' were not mentioned anywhere at all in the minutes. Why exactly should the manufacturers be in such fear that their current licences could be revoked? Were future orders likely to be for 'general engineering' or not? Everything seemed to be expressed in a kind of code. Clearly, that restricted group who were at the meeting and to whom the minutes were circulated, knew exactly what the Minister was talking about. And equally clearly, so did he.

But the interpretation put on the meeting in the *Sunday Times* article – that Alan Clark was giving military exporters of machine-tools a 'nod and a wink' – had been denied once: by him to the Prime Minister, John Major. It had been denied twice: by Minister Tim Sainsbury, on his behalf, to Parliament. And now it was to be denied thrice: in a statutory witness statement, each page signed by Clark himself.

'The MTTA report,' he testified, 'to the best of my recollection, does NOT accurately record the substance of that meeting.' He testified, unequivocally: 'The advice I gave the MTTA was based upon the assumption that the exports were intended for civil application.'

And he went on: 'I can recall setting out the guidelines.' He could also recall 'stressing that it was important for UK companies when seeking to supply machine tools for general engineering purposes to agree a specification with the customer which clarified the peaceful and non-military use to which they would be put'.

This witness statement of Clark's was the engine which drove on the Customs prosecution. In the end, in the hands of Geoffrey Robertson QC, it was to prove its undoing – and a body-blow to the administration his behaviour had temporarily served to protect. This document must have appeared to Customs to be a solid foundation for its case. It was true that Clark was unpredictable and cocksure: he had once scandalised liberal opinion by referring to the Third World as 'Bongo Bongo Land' and kept a dog at his stately home, Saltwood Castle in Kent, which he delighted to tell right-thinking visitors was named 'Eva Braun' after Hitler's mistress.

But it was natural for Customs to assume that the word of a Minister of the Crown was going to be worth infinitely more to a jury than the word of someone like Paul Henderson.

★   ★   ★

BETRAYED

Customs was not confining its pursuit of wrongdoing to Paul Henderson and Matrix Churchill. It was scouring the entire British machine-tool industry for evidence, for all the firms seemed to have made a killing out of Saddam. In April, a fresh wave of arrests was reported of executives from two other big machine-tool companies in the Midlands, Wickman Bennett Ltd and BSA Machines. The charges were similar – export of automatic lathes and grinders to make munitions in Iraq.

But Matrix Churchill was certainly the company most squarely in Customs' sights: the one which had been secretly bankrolled by Iraq itself. A 1987 'management buy-out' had been largely achieved with Iraqi funds, and an Iraqi chairman lived in a £1 million house in Hampstead, directing operations on behalf of Baghdad.

This made the prosecution seem doubly unfair to Paul Henderson. For it was also as a result of Iraqi ownership that he had been re-enlisted as an agent of MI6, the Secret Intelligence Service. He and Mark Gutteridge had both done things for Her Majesty's Government, by way of spying on the Iraqis. They might have been thought to have taken risks with their necks. And they had not been paid.

For the second time, in April 1991, the *Sunday Times* was given and printed a story which fired a shot across the bows of the Matrix Churchill prosecution. Previously, the defendants had been said to be threatening to reveal that Trade Minister Alan Clark had given them a 'nod and a wink'. It was, as MI6 had world-wearily described it, the 'HMG knew' defence.

This time, Customs was facing the prospect of the 'British Intelligence knew' defence. The *Sunday Times* reported: 'MI5 "KNEW OF BRITISH ARMS TRADE WITH IRAQ".' The story said that two of the men facing charges – presumably Henderson and Peter Allen, who had occasionally given 'Balsam' a lift – met regularly with an intelligence agent from MI5.

The businessmen plan to subpoena their intelligence case

officer in their defence . . . One former Matrix Churchill director said: 'He knew what we were doing and it gave him no concern.'

Prominent among the article's details was an account of the entries in the Matrix Churchill factory gate book mentioning the visits of 'Mr Balsam from the DTI'. The story was a little garbled – mixing up MI5 with MI6, for example – but at Century House, MI6 headquarters, it was obvious that somebody was talking seriously out of turn.

This impression increased twelve days later, when one of the phones buzzed at Century House. As MI6 recorded: 'Gutteridge rang his agent telephone number . . . Not knowing his status in the Matrix Churchill case, we briefed the switchboard that neither "Eacott" nor "Michael Ford" was available.' Eventually contact was resumed. Mark Gutteridge told his MI6 officer that 'It would be a good idea to talk through his concerns and what he knew about the *Sunday Times* article'. Gutteridge appeared to be hinting that one of the defence lawyers was becoming aware of his intelligence connections. '528 wanted instruction on what to say if asked directly whether he is in touch with us.'

Customs had not made any attempt to prosecute Gutteridge: in fact, a lengthy statement had been taken with a view to using him as a prosecution witness. Gutteridge dutifully made no mention in his statement of his intelligence connections – and the Customs men in turn had made no mention to Gutteridge that they already knew all about him. They had been shown his file. MI6 now called Customs. They explained that Gutteridge was becoming a little difficult, and something fresh had to be worked out.

On May Day morning, 'Ian Eacott' rang Gutteridge at his office in Coventry: 'It will be possible to arrange a discussion with Customs late this afternoon in London. Can you make that?'

'I'm keen to do it,' replied Gutteridge. 'There shouldn't be a problem about getting away. I can get a train arriving at Euston at 16.30.'

'I'll meet you at the station.'

This exchange was carefully recorded in 'Eacott's' subsequent report. So was the way they had a cup of coffee at Euston; rode south in a taxi to Bouverie Street by the Thames; and were greeted at the Customs reception desk at 17.10 by lawyer Cedric Andrew, without having to breach security by giving names. 'Eacott' seemed in a suspicious frame of mind about Gutteridge, 'Agent 528'.

> I should record that before we started our discussion, he asked to visit the lavatory. It occurs to me that he could have created this opportunity to switch on a tape-recorder in the briefcase he was carrying. Not impossible under the circumstances . . .

But the agent handler then relapsed into a more trusting mode: '. . . Unlikely, and I do not think he sees the situation with regard to ourselves and HM Customs as combative.'

The three men spent an hour together in the bleak office at Harmsworth House. The atmosphere started out stiff and cautious. 'I am choosing my words with care,' said Andrew. Riposted Gutteridge: 'I thought we were all on the same side.'

Afterwards, 'Eacott' had a very long and detailed secret meeting with his boss, describing Gutteridge's approach. According to the MI6 minute, Gutteridge thought that he might be asked in or out of court whether he too had had contact with the intelligence services. His business standing and his safety could be jeopardised. What should he do? 'His repeated theme was that there was bound to be much more publicity of one kind or another about the charges against Matrix Churchill, and it could not be said where all this would lead.'

Andrew told him to give a flat denial unless he was formally interviewed by defence lawyers, as was their right. However, said the Customs lawyer, Gutteridge, who was technically a prosecution witness, need not speak to defence lawyers unless he wished. Andrew also said: 'It would not be possible for the case to be held in camera.' What he did offer, according to the minute, was a more dramatic form of assistance.

There was a method which could be used to stop defence lawyers asking Gutteridge in the witness-box whether he worked for MI6. Customs could go to a Minister – in this case the Foreign Secretary – and obtain a 'Public Interest Immunity Certificate' from him. This document would forbid disclosure of such evidence.

The only source of potential problems did not seem to be getting a signature from the Minister, in Andrew's account, but the judge. The trial judge might refuse to accept the certificate. But then, said Andrew reassuringly, 'in previous cases HM Customs, in order to protect sources, had dropped proceedings altogether'.

The Customs lawyer did his best to field Gutteridge's other fears. The *Sunday Times* piece had been 'just about on limits' because of the *sub judice* rule, he promised. This restricted what the papers could say. But Gutteridge painted a colourful picture of his old friend Paul Henderson as a man at the end of his tether and capable of desperate acts:

Henderson felt very bitter about the whole affair . . . he felt he had been entirely open with the authorities (either to the DTI or indirectly via his 'British Security' contact) and that he was now being pilloried for dubious reasons. Henderson was not an intellectual but a clever man, said 528, who would pull every trick he could to get off the charges against him. He was a broken man and in a state of great agitation and depression. In becoming chairman of Matrix Churchill he had achieved a lifetime's ambition, working up from the bottom, and had now been thrown down to the ground again.

The Customs lawyer responded. The case against Henderson and his colleagues was that, at their January 1988 meeting with Alan Clark, the Minister had given them specific guidelines. Those guidelines had been broken by the export of machine-tools 'specifically designed' to make weapons.

Mark Gutteridge's reaction should have given Customs pause: '528 pointed out that during 1987, he had given his case officer copious material on *certain equipments* being exported.' [author's italics]

If this was a hint, Customs and MI6 apparently failed to pick it up. Nonetheless, such an encounter with an apparently wavering Gutteridge, coupled with the accurate details in the *Sunday Times* piece, could only have made Cedric Andrew and the Customs team uneasy. It did not frighten them off. If MI6 had wanted to avoid all danger of exposure and publicity, they would indeed have tried to stop the case at this point. They were in a position to make the attempt. But there is no evidence that they did so. 'Eacott's' MI6 superior instead wrote an internal memo: 'SIS should note . . . the general tenor of 528's comments about Henderson, but we should not prejudice our collective position by attempting to contact him.'

Perhaps it was thought that Henderson and Gutteridge simply would not dare reveal in public their history as intelligence agents. Such a disclosure risked not being believed. If it were, it might shock their families; alarm their colleagues; damage their future business activities; and worst of all, lay them open to reprisals from the Iraqis. The Iraqis hanged spies.

It began to look to Paul Henderson, however, as though there were no way out of the case. He was going to have to fight it to a finish. Henderson took a deep breath and told his lawyers what had really gone on at the notorious January 1988 meeting between the machine-tool manufacturers with Alan Clark; the meeting which had already caused so much newspaper controversy and so many Ministerial denials.

Matrix Churchill and the other machine-tool firms had obtained contracts from Iraq for machines to make mortars and artillery shells. The Iraqis might well have planned to convert the machines to other peaceful uses in the misty future, but they were in the middle of a war and their orders were for military production-lines. Samples of the shells were machined at Matrix Churchill in the normal way, to show the Iraqis that the machine-tools worked properly with the shell-manufacturing tools and computer programs installed.

The DTI, after issuing export licences for 'general engineering', had rung up to say that they might now be revoked. At the protest meeting with Clark, the Minister, however, had addressed the delegation in an 'arrogant and bombastic manner'.

> He opened the meeting with words which are engraved on my memory. 'Let's not waste time. You know what the machines are used for. We know what the machines are used for . . .'

As was recorded in Henderson's statement to his lawyers, Clark had then gone on to give advice on how to deal with future applications for licences 'which seemed to amount to the creation of a smokescreen'. These were the allegations which Clark himself now so strenuously denied in his statements to the Prime Minister and to Customs.

That was only the first half of Henderson's story. The second was that he and Mark Gutteridge between them had covertly given MI6 many details of Iraq's original purchase of machines for munitions projects in 1987, and thereafter for the Cardoen and ABA projects in 1988 and 1989.

Henderson explained that he had been an intelligence service 'agent' on and off for twenty years. Contact had begun in 1970, when he was export sales manager for Matrix Churchill's predecessor, Coventry Gauge and Tool, travelling all over the Eastern bloc and China. The original man 'from the Ministry of Defence' told him about the Official Secrets Act. 'I was made to say some form of words which I was told bound me to secrecy.' The man gave him a phone number and a contact name in order to pass on information about various 'Sovbloc' individuals and the technology being sold.

Targets, to be observed and if possible compromised, included Poles and Russians at the Trade Delegation in Highgate. Visiting Soviet trade contacts were informed on by Henderson, to be bugged in their hotel rooms. Abroad, Henderson absorbed what he saw in Soviet factories, and passed it on when he got home.

Two officers from MI5 came to the firm to give a standard lecture in the 1970s to a group of staff involved in travelling to the East, about the dangers and perils of compromise and espionage while they were there. Henderson said he had listened in amused silence. By then he was a seasoned agent, who had been spying for years.

The contacts ebbed and flowed as he changed jobs. In the 1980s, for example, a man called 'Richard Stanbury' contacted him when he was selling fork-lift trucks. Stanbury wanted to find Poles and Russians with weaknesses, to compromise or 'turn'. Which of them went to nightclubs? Did they drink? Womanise?

Then, after Mark Gutteridge had moved on from his job at Matrix Churchill as export manager, and Henderson had been installed by the Iraqis as managing director, the phone rang in Coventry. It was 'Balsam' – a fresh-faced and intense Middle East expert. Gutteridge had hinted that his friend and colleague might be hearing from someone after his departure, so Henderson was not particularly surprised.

'Balsam' mentioned a name. When he arrived, he showed a card that said he was from the 'Ministry of Defence'. Henderson had already signed him in at the factory gate as 'Balsam of the DTI'. So that was the cover they used from then on.

The Cold War was petering out, and Henderson was now

part of the new wave of espionage with which MI6 and MI5 hoped to justify their existence – not to the taxpayer, from whom their cost was concealed, but to the Treasury and to 'PSIS', the Permanent Secretaries Committee on the Intelligence Services, which set the budget.

Henderson said 'Balsam' wanted to know about Iraq and the Iraqis. Henderson had told him, in an intensive series of twenty meetings over more than a year. Henderson reeled off dates and locations – the lobby of the Inn on the Park hotel in London; Heathrow airport; his brother's pub, The Malt Shovel, in Warwickshire. He quoted the London telephone number he had been given for emergencies – 499 9155.

Dramatic though these intelligence disclosures to the defence lawyers were, the prospect of them was not enough to frighten off the Customs team. Peter Wiltshire of Customs was a determined investigator: and his friendly co-operation with MI6 was about to pay off. In July, along with a batch of prosecution witness statements, Customs sent the defence an additional letter. It was a pre-emptive strike. 'Please now find enclosed a further witness statement . . . You will appreciate that this is particularly sensitive.' The document had no name at the top. But it began:

> I am an officer of the security and intelligence services. . . . I first saw HENDERSON on 24 April 1989. I told him I was interested in any knowledge of Iraqi procurement of nuclear, biological, chemical and missile technology which he might obtain through his business dealings with the Iraqis . . .

The defence bluff – if it had been a bluff – was called. The Customs team had had a statement from 'Balsam' in their pocket all the time: certainly since the beginning of the year, when they had put together the basic structure of the case. Far from being embarrassed out of the prosecution, they were prepared to call an officer of MI6 as a witness to contradict the defence – something which had never happened before in a British court. And MI6 was prepared – unprecedentedly – to come. Instead of Henderson playing the MI6 card in court, Customs would play it themselves. If Henderson insisted on fighting the case, he would be thoroughly exposed as a spy and a British intelligence stool-pigeon. And it would do him no good.

For, according to the statement, the MI6 officer would testify that he had not met Henderson until after Matrix Churchill had already signed the 'illegal' arms contracts; that Henderson had concealed them; and that MI6 itself was simply another government department deceived by Matrix Churchill and its unscrupulous merchants of death. The statement declared:

> HENDERSON provided a certain amount of useful, though not high-level information . . . and a few technical snippets . . . At no time did he give me any indication of impropriety by Matrix Churchill . . . at no time did Henderson discuss with me the contracts.

At the time of the Customs raid, wrote 'Balsam', 'He made no suggestion that these applications had ever been discussed with me previously.' There were, though, a few apparently inescapable admissions in the three-page statement. It seemed that Henderson had in fact handed over entire drawings, including some of a projectile marked 'ABA' which, he said, the Iraqis had asked Matrix Churchill to manufacture. He had also, without being specific, given information of some kind about the Chilean arms manufacturers Cardoen and their dealings with the Arabs. But all in all, the statement minimised Henderson's intelligence role. In court, such unadorned evidence might leave the Coventry company director looking guiltier than ever.

What saved the Henderson case was the loyalty of his old friend Mark Gutteridge, sales director and secret agent extraordinaire – the man who would spend seven or eight hours at a time being debriefed by his original MI5 case officer; and a spy whom no one would accuse of providing low-quality information. If it was essential in order to save Henderson, said Gutteridge reluctantly, he would also tell all that he knew.

> The only reason I did it was to help a friend who was going to be prosecuted. I didn't want to reveal it. I had to examine my conscience, I must admit. I felt a certain amount of loyalty, to my MI5 case officer and to my country. I'd signed the Official Secrets Act: although I wasn't aware what that meant, legally, I knew not to talk about my work. And I didn't. But there was loyalty to the country on the one hand, and on the other, loyalty to a friend, a friend of 30 years. The prosecution was ridiculous, ludicrous, when the Government already knew.*

Paul Henderson might have known what Trade Minister Alan Clark had really said at the much-disputed January 1988 meeting with the manufacturers, but Gutteridge knew the reason why he had said it. He knew of a layer of duplicity that none of the newspaper articles had even hinted at. He knew exactly why Whitehall had panicked and threatened to revoke the companies' export licences. And he knew exactly what secret service channels had been used to try to persuade them to let sleeping dogs lie. He possessed the classic secrets which unsettle governments – he was aware of what they knew; and when they knew it.

Mark Gutteridge made a 25-page statement to Henderson's solicitors. He could not tell them, because he did not know, that his secret agent number within MI5 was '528'. But he could reveal the cover-names of his eventual MI6 controller, and of his plump original case-officer from MI5, the man the

---

* Interview with author.

defence team referred to from then on, in their own code drawn from the children's story *Thomas the Tank Engine*, as 'The Fat Controller'.

The disclosure of the cover-names 'Ian Eacott' and 'Michael Ford' would reveal to the intelligence services that Gutteridge was really spilling the beans. He hoped that his name would not come out and that his evidence would never have to be used; and he probably assumed – correctly – that he would be unlikely to have to testify in open court. It seemed inconceivable that a trial as explosive as this would be allowed even to begin – let alone run to a finish.

4

REPRESENTED

Geoffrey Robertson QC and the legal team, summer 1992

Henderson gets to the point straight away.
MI6 report, 14 July 1989

It can be hypnotically fascinating to watch one of Paul Henderson's CNC machines – a Computerised Numerically Controlled lathe – in action. Through the safety window, its operator can observe the small block of metal on the rack, clamped tight and revolving. With robot hisses and whirrings, drills and tools protrude in an order determined by the computer program, and advance on the spinning piece of steel. As coolant and lubricant sprays switch on and off automatically, the drills gouge – withdraw – score – withdraw – shape, and grind. The waste metal swarf peels away in bright ribbons. After a few minutes, the piece of steel falls off the spindle and joins its finished companions. It has been shaped into whatever the purchaser asked for in the first place – a pump for a washing-machine; a piece of a car back-axle; or an artillery shell.

BETRAYED

Paul Henderson must have felt like one of his own components. He might have been made of tough material, but a powerful government machine was being programmed to shape and turn him into its own pattern. He was to be moulded into a criminal.

In this situation, a great deal depended on Henderson finding the right kind of lawyers, who would take on HM Customs and its large legal team. His colleagues, Abraham and Allen, employed local Midlands solicitors. Henderson was more decisive: he went to Sheffield. During the Supergun affair, the Sheffield steel firms which had made the gun-barrels, and Christopher Cowley, whose team had assembled them in the Mosul mountains of Iraq, had engaged Kevin Robinson as a solicitor. Although a provincial practice, Robinson's firm in Sheffield, Irwin Mitchell, was large and highly professional.

Robinson had achieved a brilliant result in the Supergun case – the Customs prosecution had been dropped before it had ever came to court. Robinson and his firm understood Iraq; export licences; and the peculiarities of the behaviour of the DTI and its Ministers. They were also familiar with some of the history of intelligence-gathering that had surrounded the Supergun affair. There were practical difficulties in running a case where the solicitors were in the north of England, the client lived in the Midlands and counsel practised in London. But they were overcome. Kevin Robinson was to serve his client formidably well.

One of the most significant questions Robinson had to decide was which team of barristers to field against the Crown in the courtroom. Customs initially – and as early as 1990 – called on Treasury counsel, who are expert prosecutors based at the Old Bailey, to prepare the case. They chose counsel involved in prosecuting Randle and Pottle (the pacifists who helped *KGB* spy George Blake escape) but later in 1991 (perhaps after that case, in which attempts to make use of Public Interest Immunity Certificates had failed), they brought in Alan Moses to lead their team.

He had by this stage earned an impressive reputation, and had become Customs' most sought-after QC. He had had a starred career at the Bar, becoming counsel to the Inland Revenue and succeeding in highly complex tax cases. He had established a very prestigious and lucrative Chancery practice, turning on an ability to play intellectual chess by making fine distinctions even finer.

Now, on the road to becoming a High Court judge, he was the most trusted and successful of prosecutors, thanks to two earlier triumphs. The first was the nuclear triggers case, in which he had put behind bars for five years an 'evil Iraqi' named Daghir. This case attracted extensive and favourable publicity for Customs, beginning as it did shortly after the Gulf War ended. Moses had conducted it brilliantly, and much as a PR exercise, producing bundles of documents for the press, who loved him for it. So had Customs, whose officers often posed for press photographs with a Daghir capacitor on their desks, to remind the world of their greatest recent triumph. This they owed to Alan Moses.

Moses was also responsible for a remarkable prosecution success in the case of 'Preston', in which he convinced the Court of Appeal that telephone tap evidence should not be presented to the defence. Prosecutors like himself could be absolutely trusted to read it and disclose whatever would assist the bugged defendant. It was a devastating precedent for civil liberties and a powerful legal support for secrecy. But Moses was still respected by defence lawyers: he had acted for left-wing solicitor Brian Rose-Smith, who had been cleared of attempting to pervert the course of justice.

Moses carried all before him at the committal proceedings of Matrix Churchill in November 1991. Henderson had to find a QC who would stand up to him, and outgun him. He faced not only Moses, of course, but the government; its Ministers; its senior civil servants; and its two intelligence services. There seemed to be too much at stake for Henderson to be acquitted. Robinson advised him that there were perhaps only two QCs in the country who possessed the courage to take on this weight of opposition – Michael Mansfield and Geoffrey Robertson. Of the two, he marginally preferred Robertson, attracted by his intellectual background.

Geoffrey Robertson QC was a curious choice to defend a Midlands businessman engaged in military trade to Saddam Hussein. At the beginning of 1992, he was representing the families of 'friendly fire' victims, causing an international incident by convincing an inquest jury in Oxford to convict absentee American A10 pilots of 'aerial manslaughter' during the Gulf War. In 1990, as counsel for a Commission of Inquiry on gun-running to the Colombian drug cartels, he had risked his own safety to investigate a ring of mercenaries who had used the Caribbean government of Antigua as a 'front' for arming the drug barons.

Robertson had a close connection with Amnesty International, heading its human rights missions to South Africa and Vietnam, and had been involved with the clandestine support given by some English writers to Vaclav Havel and his Charter 77 dissidents in Czechoslovakia. Robertson had also been Salman Rushdie's lawyer during his time in hiding, successfully defending him from blasphemy charges and leading demands for UN action against Iran.

It was difficult to describe, at first, the prosecution of three directors of Matrix Churchill for arms-related trade with a subsequent enemy, as a human rights case. But Robertson appealed to the defence team as an anti-government foil to Moses. He had come up a harder way, as John Mortimer's junior in the 'political' lifestyle trials of the '70s, acting for publications such as *Oz* and *Gay News*. He had defended *New Statesman* journalist Duncan Campbell, who faced thirty years' imprisonment in the 'ABC' official secrets case; and the group of anarchists led by Ronan Bennett who had been acquitted of planning anti-state crimes in the 'Persons Unknown' case. The failure of these prosecutions had embarrassed the government. Robertson had successfully defended the 'Bradford Twelve', the Bristol rioters and the 'Winchester Three'. In 1991 he had caused headlines when he destroyed the criminal charges levelled against Arthur Scargill over his accounting for donations during the miners' strike; and secured the acquittal of Dessie Ellis, accused of being an IRA bomb-maker, and the first Irishman to be extradited from the Republic.

Many criminal barristers enjoy boasting about their lack of knowledge of the law, but Robertson owed much of his success to his intellectual interests. He was author of legal textbooks on civil liberties and media law. He could also shift from jury advocacy to the quite different task of convincing an appellate court.

Although John Mortimer had described him as 'utterly fearless' and had dedicated a *Rumpole* omnibus to him, Robertson's life and style could not have been more different to those of the fictional fat barrister. He had left his traditional chambers in the Temple to establish a modern office opposite the *Spectator* in Doughty Street; he ran a high-ratings *Hypotheticals* television series in his native Australia; and he was married not to 'She who must be obeyed', but to the sparky feminist novelist, Kathy Lette.

Alan Moses and Geoffrey Robertson were both in their mid-forties: two men at the top, respectively, of the prosecution and defence trees – which they had both climbed in unconventional ways. 'Convention' was represented, in the Rumpolean sense, by the older 'circuit hacks' who were briefed by Henderson's co-defendents, Trevor Abraham and Peter Allen; and by Judge Brian Smedley, a figure of such reliable orthodoxy that he had recently been made visiting judge to the Cyprus British military base area – a sure indication that he was trusted by the political and military establishments.

Smedley, together with Gilbert Gray QC and James Hunt QC, seemed to have come from the forensic world of heavy furniture and 'heavy' crime, their language laden with the traditional bowing and scraping of 'with very great respect' and 'I am much obliged'. The criminal law, for them, appeared to be only a game to catch felons, not a vehicle for exploring the secrets of the state. Moses and Robertson, on the other hand, had no particular inhibition about exposing MI5 and MI6 to the public, criticising Ministers severely, or treating Whitehall security classifications with the contempt they usually deserve.

For Judge Smedley, and for Hunt especially, one had the impression that this was disturbing, almost sacrilegious. Smedley would in the end overrule Ministers' Public Interest Immunity certificates, but only partly, with great reluctance and when presented with no alternative. He seemed genuinely shocked when Moses told him that an MI6 witness would be heard in open court – so much so that he had a special witness-box built to ensure that no part of the MI6 employee could be seen. When Robertson demanded – on what he said were powerful legal grounds - that the special witness-box should be demolished, it was Hunt, rather than Moses for the prosecution, who opposed him.

Hunt must have believed that he was acting in his client's interests. But Robertson was at odds with him. Hunt's approach seemed to be that of the traditional barrister defending a man whom the evidence shows might be guilty of some crime – of which other defendants are more guilty. The approach is to say little, in the hope that the jury will think that there is less evidence against him than there really is.

Robertson's deliberately high-profile and wide-ranging approach was directly opposite. In the courtroom, he was to see no problem in taking the Old Bailey on a magical mystery tour encompassing the technicalities of high-precision machine-tools; the complexities of high-level British foreign policy; and the taboo subject of the internal workings of the intelligence agencies. The others had never practised law like this, and sometimes seemed bewildered. 'The truth will set you free,' Geoffrey Robertson told Henderson at an early stage, and from his obsession with finding it out, it was clear that he believed it.

Henderson's first meeting with his QC was delayed until Robertson returned from Trinidad. There, he had secured the release from Death Row of 112 Muslims who had staged an armed attack on the parliament two years before. They had taken the Prime Minister and Cabinet hostage and had only given up their insurrection in return for a presidential amnesty, which the government refused to honour. To considerable amazement, and to the local government's embarrassment, their appeals were allowed and they were awarded damages of several million dollars for wrongful detention. It was a precedent Paul Henderson might perhaps have hoped one day to follow.

Robertson, assisted by junior counsel Ken McDonald, told Henderson that he had two good defences to the charges.

1 The government was not deceived about the nature of the machine-sales, but connived at selling some arms to Saddam Hussein.
2 The government had full knowledge of the nature of his machine-tool exports anyway, because Henderson had told a government department, MI6.

Robertson also informed the managing director that he was entitled to see all the records of meetings with MI6, to prove the second defence; and such policy documents as mentioned Matrix Churchill, to help support the first.

Working their way through the prosecution papers, the committal documents, the Supergun parliamentary committee's transcripts of evidence about licensing procedures, and all other available sources, solicitor Kevin Robinson and the defence lawyers prepared a detailed 'discovery schedule' which was served on the prosecution and the court on 15 June 1992. Not only did it refer to high-level policy and

Cabinet material. It must have shocked the Secret Intelligence Service, by referring to Mark Gutteridge's case officers by their cover-names ('Ford' and 'Eacott') and demanding details of their numerous meetings with him.

It contained a demand for:

> . . . a report prepared by 'Michael Ford' in 1987/88 and allegedly seen by the then Prime Minister, Margaret Thatcher, detailing, *inter alia*, British machine-tool industry involvement in Iraq and the potential effect on Matrix Churchill of its contracts being frustrated by the revocation of export licences.

This demand (based on Gutteridge's disclosures) was for what turned out to be a devastating MI6 intelligence document – Secret Telegram 894 of 30 November 1987. The demand must have sent a chill not only through MI6, in their tower-block Century House alongside Lambeth North tube station, but also through Ministers. At first, the authorities denied the existence of anything like it. They did not, in the end, disgorge it until the trial was virtually over.

When the trial eventually collapsed, and recriminations were coming thick and fast, the Attorney-General, Sir Nicholas Lyell, wrote a letter to *The Times* on 12 November 1992. He claimed that the existence and nature of the documents in question, i.e. documents covered by the Public Interest Immunity certificates that Ministers signed to try to conceal the truth:

> . . . were declared by the prosecution to the defence in accordance with its duty to disclose unused material. For this purpose, the prosecution had required a trawl of files by all relevant departments to identify potentially disclosable material.

In other words, it was Customs, the prosecution, Whitehall

and the government which had voluntarily joined forces to bring documents to light which might aid the defence and ensure that justice was done: a touching picture of democracy in action.

The facts of the trial proceedings show that this claim by the Attorney-General in support of his beleaguered political colleagues was wholly incorrect. It was the same claim that Alan Moses, acting, he said, for other Whitehall departments involved and not for Customs, implied at the Old Bailey on 30 September:

> Consistent with its duty to disclose unused material, we the prosecution have requested different departments to search for and find certain documents which we, the prosecution, consider may be material . . . I took the view that it was our duty to make requests of those different departments to seach through those files.

Moses took these punctilious steps when he was left with little legal alternative. The documents which won the case were never voluntarily disclosed to the defence at all. They were not mentioned in any of the 2,000 pages of committal exhibits or in any of the 'unused material' that the prosecution was prepared for the defence to inspect. They would never have been produced had not Henderson's lawyers managed to identify them, and to press time and again for their disclosure.

The original defence letter demanded, in addition to the Crown witness statements and the prosecution's 'unused material', all the following documents (the words are those of Judge Brian Smedley):

1 Minutes of the inter-departmental committee which considered the export licence applications.

This was the 'IDC'. It was made up of officials from the Trade

Ministry, the Defence Ministry and the Foreign Office – all of whom had to be consulted before sensitive licences for trade with Iran and Iraq were awarded.

2 Any written communications between named senior officials of the DTI and the FCO regarding the applications.

Tony Steadman of the Export Licensing Unit and his boss Eric Beston were the two chief civil servants in charge at the DTI.

3 Notes or minutes of meetings referred to by Lord Trefgarne or Mr Alan Clark, and any departmental communications including briefing notes coming into existence as a result of those meetings.

This category would include the Whitehall minutes of Alan Clark's notorious meeting with the machine-tool manufacturers – the 'working papers' which Ministers had refused to reveal to Parliament.

4 All notes, minutes or communications prepared by Special Branch officers whose pseudonyms are given, as a result of their meetings with a Mr Mark Gutteridge.

This request was the first indication to MI6 that 'Agent 528' had decided to break his promise of silence.

5 A report allegedly sent to the then Prime Minister from a Mr Ford.

This was the explosive demand that would – after a hard struggle – unearth Telegram 894.

6 All records relating to meetings between the accused Mr Henderson and the Security Services.

At first, the Customs team were not going to engage even in courtesies. They made no reply to Kevin Robinson's letter, despite a reminder. At a 'practice direction' hearing held before Judge Smedley at the end of July, Robertson mentioned the recently-decided appeal of Judith Ward – the supposed IRA bomber who had been wrongfully convicted and was released only after it was disclosed that the prosecution had withheld important documents and witness statements from the defence at the time of her trial. Robertson criticised the prosecution in the present case for 'failing to do its duty'.

Gibson Grenfell, standing in for Moses, said that it was likely that Public Interest Immunity certificates would be issued by Ministers. Robertson declared that he would oppose them. Judge Smedley agreed to hear argument on the subject in September, the week before the trial was scheduled to begin.

In fact, the prosecution replied to the defence request of 15 June for the first time on 10 September – some three months later. They disclosed a handful of documents, and claimed PII for all the rest. So far as the report by 'Michael Ford' was concerned, Gibson Grenfell stated in writing: 'As far as is known, no such report was prepared, or exists.'

One week before the trial was due to begin, the prosecution – or the security services – were still withholding many papers, including Telegram 894, the report which would explode the whole proceedings.

'Bobby Lee Cook here . . . It's Bobby Lee Cook.' A telephone call from the United States to a speck in the middle of the Indian Ocean was always going to be problematic. On Bird Island in the Seychelles, the background screeches of three million fairy terns are exceptionally noisy. But eventually Cook made contact with his man. Bobby Lee Cook, celebrated trial lawyer and a friend and supporter of Bill Clinton, who that August was running hard for the presidency, was returning a call from Henderson's QC, at work on a case in the Seychelles. Geoffrey Robertson and Bobby Lee Cook had certain matters of common interest to talk about.

Faced with a lack of candour and co-operation from Customs, the Henderson team were doing their own research. Robertson had for many years been overseas counsel to the *Wall Street Journal* proprietors, Dow Jones. The defence team were intrigued when he returned from New York in August with a pile of material which had recently been published about 'Iraqgate' and the involvement of Matrix Churchill's US subsidiary (of which Henderson had been a director).

Robertson told them that he was also making applications for CIA material, under the US Freedom of Information Act, and had linked up with researchers on the Gonzalez Congressional banking committee. This was investigating the astonishing story which had first, in 1989, publicly exposed the name of Matrix Churchill and linked it to a secret Iraqi procurement network.

An overseas branch of the Italian State Bank, Banco Nazionale Lavoro (BNL), was operated in Atlanta, Georgia, by a manager called Chris Drogoul. Drogoul was believed to have made more than a billion dollars' worth of covert and unauthorised cheap loans to contacts from Iraq (which the US prosecutors called 'one of the most uncreditworthy countries in the world'). Iraqi intelligence organisations had been using the money to fund a secret international procurement network throughout the West, buying in arms, equipment for armaments factories, components to help build nuclear weapons, and missile technology.

How much did the US government – notorious for its 'tilting' towards Iraq – know of this scandal? And when did they know it? Were they covertly funnelling arms to Iraq to strengthen it against Iran, just as they had covertly funnelled arms to Iran to gain the return of hostages? These questions were what was meant by 'Iraqgate'. The real policy of the United States – as Trade Minister Alan Clark had allegedly all but admitted – was likely to shed a good deal of light on the pressures which pushed British Ministers along in a covert pro-Iraq direction.

Drogoul was eventually betrayed to the FBI – by colleagues who said that they feared he was about to make the international monetary system totter. The US authorities discovered Matrix Churchill on the secret list of Iraqi-controlled procurement companies. They had made the fact public in September 1989, putting Matrix Churchill in the British limelight and increasing the level of subterranean controversy in Whitehall.

In the months before the US presidential election, 'Iraqgate' was a subject of major concern in the US, in a way that the Matrix trial, with its *sub judice* rule, had prevented it from becoming at the UK general election in April 1992. George Bush, at his renomination in August, had relied heavily on his record as 'Commander-in-Chief'. It was a record that would be undermined and besmirched if he were shown to have gone to war to dismantle a machine that the US had helped to build.

Henderson's defence team realised that Gutteridge's evidence might blow a Bush cover-up. Gonzalez had only established so far that the CIA knew about the procurement network in September 1989. There was no doubt that Gutteridge's information would have been shared with the CIA – and it would have been shared with them from 1987 onwards.

Robertson's research in America was concentrated on the prosecution of Christopher Drogoul. It seemed possible he was being made a scapegoat for the way US grain credits were also used to back arms sales to Iraq – some of which were going through Matrix Churchill. Drogoul's BNL had backed the ABA rocket contract which was the subject of a criminal prosecution in Britain: and at one point Henderson had been interviewed as a potential witness.

BETRAYED

The Drogoul prosecution in Atlanta alleged that he had pulled off his coup without any help from the Bush administration. This was difficult to believe. But Drogoul had 'gone quietly' into a White House cover-up, by pleading guilty in response to an offer of a lighter sentence. The press and the Democrats were most unhappy that the pleas would not allow the facts to emerge in Atlanta in the way they might do in London, if Henderson maintained his plea of not guilty.

His Dow Jones colleagues say Robertson approached them that summer to find him Drogoul's lawyer. In August, Drogoul had changed his counsel, to the well-known trial lawyer and Democrat Bobby Lee Cook. Cook's office received a fax from Geoffrey Robertson in Doughty Street on 3 September. It said: 'We have come across material which may assist your client's mitigation, and conversely, you may have evidence which would assist my client's defence.' The letter suggested they co-operate in the task of eliciting the truth. Cook was out of town. Robertson was about to take wing again, for his job in the Seychelles (he was helping opposition parties to draft a model constitution) and then for Malawi, on the east coast of Africa, on a human rights mission. On 5 September, Cook returned Robertson's call, to Bird Island in the Indian Ocean. The lawyers discussed their respective clients – two scapegoats, as it seemed they might be depicted, for the West's blunder in putting its money on Saddam.

Cook found Robertson's suggestion that the American should withdraw his plea in line with his own thinking. Cook asked for evidence from the Henderson defence as it was envisaged for the Old Bailey trial, and used it in a successful attempt the following week to change Drogoul's plea to not guilty.

Once Cook became involved, the US press were tipped off that 'Iraqgate' might emerge at the Old Bailey. The *New York Times* was preparing to send Dean Baquet – one of their best reporters – as soon as anything developed. The British press should have been similarly aware. It was only *Guardian* journalist Richard Norton-Taylor, at the end of the month, who was to discover the astonishing fact that no fewer than four serving Ministers of the Crown were about to sign PII certificates whose effect would be to prevent the truth emerging – the truth that might damage George Bush and John Major, and free Paul Henderson.

5

MINISTERS INTERVENE

Public Interest Immunity certificates, September 1992

If necessary, a 'PII certificate' would be obtained.
MI6 minute, 8 May 1991

Gradually, the legal players returned from their long summer breaks. The judge, Brian Smedley, came back from Kenya on 28 September; and Geoffrey Robertson had returned from Malawi the previous week. He notched up a big public success on 25 September at the Old Bailey, when his client Karanjit Ahluwalia was freed, to much singing and dancing by supporters in front of the court. She had been jailed for life some years before for setting alight the husband who had brutally beaten her throughout their ten-year marriage. Robertson had taken on her case and convinced the Court of Appeal that her first trial had overlooked the 'battered wife syndrome' from which she had been suffering. Now, all the prosecution psychiatrists agreed with him. It was a far cry from post-traumatic stress disorder to the Export of Goods [Control] Order 1989, and legal interpretations of duty concerning Public Interest Immunity certificates.

Judge Smedley was showing signs of unhappiness. He was heard by one barrister to confide to a colleague that he did not enjoy having this case. He was only a circuit judge and he felt that, with its knotty political content, it was more suited to a senior judge from the High Court bench. Perhaps he was aware that he was holding a hot potato.

For Ministers to sign PII certificates, claiming what used to be known as 'Crown Privilege', was controversial even in civil disputes. In criminal cases, where the 'liberty of the subject' was endangered, they were almost unheard of – some said unthinkable. Ministers were perfectly prepared to tell Smedley that lives were at risk, and innocent civilians might be killed by terrorists if he declined to suppress the Matrix Churchill documents. They later promoted the idea that the PII certificates merely offered an invitation to the judge to choose which state documents he regarded as really important, in order to discourage damaging 'fishing expeditions'. The wording of the certificates shows this story was not so.

A Foreign Office Minister signed the main PII certificate which said that it was against the public interest to reveal Foreign Office documents, and also those emanating from MI6. MI6, the Secret Intelligence Service, reports to the Foreign Secretary, Douglas Hurd, through PUSD, the Permanent Under-Secretary's Department in the Foreign Office, and many MI6 officers abroad are attached to embassies under 'diplomatic cover'.

Curiously, the certificate was not signed by Douglas Hurd, chairman of the Cabinet Ministers' meeting which had secretly agreed to relax military sales to Iraq on 19 July 1990, a fortnight before Saddam's army invaded Kuwait. Hurd was said to be 'absent abroad'. It was signed by his junior Minister, Tristan Garel-Jones. Garel-Jones had replaced the gilded Waldegrave, now tasked, ironically, with promoting, among other things, open government. The happy absence of Hurd meant that not a single one of the Ministers formerly involved in the scandal of arms for Iraq could now be found with their fingerprints on the cover-up.

It was said afterwards that the Foreign Office Minister and the others wrote what they did on the advice of the Attorney-General, Sir Nicholas Lyell, and had no option. If that was the case, it was surprising that the Ministers were prepared to put their names to quite differently-worded statements. Garel-Jones's was one of the most extreme.

Civil servants had trawled through the departmental files as demanded, Garel-Jones certified. He recorded that Alan Moses, Customs' counsel, had decided that, under guidelines issued by the Attorney-General, the relevant Whitehall papers would normally be shown to the defence, as they had asked. Garel-Jones asserted: 'I have read all the documents.' The purpose of the certificate, he said, was 'to explain to the Court why, for reasons of public interest, such documents should not be so disclosed.'

The first group of documents ('Category A') was a small and very special collection – only two pieces of paper. The Foreign Office had a letter from an informant, and a departmental memo discussing it. This was 'a confidential informant who is a member of the public and whose personal security and livelihood may be jeopardised if his or her identity is disclosed'. (It later transpired that one of Matrix Churchill's employees had written to the government, tipping them off that the factory was making shells for Iraq. After such a risky move, the 'mole' must have been puzzled at the government's lack of interest.) Informers are protected in criminal cases by well-established law, and the defence did not challenge the Garel-Jones claim:

It is undoubtedly in the public interest that the identity of a person carrying out his duty to inform the author-ities of suspected wrong-doing and thereby jeopardising his livelihood, should as far as possible be kept confi-dential.

MINISTERS INTERVENE

The second group of relevant papers ('Category B') was the Foreign Office's working papers. 'All these documents relate to the formation of the policy of HM Government, in particular with regard to relations with and the export of military and quasi-military equipment to foreign countries.' There were letters between Ministers; memos passing between Ministers and officials; and correspondence officials had had with each other. There were minutes of meetings; and there were records of dealings with the Defence Ministry and the DTI. This was exactly the valuable material the defence had identified after painstaking research. It would, of course, show what government policy about arms for Iraq really was in that period.

'I have formed the opinion,' said Garel-Jones, '[that release of this information] would be injurious to the public interest, and that it is necessary for the proper functioning of the public service that the documents should be withheld from production.' Furthermore, no witness should be allowed to be asked questions about what went on at such meetings.

He went on to rehearse the standard Whitehall line – that British government would collapse if this kind of material was exposed in court.

It would in my view be against the public interest that documents or oral evidence revealing the process of providing for Ministers honest and candid advice on matters of high-level policy should be subject to disclosure or compulsion. Similarly, records of discussions between Ministers within or between departments should not be disclosed.

Whitehall policy on arms for Iraq, explained the Minister, started with 'detailed discussions within and between Government departments'. Then there was: 'consideration of the various possibilities open to Ministers'. Then the officials formulated advice, often in the form of drafts intended for

Ministerial approval. Finally, Ministers, generally from the FCO, the DTI and the MOD, 'decided policy at a high level'. And he quoted – no doubt on government lawyers' instruction – the famous 1968 case of *Conway v Rimmer*. The Law Lords, the nation's supreme court, had there agreed that in civil disputes there was a case for secrecy over such general classes of government documents as Cabinet papers, Lord Reid saying:

> To my mind, the most important reason is that such disclosures would create or fan ill-informed or captious public or political criticism. The business of government is difficult enough as it is, and no government could contemplate with equanimity the inner workings of the government machine being exposed to the gaze of those ready to criticise without adequate knowledge of the background, and perhaps with some axe to grind.

Particularly, Lord Reid might have added twenty-three years later, if the government was up to no good.

Garel-Jones rounded off his argument for suppressing Foreign Office policy documents by saying that those about Matrix Churchill also mentioned other companies seeking licences for arms-related exports to Iraq and Iran – 'secret or highly confidential matters relating to proposed exports of military or quasi-military equipment by companies not in any way associated with the defendants.' He wanted to make it clear that the release of any of the documents would be 'objectionable'; but if the Foreign Office lost this battle, then he asked for only 'strictly relevant' parts to be disclosed, and not those revealing the identity of the other companies.

The Defence Secretary, Malcolm Rifkind, testified in a second certificate that, as far as his own department's paper mountain was concerned: 'I have read all these documents and am satisfied they are of the nature described.' Rifkind, a Scottish QC himself, was content, like a policeman in court backing up the contents of a colleague's notebook, to agree with everything Garel-Jones had said. 'I have formed the opinion that, for the reasons described in Mr Garel-Jones' certificate, with which I agree, and whose arguments I adopt, the production of such documents . . . would be injurious to the public interest.'

Rifkind later told Parliament, in an attempt to defend himself, that he found suggestions that he was among Ministers who had signed certificates to allow innocent men to go to prison – 'deeply offensive, deeply insulting, and entirely without foundation'. He went on: 'There is no way that a Cabinet Minister who has no idea what the defence in a criminal trial might be can come to any judgement as to whether the papers before him are likely to be helpful or harmful to the defence or the prosecution.' This seems a little naïve: Rifkind was a senior lawyer who must have known that it was the defence team who were trying to prise the papers out of Whitehall, and Customs who were going about obtaining the PII certificates to stop them. What did he think the defendants were on trial for?

There was a third certificate about policy documents, from the new Trade and Industry Secretary, Michael Heseltine. Heseltine had not been a member of the Thatcher government at the time of these controversial events – he had resigned some time previously, in a quarrel with Thatcher, ostensibly over whether the firm of Westland Helicopters should link up with American or European partners. He had only returned to office with the ousting of Thatcher, and the succession of John Major. Yet it was the DTI, now Heseltine's department, which was in the firing line over the Matrix Churchill affair, because they, under various Thatcherite Ministers, had issued the apparently-fraudulent export licences. They were the department whose files contained damning evidence of 'dirty washing'. Was any of Thatcher's mud going to stick to Heseltine?

Cynics would say it was no accident that Heseltine's Public

Interest Immunity certificate, as signed by him, was in a very different form to those of the others. The result was that when things went wrong, he was able to defend himself eloquently from a charge of cover-up. He, too, he said, had read all the documents emanating from his department. They fell within *classes of documents* that are *prima facie* immune from production. He had 'been *advised as to past decisions* and accordingly *it is my duty* to assert the public interest grounds why such documents are immune'. For the reasons given by Garel-Jones, there was a public interest that documents should *in principle* be withheld (author's emphases). Heseltine insisted on spelling out that he was *not* trying to engage in a cover-up:

> In making this certificate, I emphasise that my concern is only with the question whether the documents . . . fall within classes of documents which are *prima facie* immune from production. Whether in fact all or part of any individual document or documents should be disclosed is a matter for the Court. I am aware that the Court will consider this claim to immunity at the same time as considering whether in this case and in relation to each document *there is a countervailing public interest that the requirements of doing justice in each case require their disclosure* [author's emphasis]. I recognise . . . that the ultimate judge of where the balance of public interest lies is not the person asserting the immunity, but the Court.

Heseltine said afterwards that the legal advice had been supplied by his fellow-Minister Nicholas Lyell, the Attorney-General: 'The certificate that I was asked to sign did not ask me to become involved in investigating, or even understanding the nature of the prosecution – I was advised it was my duty to sign them, and I did so on that basis . . . On the legal advice available to us, there was no discretion.' He said: 'I did not try to conceal the facts from the court.' However, there was one question which Heseltine dodged afterwards in the

House of Commons. Did he know that Paul Henderson had been supplying intelligence information to the government when he signed the certificate? Rather than answer, Heseltine said it was for a judicial inquiry to find out. 'What I knew, what I should have known, the questions that I asked and the questions I should have asked, are matters which will be properly examined.'

Was it true, that Ministers had no discretion, and were required to sign certificates about such documents, whenever a passing prosecution lawyer demanded? This was a very questionable point. Critics pointed to the way Heseltine himself had insisted on the release of sensitive intelligence documents about the sinking of the Argentinian cruiser *Belgrano*, when he thought it might help to convict Clive Ponting, a civil servant in his department accused of leaking the truth and breaking the Official Secrets Act. Was it true, in fact, that Ministers were even *permitted* to claim PII in a criminal case? To do so meant there was a legal possibility that innocent people would be jailed in order to avoid disruption to the administrative machinery of the state. And, for all Heseltine's words, what he had in fact done was to add his voice, demanding suppression, to those of two other Ministers calling for the concealment of what were, in many cases, identical sets of documents.

The Ministerial certificates about policy documents were clearly designed to conceal knowledge from the defence. But there was a third group of documents about intelligence, listed as 'Category C'. Certificates covering the intelligence material were in a different form altogether. They were written in such extreme terms that it would have taken an exceptionally tough-minded judge not to have been overawed. In tone, they were compilations reminiscent of the more hysterical documents presented by the government to Australian and British courts in the *Spycatcher* case, during the failed attempts to prevent publication of the old MI5 officer's memoirs. The implication was that if Paul Henderson was allowed to see reports of his own meetings with his handler, for example, then intelligence officers would be assassinated, and innocent passers-by would be blown up by terrorist bombs. All this carnage would be attributable to the irresponsibility of Judge Brian Smedley in overturning the certificates.

Kenneth Clarke, the Home Secretary, and a QC himself, signed a certificate to suppress MI5 documents on Tuesday 29 September. The Home Secretary has Ministerial responsibility for MI5, whose main offices are in Curzon Street, near Berkeley Square, and whose new head has been officially revealed by name as Stella Rimington, in a recent move towards *glasnost*. Clarke said: 'The contents and subject matter of the documents are such that their disclosure is likely to prejudice national security.' They would do this, he certified, 'by revealing matters, the knowledge of which would assist those who further wish to injure the security of the United Kingdom, and whose actions in the past have shown that they are willing to kill innocent civilians'.

Tristan Garel-Jones, the Foreign Office Minister, signed a similar certificate to suppress MI6 documents. He said:

> Category C documents include material relating to secret intelligence emanating from the Security and Intelligence Services, primarily relating to Iraq and other Middle Eastern countries . . . Evidence about the identity of members of the Security and Intelligence Services could put their lives at risk.

The Garel-Jones certificate, in its determination to adduce every imaginable reason why the state would totter if intelligence documents were released, read like an old-fashioned *Spycatcher* special. It made some of the very claims that had been disproved and laughed out of court in Sydney. And its vehemence seemed to overlook the fact that it was the Crown which had decided to put an MI6 officer for the first time in the witness box, for purposes of its own.

The very nature of the work . . . requires secrecy if it is to be effective. It has for this reason been the policy of successive governments not to disclose information . . . and neither to confirm nor deny matters relating to their work.

Evidence about identity could 'substantially impair' officers' efficiency. Talking about MI6 could 'substantially impair' its work in protecting the UK and its allies from foreign threats.

The disclosure of any sources of intelligence information . . . the means by which it was gathered (including dates and times) would cause unquantifiable damage . . . in the UK and abroad. Any evidence . . . would tend to reveal aspects of the *modus operandi* of these services.

All this, asserted Garel-Jones, would make MI6 less effective in the future, and less successful at gathering information. 'Human sources' expected confidentiality, and not to have their identities revealed. Otherwise, there was 'a real and serious danger' of information drying up, as well as the prospect of 'grave danger' to informants. Kenneth Clarke repeated all these claims on behalf of MI5, adding that any information at all about things that MI5 did was 'likely to cause serious and unquantifiable damage' to its functions and 'would damage intelligence operations'.

At the Old Bailey on 30 September, there was a distinct edginess in the courtroom. To what extent would the government's certificates overawe the Court? Counsel, solicitors and assorted Customs officials packed the modern, wood-panelled room in preparation for what they knew would be highly charged and politically sensitive pre-trial hearings. The government was going to attempt to suppress evidence about its policy on exports to Iraq.

The court clerk approached the few journalists present –

from the *Guardian*, the *Independent*, the *Financial Times* and Channel 4 News. He advised them that it was not worth their staying. There was only going to be a tedious discussion about what evidence could be admitted during the trial itself. In case distraction failed, however, Customs had brought a legal truncheon in their briefcase. They made an attempt to prevent Parliament and the public – and the jury – from knowing about the government's initiative. Judge Smedley acceded to a demand from Alan Moses, the Customs QC, that a 'contempt order' should be imposed preventing media reports of any of the pre-trial argument until the case was over – reporters cannot afford to stay to cover 'unreportable' copy, and such a 'postponement' in effect means an almost total concealment. Both barrister and judge were unaware that that morning's *Guardian* carried a report already, headlined: 'MINISTERS SEEK GAG ON IRAQ EXPORTS'. Perhaps they studied only *The Times* over breakfast.

Geoffrey Robertson, on Paul Henderson's behalf, protested at the proposed gagging order, signalling a confrontational approach to the case which in the ensuing weeks was sometimes to discomfit not only the judge but the counsel for other defendants as well. The atmosphere was acrid. Robertson said: 'A few mumbled words by my learned friend that we are going to discuss things, and we have a jury coming in on Monday, falls far short of the constitutional principles set out as required . . . Ministers are trying to stop relevant evidence being admitted in the defence of these men.' Moses riposted: 'The Court is seeking to protect the jury from reading, for example, some of the inflammatory and incorrect remarks made by Mr Robertson . . . It is not a question of the government seeking to gag the production of documents. If that were to be reported and a potential juror were to read it, it would be wholly wrong . . .'

Robertson said a 'contempt order' stifling public comment both about the existence of the PII certificates and the legal argument as to their validity flew in the face of 'the fundamental constitutional principle that every court in the land should be open to the subjects of the King'.

Citing the 19th-century political philosopher Jeremy Bentham, he said the principle of open justice was designed to keep the judge under trial, to act as a safeguard against judges who might otherwise be tempted to ally themselves with the interests of the state. The prosecution had given no warning that it would demand a contempt order. It had provided no explanation. In previous cases, judges had ruled that reporting should be banned only when there was a 'substantial risk' to the administration of justice. Here, the substantial risk was simply that of embarrassing Ministers. The 1979 Leveller case had established that whenever there was an attempt to gag the press, the argument should be aired in public to safeguard against arbitrariness and idiosyncrasy. It was not a question at this stage of revealing the substance of the evidence the government did not want disclosed – the defence did not even know the contents of the documents.

On this, Gilbert Gray QC, counsel for Trevor Abraham, agreed. It was outrageous, he said, if the jury could never be told that, in the government's view, there were 'forbidden areas' which the defence was being prevented from exploring. It was an abuse of the judicial process. James Hunt QC, counsel for the third defendant, Peter Allen, joined this alliance.

Judge Smedley was for suppression. 'The jury must start with fresh and open minds,' he said. There should be no risk of their being prejudiced in advance, particularly by reading in the papers 'remarks such as those made by Mr Robertson'. His order was designed to conceal not just from the jury, but from the public, what the government were trying to do.

Richard Norton-Taylor of the *Guardian* had, however, revealed the Ministerial moves in that day's newspaper. He now urged a willing Jonathan Foster of the *Independent* to join him in contesting the contempt order. They contacted their editors who gave the green light. The newspapers' lawyers were approached. But they were informed by Smedley that any challenge to his order would have to be made, not to him, but formally to the High Court. That would have meant delay – and expense – that would have defeated the object.

The *Guardian*'s original report was followed by a short account by Norton-Taylor of the attempt to contest the contempt order published the following day, 1 October. Both these disclosures were seized on by Moses who complained to the judge. Smedley announced that he would refer the reports to the Attorney-General: and he subsequently described them as a 'flagrant breach' of his contempt order. But the Attorney-General, Sir Nicholas Lyell, was eventually to tell the judge that there was no basis for any action to be taken by him. Smedley had not made it clear that the very existence of his contempt order should itself be the subject of a reporting ban.

Alan Moses now rose to his feet, in the absence of the press, to make what was to turn out to be the most controversial claim of the trial:

> I have read these documents. So has my learned junior . . . We do not consider they assist the defence in relation to any foreseeable issue . . . These documents do not assist in any way the defence. And it is for these reasons that your Lordship should not order their disclosure.

He admitted that the files 'touch on the circumstances of the case'. This made them relevant, but not, he claimed, relevant enough. The files certainly did not help show, he said, that the DTI:

> . . . connived at concealment by the defendants of the true purpose for which machines were to be used . . . There is nothing in the documents to suggest that the DTI . . . knew that there had been concealment, or that assurances the machines were for civilian or general use were false.

There is no reason to think Moses' opinion was not genuine, but in the end, these claims were to look like the exact opposite of the truth. To make such statements, he was acting on instructions and he was acting on behalf of Ministers. He did go on to add that he wanted the judge to make the decision after reading the papers himself. But – despite these qualifications – he had made extraordinary claims. They had a public relations virtue: if disclosure were withheld, there was a statement on the record saying that no 'dirty washing' existed in the government's locked closet. Were disclosure to be granted, then the dirty washing would come tumbling out. Moses' statements to the court – like the Attorney-General's letter to *The Times* – were later to seem prime material for close examination by Lord Justice Scott when his inquiry into the affair began.

It turned out that Moses was playing a tactical game. He knew very well that there were questionable items revealed in the documents. But he told the judge he was going to mention them in his opening speech. Therefore, he hoped the judge would consider this was enough of a concession to fair play, and not order disclosure. Moses offered to make the following peculiar, but blandly worded, 'concessions' in his opening speech, in return for the judge agreeing to suppress the documents:

1 The documents do confirm that Government departments and the DTI were aware that, in the past, before 1988, machines had been exported which had in fact been used for military production.

2 The documents disclose discussion of policy as to whether to permit the export of dual-use equipment which might in fact be used for military production.

At its kindest, this was to prove a pair of astonishing under-statements.

BETRAYED

To stake his general claim to a right to PII, Moses took the judge through the well-known civil cases, starting with *Conway v Rimmer*, which showed how, since the overturn of the old concept of 'Crown Privilege', the civil courts had increasingly been prepared to perform a 'balancing act' between the interests of justice, on the one hand, and the legitimate interests of Whitehall secrecy on the other. But this was not the issue. Should such a notion be allowed any place in a criminal trial? It had never happened in a clear case before. Moses produced three cases in which criminal questions were involved, and claimed that PII could indeed be used to withhold evidence in a criminal trial. He urged the judge to accept the certificates, and the invitation, spelled out by Michael Heseltine and implicit in the other certificates, to look at the documents and decide personally which had enough importance to be released.

Moses said that there was no difference between civil and criminal trials. The Appeal Court had considered it that very year, 1992, in the Lorrain Osman extradition case. There, Lord Justice Mann had said:

> The seminal cases in regard to public immunity do not refer to criminal proceedings, but the principles are expressed in general terms. Asking myself why those general exposi-tions should not apply to criminal proceedings, I can see no answer but that they do . . . I acknowledge that the application of the public immunity doctrine in criminal proceedings will involve a different balancing act.

Mann made it clear that, in a criminal case, he thought a judge ought to tip over a long way towards disclosure: 'Where the interests of justice arise in a criminal case, touching and concerning liberty or conceivably on occasion life, the weight to be attached to the interests of justice is plainly very great indeed.' Why were there so few criminal cases where the issue had come up? Mann said he assumed either that prosecutions had been dropped in the past, rather than risk exposing material, 'or it may be that the force of the balance is recognised by prosecuting authorities, and the immunity is never claimed'.

Moses certainly wanted to claim it now. He went on to quote the Appeal Court in the recent Judith Ward miscarriage of justice case. The case, in which the prosecution stood accused of withholding vital evidence, was, in fact, powerful support for full disclosure. The reverberations of the Judith Ward case had forced Moses to order the 'trawl' for departmental documents in the first place. But there, Lord Justice Glidewell had said: 'The common law has always recognised that the public interest might require relevant evidence to be withheld from the defendant. Obvious examples are evidence dealing with national security, or disclosing the identity of an informant . . . The ultimate decision as to whether evidence which was otherwise disclosable should be withheld from disclosure on grounds of public interest immunity was one to be made by the Court.' Naturally, said Moses, the judge should consider the much greater risk of damage to the public interest if intelligence documents came out. This meant that the burden on the defence of proving 'relevance' ought to be much higher.

PII was a duty on certain 'classes' of material, such as advice to Ministers. Ministers had to claim it: 'Even Mr Robertson might begin to understand that it is because of the Law . . . and not because the DTI do not want Mr Robertson or his client to see those particular documents.' Robertson rose far enough to the bait to interject: 'If my learned friend is going to make offensive remarks like that, I should make it clear that I am suggesting it is not the Law at all. It is he who has misadvised the Minister as to what the Law is.'

Robertson attacked the whole notion that Ministers could claim the right to keep evidence secret in a criminal trial. 'One of the mistakes my learned friend has made is in advising these Ministers that they have a duty to claim PII. It is simply not so.' Robertson's challenge was of vital constitutional significance. Lord Kilmuir, then Lord Chancellor, had said in 1956 that

'Crown Privilege' would not be claimed in criminal cases. Had the constitution changed?

There was another large problem. How on earth would a trial judge know how relevant the documents were to the defence? In a civil case, both sides laid out in their 'pleadings' what their case was. In a criminal case, the balance was very different. In the interests of protecting individuals who were at risk of going to jail, the Crown had to disclose its case in advance. They had to serve the evidence on which they wished to rely; and any other relevant information in their possession. But the defence were not under any such duty. Apart from a few 'ambushes', which were outlawed – such as sudden alibis and expert witnesses – the defence could keep its cards close to its chest until the prosecution had laid out its case. So how could the judge rule in advance on what was important?

Robertson did not want the judge to read the documents and decide what evidence the defence should and should not be allowed to have. 'It's a meaningless exercise,' he said. How could the judge know what case the defence counsel were planning to make? 'You have no idea what the defence case is.' The only way would be if Robertson disclosed to him the nature of Henderson's defence. He did not particularly mind revealing the 'HMG knew' defence – it was obvious. But the second leg – that Mark Gutteridge was prepared to come and testify for his friend – needed to be a surprise. Moses was saying that if the defence wanted the documents, the defence must disclose its case. To be forced to do so was, maintained Robertson, a back-door way of attacking the 'right to silence'. What, too, if the judge looked at the documents and decided that they were useless to the defence – when they might be fabricated or full of lies – and the defence could prove it, given the chance?

'Balancing exercises' had no place in a criminal trial, he said. The only true principle at work should be that the prosecution had a duty to disclose all information in their possession to the defence, whether it was part of their case or not.

His fellow-defender, Gilbert Gray, QC for Trevor Abraham, also spoke, but did not support Robertson's arguments from principle. He would be content, he said, to accept Moses' proposal that the judge should read the documents. Judge Smedley found the invitation to do so irresistible. The words of Lord Justice Mann he found 'highly persuasive'; the remarks of Lord Justice Glidewell he considered binding and clear.

The claims made are proper claims to be made in a criminal trial . . . I would not myself consider the right not to disclose a defendant's case as an extension of the right to silence. Indeed, it seems to me that where a defendant seeks to challenge a PII certificate, it is incumbent on him to show the court why the documents which are sought to be disclosed are relevant to the case which he wishes to present . . . I have to perform, however difficult it may be, the balancing exercise.

The documents in question were solemnly brought to the judge's room. There were three fat folders of Iraq policy documents from the DTI, the Defence Ministry and the Foreign Office. The sections that officials considered 'relevant' – not the embarrassing lists of other companies which had applied for or received military export licences – were highlighted in yellow. The departmental papers mentioning intelligence, along with the MI6 documents from the Century House tower block in Lambeth and the MI5 papers from the secret Registry in Curzon Street, were delivered to the judge's room in safes, under guard. And a guard remained outside while he studied them over the weekend. Those papers too had allegedly relevant passages, highlighted in green for the judge to see. The 'sealed containers' – as Smedley portentously described them in his judgment – were an example of the mystique around intelligence and Whitehall policy-making.

*　　*　　*

Robertson and Gray won half a victory. Smedley came back from his lengthy reading session and said that he would permit them to see all the 'Category B' documents, including the alleged 'irrelevancies' discussing other British companies and their military exports:

> I am invited to restrict disclosure to those passages marked in yellow, which are said to be the only ones relevant to the present case. I am not prepared to do so . . . the policy of the DTI is said to be central to the defence case. Mr Robertson argues the granting or refusal of licences to other companies may reveal what he calls the 'true policy'. Mr Gray says 'The formation of the policy, its variation, implementation, and countless departures from it' are crucial to his defence. I can well understand that argument . . . It may be unfortunate that the commercial interests of others may in the result be made public. That cannot outweigh the disadvantage to the accused of being prevented from a full explanation of what the policy was.'

Smedley had been given the prosecution side's opening statement to the jury, written out in advance by Moses. And there were some lines of defence which had emerged already, and which he said he had taken into account, or perhaps guessed at, in coming to his overall decision. 'Henderson's case is that although the terms in which export licence applications were made might have been misleading to the casual reader, that was done with the complicity of the DTI for policy purposes.' Counsel might well want to cross-examine Ministers and officials to say that their assertions about DTI policy were false: 'To prevent access to those documents may well result in a miscarriage of justice in an important criminal case.'

This was a strong ruling. On the relatively unimportant 'Category A' documents – the letter from an informant and a memo about it – Smedley was unopposed: 'This class of document has long been protected from disclosure save in the most exceptional circumstances, and having read both of them I am quite satisfied there is nothing in them which would assist the defendants in this case. I shall uphold the claim to Public Interest Immunity.'

But then he turned to 'Category C'. On every single one of the 'Category C' documents, his ruling was disastrous to the defence. He seemed indeed overawed by the certificates of Kenneth Clarke and Tristan Garel-Jones, with their talk of the deaths of innocent civilians. 'The court is not really in a position to weigh the effect of disclosure . . . The Home Secretary and the Foreign Secretary can be the only judges. I have therefore read their certificates with added care. They present powerful and weighty arguments . . .' Smedley had in effect ruled that Ministers could be judges in their own cause, if they invoked the magic phrase 'national security'. What he said destroyed the claim the Attorney-General and Ministers were later to make – that they had encouraged the Old Bailey judge to decide what should and should not be disclosed.

Smedley said he might still be prepared to order disclosure if there was clear material to assist the defence. But he did not see how it would. 'Balsam', the MI6 officer was going to testify about meetings he had had with Henderson, and would refresh his memory by looking at his records. But this did not mean that Henderson could be allowed to see the records himself. 'If Mr Henderson wishes to give evidence about those meetings, then he can do so. The evidence may be unchallenged. If there is any advantage to him in seeing these records, which I doubt, it does not outweigh the objections put forward in the certificate.'

The request for intelligence records relating to Gutteridge was dismissed abruptly as – on the available evidence – a 'fishing expedition'. Gutteridge, said the judge, seemed to be somebody who had given a prosecution statement to Customs, but now was not going to be called by them as a witness.

No reason has been advanced to explain the relevance of any such information to any issue likely to arise in the case . . . no other reason has been put forward to justify the disclosure of this highly-sensitive documentation, and I can see no way in which preventing its disclosure could have any adverse effect on the fairness of the trial. So I am not prepared to override the certificate.

This ruling was heard with gloom by Henderson's defence. James Hunt, QC for the defence of Peter Allen, and Allen's solicitor subsequently wrote a letter to *The Times*, on 13 November, supporting Conservative Ministers and claiming that the judge had ordered complete disclosure.

The plain fact of the matter is that counsel for the Crown said at the outset . . . that disclosure was a matter for the trial judge . . . PII cannot be waived by either the prosecution or Ministers . . . There was no question of anyone attempting to suppress evidence. In the event, the judge decided in favour of disclosure, and the documents were immediately produced.

After *The Times* letter was published, a beleaguered Michael Heseltine told the Commons: 'I want to express my gratitude to Mr James Hunt QC.'

The Henderson defence were a very long way indeed from having got the documents they considered necessary; after battles, they were to get many more, but there were some documents they only extracted halfway through the trial, when it was already too late to use them in cross-examination. There were others, pursuing the trail of deception up to the level of the Cabinet and the office of the Prime Minister herself, that the judge simply refused to have disclosed.

After scouring the bundles of policy documents through Tuesday 6 October, the defence realised that there were many referred to in the existing texts which had simply not been supplied. The following morning, they presented a request for more than thirty missing documents. These included letters between Ministers; a military intelligence report on the growth of the Iraqi arms industry; and Joint Intelligence Committee, Cabinet Office, Prime Ministerial and Cabinet Committee minutes which would reveal how complicit Margaret Thatcher herself might have been in decisions to help arm the 'Butcher of Baghdad' right up until the day he invaded Kuwait.

By the end of the week, Henderson's solicitors wrote to Customs, complaining that, on the eve of the trial, they had still had no reply. On the basis of what they had read of the available policy documents, they protested at the planned opening prosecution speech, which Alan Moses had provided in advance:

> We must say, having now had the opportunity to examine the 'Class B' documentation in detail, we are astonished that any prosecution could present this case to a jury on the basis that the original prosecution opening painted a truthful picture of the decision-making process in respect of the licence applications.

It was only two days after the trial actually began, on 14 October, that some of the 'weeded' files were supplied. The Cabinet-level material was never handed over.

The biggest decision of the Henderson team was whether to admit defeat on the 'Category C' intelligence documents. Many barristers, registering the judge's hostile attitude and reflecting that no one in forensic history had ever succeeded in having MI6 intelligence reports turned into courtroom exhibits, would have given up at this point. Geoffrey Robertson would not.

Judge Smedley had committed himself to saying that he would order disclosure 'if there is in those documents material which would assist the defence in putting forward its case'. The Henderson team decided to call the judge's bluff, by taking a considerable gamble. On the Wednesday, 7 October, Robertson told Smedley that he was being forced – unprecedentedly – to disclose the hitherto hidden part of the defence case, so that the judge would see he had no option but to release the papers. Robertson revealed that Mark Gutteridge was going to be called for the defence, not the prosecution. He would say that Paul Henderson, his colleague, knew all about his spying activities for MI5 and MI6.

This was to be the essence of the 'MI6 knew' defence. Henderson was aware in all he did that Gutteridge was secretly passing on to government departments every detail of the early history of the company and its dealings with Iraq. Gutteridge was Matrix Churchill's export manager in 1987 and 1988, and knew everything about the signing of the original arms-related contracts. After he left Matrix Churchill, it was Henderson who had taken over his 'reporting' role to the intelligence services. Far from deceiving the government, Matrix Churchill had been playing an intelligence role throughout.

If the documents supported Gutteridge's claims that he had reported on the arms contracts from the beginning, and so long as Gutteridge was prepared to testify in support of Paul Henderson's claims that there was an arrangement between the two men, then there was a new and excellent defence to the charges.

Had it ever come to trial in the witness-box, this defence might have involved some strenuous cross-examination of Gutteridge. When MI5 originally approached the company, before Henderson's time, their request to recruit Matrix Churchill's export manager for 'Sovbloc' spying had been turned down. They had subsequently recruited him, as Gutteridge put it, 'through the back door'. According to MI5, Gutteridge had often said during his spying days that it was quite important no one at Matrix Churchill found out just what he was doing with respect, at any rate, to Iraq.

MINISTERS INTERVENE

This was a defence which clearly entitled – or so Robertson thought – defence lawyers to see the intelligence records. On 7 October, he told the judge that Henderson's denial that he had had any intention to deceive the government was supported by evidence that:

> the security and intelligence services were supplied by Paul Henderson himself, and (to Henderson's knowledge) by Mark Gutteridge, with detailed information about Matrix Churchill dealings with Iraq, including details of the true nature of the Cardoen and ABA contracts.

Robertson continued:

> Paul Henderson believed that the information he and Gutteridge were supplying to the intelligence services was being transmitted to the DTI and to Ministers. This belief was based on information given to him by the security services and by Mark Gutteridge. He had a number of conversations with his main security service contact relating to the export licences, and [Henderson's contact] purported to assist him in speeding up their issue.

Henderson had provided his contact 'not only with oral information about the Cardoen and ABA contracts, but even with drawings of a section which is of particular interest to the prosecution'. Ministers were under a legal and moral obligation to disclose intelligence records relating to Henderson and Gutteridge, Robertson insisted.

> The legal obligation arises from their relevance to a criminal prosecution; the moral duty arises from the fact that Henderson was prevailed upon, despite the risk to his life and his job, to provide detailed information about the activities of senior Iraqi intelligence officers and about the company which employed him in a position of trust. He

cannot now be denied the evidence, arising from his loyal work for the Crown, which is necessary for his defence to a serious criminal charge.

The pre-trial argument over the intelligence documents had led to the first open division in the defence camp. Apparently accepting the view that intelligence documents should be withheld, Gilbert Gray quoted Churchill's dictum: 'Truth is sometimes so precious it needs a bodyguard of lies.' This remark of the wartime Prime Minister was in fact a justification of Second World War propaganda and deception to conceal matters like the location of the D-Day invasion of France. The guarded truths of modern Whitehall intelligence work were to turn out in the end to be far from Churchillian in their import.

However, prosecution counsel was Robertson's real opponent: and he made a historic surrender. Alan Moses told the judge: 'We can well see . . . how the balance tips clearly in favour of the defence seeing the records of those meetings.' His concession was decisive. Judge Smedley took it on board: 'It seems to me now that these accused, contrary to what I said yesterday . . . could not be fairly tried if I were to uphold the class objection to the documents . . . I shall order their disclosure.' He insisted that the MI5 and MI6 files should be heavily edited, so that only the green-marker references of absolutely direct relevance remained. Both Smedley and Moses for Customs had seen the unedited files. The defence would see only a heavily blacked-out 'redacted' version. Smedley said he was satisfied this could be done in a way which would not produce a meaningless result. How much of a farce that made some of the documents, the defence was yet to discover: some were merely sheet after sheet of blacked-out paper. And Robertson was yet to find out through detective work that the files had been mysteriously 'weeded' of Telegram 894.

Nonetheless, at 4 p.m. on Thursday 8 October, four days

after Smedley's initial refusal, and with only Friday and the weekend before the trial was due to open before a jury, the file of 'Category C' intelligence documents was solemnly handed over at the Old Bailey to Geoffrey Robertson and his team. In a nation as obsessed with secrecy as Britain, the event was a landmark. It was typical of Britain that, however, because of Smedley's order under the Contempt of Court Act, the press were then forbidden publicly to reveal the news. The prosecution surrender at least improved relationships thereafter between the duelling QCs. 'My learned friend, who is *almost* always fair . . .' was Roberton's concession to Moses on the day of the hand-over.

The secret service and Whitehall papers, in the grey files that came to be known as the 'defence bundle', were from now on going to dominate the process of the trial. They ended up being referred to far more often by judge and counsel than the piles of technical drawings amassed by the prosecution to help prove a much more narrow case. Those secret intelligence records might show that Paul Henderson and his colleagues were innocent. They would, without a shadow of a doubt, prove that the government was guilty.

6

PROSECUTED

Alan Moses QC opens the trial, 12 October 1992

The businessman believes ABA to involve artillery rockets.
MI6 telegram, 5 March 1990

The team worked all weekend. Pete Weatherby, Ken McDonald's pupil, stayed up until 3 a.m., photocopying thousands of pages of duplicates. He and the Doughty Street clerks were eventually to arrive like a line of native bearers in court in the morning, with the twenty grey files. Because solicitor Kevin Robinson's office was in Sheffield, all the typing, copying and preparation had to be done in the barrister's chambers. As a rule, chambers would turn up their noses at such a novelty; fortunately, Doughty Street was 'progressive', and Robertson its head of chambers, so he was able to do the job – but not, however, under archaic legal aid rules, get paid for it. (Barristers receive fees, not expenses.) The nerve centre of the defence became, for six weeks, the conference room and clerk's room at Doughty Street.

The chaotic pile of documents from five different government departments eventually became 427 pages – as long as the thickest of spy sagas on an airport bookstall, and at first sight, much less fun to read. The files were liberally stamped with the Whitehall security classifications that limited who could see them and how carefully they had to be locked up: RESTRICTED, COMMERCIAL IN CONFIDENCE, CONFIDENTIAL, SECRET, SECRET AND PERSONAL, SECRET UK EYES ALPHA.

Into the defence bundle also went some documents which Kevin Robinson had found in his trawl through available ECGD files, documents obtained from the Gonzalez committee in the US, and a collection of press articles which had triggered particular action. For the first time, it might be possible to find out what had really happened, as it happened.

Although the contents of this bundle were explosive, there was no certainty that all the documents would be accepted in evidence. The rules of evidence meant that each document on which the defence wished to rely had to be 'identified' by a witness and read to the court. The press, including the US reporters in the gallery, were not to be allowed copies, but had to make the best they could of the documents as read by counsel.

Robertson and the defence team were still sitting up at night sorting out the chronology and seeking to make sense of it as the trial itself began. Their learning-curve about Whitehall intrigue was steep, but civil service witnesses were being cross-examined as further documents were still being obtained.

This was not the ideal way to conduct a trial. Why did the defence team not seek an adjournment for a few weeks? The reason was probably tactical. The prosecution were off-balance: if the defence were having trouble sorting and digesting the new documents, then the problem must have been even greater for Customs. Moses was now aware what the 'MI6 knew' line of defence would be – an adjournment would give him the opportunity to devise a way to discredit it, and for prosecution witnesses to rehearse their thinking. Every legal instinct must have told Robertson to press home his advantage, insist on a Monday start and not allow the trial to go off the boil.

There was perhaps another, unspoken, impulse as well. Probably no one in Whitehall had expected the judge to hand over intelligence documents. Robertson's coup in forcing the judge's hand by disclosing Gutteridge's intention to testify for the defence had been sudden. The defence had only received the secret papers the weekend before the trial was due to commence. Once a round of anxious Whitehall meetings began on the Monday morning, there was bound to be pressure to reconsider the whole prosecution. Did Henderson want the case to be hastily dropped, Supergun style, by an embarrassed government? It might be better to see one's position vindicated than merely swept under the carpet.

As Robertson insisted, the trial began on time, on 12 October, with the swearing-in of the jury in Court 16 on the first floor of the Old Bailey.

The ushers brought a large jury-panel into court, of people who had presumably been 'vetted' for their loyalty, under guidelines the Attorney-General uses for cases such as these. These twelve men and women would hear MI5 and MI6 evidence and pore over the most secret of documents. The state would have the advantage of checking MI5 files on them to see whether any were known to harbour 'subversive' ideas.

Most of the subversive ideas harboured by jurors that morning were about their holidays or their jobs. As their names were called, quite a few approached the judge to be excused on those grounds. He had told them that the trial ought to last ten weeks, or even until Christmas, and there were many excuses offered to escape what they could not have realised would be a shorter and interesting – if not historic – experience.

Should the jury be asked about their background? There was some discussion by counsel. Robertson did not want civil servants who might feel obliged to support stories told by their senior officials. Gilbert Gray evinced a wish to avoid 'long-haired left-wing hippy pacifists' who would be opposed to the arms trade: Robertson, perhaps aware of the impact of the secret documents, said he did not mind such people. Gray and Hunt suggested that the jury should be asked whether they were of Iraqi or Iranian descent. Robertson was concerned that people with relatives in Israel might be prejudiced against men involved in the arms trade with Iraq. And Moses accepted that there would be problems for jurors whose relatives had fought in the Gulf War. Judge Smedley was reluctant to limit the jury panel in all these ways:

> If any of you are employed by the Ministry of Defence, the Department of Trade and Industry, the Foreign and Commonwealth Office, or indeed any of the security services, let me know immediately, before going to the jury box.

As soon as the jurors were sworn, the judge told them that the trial was likely to provoke considerable political interest and press comment. He told them to ignore press reports on the case. If they saw a headline relating to the trial, they should ignore it. He reminded them to avoid discussing the trial with their family and friends. Only what they heard in the courtroom was relevant.

In fact, there were fewer journalists present than Whitehall might have feared. BBC Television and *The Times* managed not to cover the case at all until it was over. The Press Association, whose reports used to be the backbone of newspaper coverage, were providing a shrinking courts service – which did not include daily reports on Matrix Churchill. From the *New York Times*, Pulitzer Prize-winning reporter Dean Baquet was refused entry to the Old Bailey because he did not possess a British press pass. He had to sit in the public gallery, from which he filed a front-page piece about the revelations in Britain's 'little-noticed trial'.

Alan Moses delivered his printed opening speech for the prosecution exactly as he had promised. The newly sworn-in jury paid attention to the case which Customs hoped to prove. His speech was long, thorough and dull. Moses gave no hint of the trial dramas to come, and read word-for-word from the unchanged agreed text, despite the protests of Henderson's solicitors that the prosecution script bore little relation to the world suddenly disclosed in the secret Whitehall documents.

Matrix Churchill machines had physically left the country in 1989 and 1990, he said, equipped with special tools and computer programs. They had been shipped to Iraq under two contracts – 'Cardoen', via a Chilean firm, was for machines to make parts of fuses for mortars, rockets and shells; and 'ABA' was a deal to make parts of a missile. Machines for both went to the Nassr organisation in Baghdad. The three men in the dock knew the contracts were military, but they had deceived the DTI: to get export licences, they had pretended they were for 'general engineering' or for 'dual-use' (civilian or military, depending on the customer's preference).

He was going to prove three points, Moses said:

1. The machines needed export licences, because they were 'specially designed' to make military items: licences which would not have been granted.

2. The three defendants did indeed export them.

3. The three 'fraudulently evaded' the requirements by deceiving the DTI, because the contracts were worth a lot of money.

The only real issue in the trial was going to be whether the government knew what was going on. No one was to dispute that the machines were intended for making munitions, or that the three had been involved in exporting them. There was to be only one other, secondary, issue – were the machines really 'specially designed', and would they really have been banned from export under the Geoffrey Howe guidelines? But Moses was required to lay out his whole case.

Paul Henderson had flown to Miami in 1988 and signed £6.5 million contracts with Cardoen representatives from Chile for eighty machines to equip an Iraqi fuse factory. The prosecutor took the jury through the contracts, labelled 'Fuse Project', showing how the purchase started with a set of drawings from the customer. These showed what they wanted the machines to manufacture – M904 and M905 fuses. Matrix Churchill had to produce finished samples of shell and mortar fuses to demonstrate that the machines would do what they were supposed to; they had to demonstrate the fuses could be produced at the agreed rate; and they had to train Iraqi engineers to carry out the fuse-making operations. They had to devise a factory lay-out for the fuse production-line. The drawings had not been in evidence at the Coventry premises, but Customs had retrieved them from Matrix Churchill's sub-contractors.

Moses flourished a telex dated January 1989, in which Abraham told its sub-contractors that the fuse items to be produced were 'parts for inclusion in measuring instruments'. This was, Moses asserted, so the DTI would not find out the truth. He told the company's credit brokers the parts were 'general measuring instruments', so that the government's Export Credits Guarantee Department (ECGD) would not find out. And he used the same 'positive misdescription' to obtain clearance for sub-contract machines from Japan. Sometimes they said the Iraqi end-user was the Fao establishment; or the State Electrical establishment. There was clear deception of the Japanese authorities. One letter used the damning handwritten phrase: 'Nothing military to be stated'.

Henderson was shown writing to DTI Minister Lord Trefgarne in August 1989, complaining of his failure so far to receive export licences – for Cardoen, among other contracts – and arranging a meeting with him in September. He talked to Trefgarne misleadingly, about dual-use machines. Later he talked about 'general engineering principally for the production of automotive components'. Moses concluded: 'The pressure and the deception succeeded, and on November 2nd 1989, the outstanding licences . . . were granted.'

The prosecution originally prepared evidence to show the jury how identical M904 and M905 fuses had been brought back by the British military, removed from Iraqi bombs captured in the Gulf during Operation 'Desert Storm'. The evidence may have been prejudicial and/or inadmissible, for it was never used. But it would have been a telling point. 'Our boys' faced British-made bombs. Whose fault was that to turn out to be?

As the court rose for lunch, there came the first drama of the trial. One juror was heard speaking anxiously to the usher about his strong feelings and his concern about whether he could fairly try the case. When the court reconvened, the juror was sent for. He explained that he was a Jew, with close connections to Israel, and he could not put his personal prejudices aside. The juror was excused, with gratitude for his honesty: leaving the court with the uncomfortable suspicion that perhaps there was something to be said, after all, for American-style questioning of jurors in cases with strong political overtones. Another juror was sworn in, and the rest of the panel had to endure Moses rereading his original speech for a full hour, before he reached a machine-tool contract which was novel.

The second £9 million contract, Moses said, was for the ABA missile. The contract, of August 1988, again commenced with drawings and lists of the missile parts to be produced. Special drills had to be installed on the machines to make parts such as a fin-carrier. The firm applied for licences for the 'production of metal components'. They went through in February 1989.

In April 1990, some of the licences had lapsed after twelve months and needed to be reapplied for. This was in the weeks following the discovery of the Supergun. Lord Trefgarne again met Henderson and other members of the MTTA: 'It was not suggested or disclosed,' Moses contended, that Henderson's applications covered equipment 'specially designed for military use.' Moses concluded: 'On 1st August 1990 Henderson heard that licences were to be granted for the outstanding machines. Again, the false details given . . . had proved successful.' The next day, Saddam Hussein invaded Kuwait.

To the irritation of Henderson, listening in the dock, Moses kept repeating the terms 'specially designed' and 'dedicated'. These were technically inaccurate – Henderson's machines could be converted to make other items than fuses at a future date, unlike some machine-tools, which would be sold with 'dedicated' multi-spindles capable of producing only one thing at a high rate. But Moses' tactic was to impress on the jury that these were machines intended from the outset to make munitions. And that was true.

'The pretence that these machines were "dual-use" lies at the heart of the deception,' Moses said. Henderson had at the time assured the Department of Trade and Industry that the machines were for civilian use. Although the DTI, in Moses' version, 'suspected' the machines might be diverted to military purposes in Iraq, because they were 'dual use' they swallowed Henderson's assurances that they were for 'general engineering' and gave him licences.

Henderson had not given 'proper and honest' information, said Moses, but 'dishonest information designed to get round the system . . . The system depends upon truthful information being given by an exporter.' If he had told the DTI that the machines were for military use, applications would have been considered under the DTI's Military List, rather than its Industrial List, and treated differently.

An exporter, if he wants to get round the system but knows that the equipment he wants to export is specially designed for military use, has a powerful incentive to conceal that fact and suggest it is for civilian use . . . Thus export was considered on a wholly false basis.

Moses then proceeded to tackle some of the 'dirty washing' – not that he disclosed this telling phrase of his governmental clients. He knew what was in the documents. He knew the defence was certainly going to allege that machine-tools originally went for military purposes to Iraq in 1987 and 1988 with government connivance. The defendants had promised to use this tactic in the *Sunday Times* article in which Trade Minister Alan Clark had been subject to, in his words, 'highly defamatory' accusations. So it was necessary for Moses, like all prosecutors, to get his retaliation in first.

Moses did admit that an earlier batch of Matrix Churchill machines – which was not the subject of charges – might have gone to Iraq for arms production. The DTI and other government departments had come to believe that these dual-use machines had been used for military purposes *after* export. But the DTI had awarded the licences in the first place because 'they were assured the contracts were for civil use'. Because of those assurances: 'The DTI was never given proper information as to the machines with their associated tools . . . and software, they were never even given the opportunity to consider them under the Military List.'

Moses was asking the jury, who must have been puzzled by this lengthy and apparently pointless digression, to believe that the DTI had been naïve. None of its officials had grasped at the time that they had been made fools of, and even when they discovered the machines were being used for military purposes, they had concluded that the Iraqis had converted to military purposes some general-purpose dual-use machines exported in good faith. The DTI had apparently made this unhappy discovery only after the machines had arrived in Iraq.

Such an approach enabled Moses to offer an explanation of the infamous January 1988 meeting with Alan Clark:

> Exporters were concerned that export of dual-use equipment might be prohibited . . . that its members would be prevented from exporting machines for *general engineering purposes* [my emphasis].

And so, continued Moses smoothly:

> It was realised that machinery could be used for military purposes by a customer after export. Accordingly, exporters were told that they should agree in advance the non-military use of the machines.

It was a complete explanation. The DTI and machine-tool exporters were both troubled by the behaviour of the wicked Iraqis. Therefore, to solve the problem, the companies were to tell the wicked Iraqis to promise in future not to convert their imported machines to war-like uses.

If there was any trouble, the DTI was in the clear. As Moses explained:

> It may be suggested that the DTI could have done more to discover to what use the machines and associated equipment were going to be put . . . The DTI did believe that machines had been exported from this country which had in the past been used for military production. But they were entitled to act upon the positive assurances given on behalf of Matrix Churchill.

Henderson had been present at the meeting with Alan Clark, and had told his lawyers that what happened there was very different indeed from the Customs QC's account of it to the jury. He had said that the Minister had given the companies an unmistakeable 'nod and a wink'. But what was his word worth against a Minister's?

7

DIRTY WASHING

Documents behind the Clark meeting, January 1988

They are buying machines specifically tooled up for arms production.

MI5 report, 11 May 1987

Once sorted into order, the 400-odd pages of secret documents now being collated by the defence brought the true Whitehall narrative into clear focus. As the files from different departments slotted together, they supported Henderson's version, and told an astonishingly different story. Nothing was the way the Customs QC had painted it to the jury.

It was clear from the documents that:

• Whatever the public thought, Geoffrey Howe's original 1985 guidelines banning significant military sales to Iraq were no longer in force – secretly, they had been by this time breached, stretched, twisted, and virtually abolished.

• The DTI had insisted on giving licences to Matrix Churchill despite repeated opposition from the Foreign

Office and evidence that they were part of a nuclear procurement network.

◉ MI6 intelligence had been supplied to the DTI from the outset, detailing that Matrix Churchill was secretly Iraqi-controlled and equipping munitions factories. This had been deliberately hushed up.

The true story that the documents told began one spring in the lobby of the De Vere Hotel, next to Coventry Cathedral. The lobby has a very small fountain in one corner, but apart from that the atmosphere is utilitarian – Coventry is not a tourist centre, but an engineering town. Swinging his heavy black briefcase, export manager Mark Gutteridge asked the receptionist in his deep voice for the room number of Mr Michael Ford. 'Ford' was waiting in one of the 'executive bedrooms', slightly larger than standard, but by no means extravagant. Gutteridge went to the lift: this way, no one ever saw them together. These two men had been meeting in cramped hotel rooms since the previous December.

Five days later, the MI5 case officer typed up his paperwork. The standard 'Contact Note' form came classified SECRET: the classification was printed in a box at the top and bottom of each page. Under the section 'Contact date and time', he typed: 'Wednesday 6 May 1987, 1730'. Referring to Gutteridge by his agent cypher, 528, he typed an account of Gutteridge's recent intelligence activities with Eastern bloc businessmen, and then added:

Lastly, and much as an afterthought, 528 told of TI Matrix dealings with a London-based Iraqi company. This company is buying milling machines specifically tooled-up for arms production. He was concerned that we should not interfere with this business since it is of high value.

This was the first occasion on which a British intelligence

service was given accurate details, by one of its trusted agents, of the purchase of machine-tools by the Iraqi arms procurement network. The intelligence arrived a full seven months before the DTI gave Gutteridge's own company, by then renamed Matrix Churchill, the first Iraqi export licence.

Over that summer and autumn, a whole sheaf of monthly reports came in from Gutteridge, to be transcribed on to 'Ford's' MI5 contact notes. As they leafed through them, the defence team realised that they confirmed every detail of the story told by Henderson and Gutteridge of how it had all started. Gutteridge's career as an overseas sales manager gave him good access. The notes recorded him flying off to bid for contracts in Bonn, where the procurement network was based. He was promoted, and took over all Middle East deals, as well as the work in Eastern Europe which had originally led 'Ford' to re-employ him on MI5's team of businessmen.

Gutteridge was abroad so much that, at home, his wife and the secret meetings with his case officer competed for his time. The contact notes record how a compromise was reached: 'Ford' could have two hours of debriefing, and then Gutteridge's wife would join the two men for a sociable dinner. She was, of course, to be kept in ignorance of their real relationship.

The rapport blossomed. Gutteridge was collecting sheaves of drawings from the company for 'Ford' to photograph. By October, Gutteridge was inviting 'Ford' home to his house in Tile Hill after the sessions, for his wife to cook supper for the three of them. (When she came in from the kitchen, the men would fall silent or change the subject.) 'Ford' practised simple psychology to keep his agent co-operative, going so far as to buy Mrs Gutteridge a Christmas present. It may have been purchased on expenses, for he minuted: 'It is important to keep Mrs 528 on-side . . . because 528 spends so much time out of the UK. Without her support, 528 might be much more reluctant to spend time with me.'

Gutteridge's story was that a team of Iraqis arrived in Britain in 1987, touring machine-tool manufacturers with a list of requirements for munitions. They were operating through a company, MEED International, run by an English entrepreneur, Roy Ricks, and an expatriate Iraqi, Anis Wadi. They gave a contract to one of Matrix Churchill's rivals for machines to make mortar shells, and there was bitter rivalry to get such lucrative work. Gutteridge had been pursuing the prospect of more business that May, when he mentioned it to his MI5 handler.

Eventually, the Iraqi embassy in Bonn conducted an auction, with bidding companies lining up in the corridors from Britain, Switzerland and Germany. The head of the procurement ring was there – a man called Dr Safa al-Habobi. He was setting up full-scale armaments factories in Iraq at two locations – the Nassr plant outside Baghdad, and Huteen. That autumn, Matrix Churchill got three contracts worth £19 million, for nearly 150 sets of heavy machinery. They were to manufacture mortars; and 122mm and 155mm big howitzer shells. Henderson applied for export licences for 'general engineering', got them from the DTI at the end of 1987, and delivered the machines all through the next year, 1988.

Paul Henderson was having dinner in Bonn with Anis Wadi and Safa al-Habobi, when Habobi first mentioned he also wanted to buy control of a British machine-tool company. The deal rapidly went through and the impression was given that it was a Coventry management buy-out. On 26 October, the *Financial Times* reported from a publicity handout:

TI Group, the engineering company, will today sell its remaining machine-tool interests to TMG Engineering, a newly-formed UK company in which management has an equity stake of up to 20%. Mr Paul Henderson . . . will become managing director of TMG. The buy-out is backed by a consortium of European banks, including one from the UK.

Gutteridge reported a truer picture to MI5 only two days later:

> TMG own about 90%: it is a holding company specially set up to purchase TI Machine Tools. The parent company is TDG, which was recently surreptitiously established by MEED International with money from Iraq, Saudi Arabi and Kuwait . . . The main account is held by the Dresdner Bank in Bonn . . . It is believed the Iraqis are a major shareholder. The contract prohibits MATRIX CHURCHILL from selling machine-tools to either Iran or Israel.

MI5's official name is the Security Service. The organisation were professionally interested in communists, subversives and terrorists. Their only concern about Iraq and machinery would still have been about technology transfer to a Soviet client-state, even at this late stage in the Cold War. The documents showed that Gutteridge's case officer wrote up what the export manager told him into a series of 'Source Reports'. These were 'sanitised': they concealed the background of the informant. The Source Reports were sent to 'Ford's' analyst colleagues in MI5.

'Ford' sent the first Source Report on 11 May 1987, detailing the way MEED was buying machines for Iraq 'specifically tooled up for arms production'. The next substantial batch of four Source Reports was sent together on 9 September: they were to prove crucial. And they were not originally disclosed by the Crown. The reports itemised the contracts British and foreign companies had obtained so far, and provided key details, based on a visit to Iraq by Gutteridge, of what the Nassr and Huteen armament factories were to produce.

They noted 'Date information gained from source: 6.8.87'. There were four subject headings:

BETRAYED

IRAQI MACHINE PURCHASES

IRAQI ARMAMENT PRODUCTION

MEED INTERNATIONAL LTD

MR ANEES M. WADI (sic)

The first report said that Iraq was buying heavy machinery through its Commercial Councillor in Bonn. Top of the list of companies was TI, Matrix Churchill's original name. They were to sell '£19m worth of multi-spindle and CNC lathes'. The second report was very detailed. It described how Anis Wadi had produced drawings for the machine-tool manufacturers, explaining they were for mortars, projectile nose-cones, cartridges and shell-cases, which Iraq now wished to build instead of buying from the Soviet Union. He had explained that arms production would take place at Huteen and Nassr, giving locations. Businessmen had visited Nassr already, and found 'production lines for a 122mm missile'. All the factory drawings were in Russian, except some American plans for a 1,000lb bomb. Wadi had disclosed production plans while in London and Iraq. Iraq wanted to have annual production under way in twelve months, as follows:

NASSR:	
122mm missiles (rockets)	10,000
130mm shells	150,000
Mortar shells	100,000
Fin-stabilised 155mm shells	300,000
HUTEEN:	
122mm shells	
130mm shells	
155mm shells	'large numbers'

The third Source Report described the structure of MEED

International and the European purchasing arrangements through the Bonn embassy and the Dresdner Bank: 'By July 1987, £167 million worth of contracts had been signed.' The final report was a personal profile of Anis Wadi. He had been telling British businessmen: 'Money is no problem. Iraq has been paying over the top for finished products from the Soviet Union.' The machine-tools being bought could be adapted after the Iran-Iraq War for civil purposes. But the orders were so large that Wadi was having to scour several European countries for supplies. This Source Report specifically identified 'Dr Safa Habboby [phonetic]' as the head of the Iraqi procurement committee.

These August–September reports were eventually to form the basis of an initiative by MI5's sister-service, MI6. But before the end of the year, even more Source Reports were compiled. On 2 November, 'Ford' wrote a detailed Source Report disclosing how Iraq had secretly taken control of Matrix Churchill. 'Paul Henderson . . . is aware of the Iraqi link but is keeping the information away from the staff.' Gutteridge 'borrowed' a batch of drawings from the factory at MI5's request, and 'Ford' spent two and a half hours photographing them. This was also Source Reported – the drawings were part of Matrix Churchill's 122mm and 155mm shell contracts. Some of the drawings still had original Soviet Cyrillic script on them.

In November, the foreign intelligence service MI6 expressed positive concern – apparently for the first time. They fired off a list of detailed questions for 'Ford' to put to his secret source. Could he get hold of the actual contracts? Could he visit the factories in Iraq? Gutteridge said that he was due to visit the closely-guarded Huteen soon, to sort out a technical problem. He would also try to purloin a copy of the Matrix Churchill contract. On 25 November, 'Ford' wrote to MI6, enclosing the batch of copied drawings and using MI5's own notepaper (it is headed 'SECRET, PO Box 500, London' with a small coat of royal arms in the left-hand corner). The mission had been partly accomplished: 'Source 528 has been able to provide details of the Iraqi contracts with UK companies . . . Source is in no doubt that all these tools will be used in Iraq for the production of armaments.'

This November interest by MI6 came slowly. Their equivalent in MI5, the domestic analysts, had had all the essential intelligence by 9 September, including the list of companies involved. Three British firms now had £37 million worth of machinery contracts in the pipeline, and the Department of Trade and Industry was merrily issuing export licences. The papers show that Wickman Bennett Ltd had been given licences in July. BSA Machines, run by Keith Bailey, was issued its licences by the DTI two days after MI5's letter. And Matrix Churchill, now secretly Iraqi-owned, was to get its licences on 2 December.

The existing machinery for handling export-licence applications seemed to be functioning in a state of ignorance. It consisted of an inter-departmental committee (IDC) which convened monthly. Here, officials from the Foreign Office, the Defence Ministry and the DTI met to chew over particularly difficult applications for Iran and Iraq, and to enforce the Howe guidelines.

A week before the IDC, a meeting would take place of another committee of officials – the Ministry of Defence working group (MODWG). This was supposed to vet applications and provide technical and intelligence advice. MODWG had representatives on it from military intelligence – the Defence Intelligence Staff. The official files show that these defence intelligence people in turn had access to, and were in communication with, MI6 itself, through a similar postal system to MI5. The coded MI6 circulation address was 'Box 850'.

The Matrix Churchill licence applications did reach the IDC agenda on 18 September. But the only files disclosed by the government show that this was for an entirely irrelevant reason – for fear that such high-tech machinery should fall into the hands of a Soviet client state like Iraq: 'There is a possibility that the USSR is the diversionary destination.' This was ludicrously wide of the mark. The committee should have been told via MODWG what MI5 already knew: that Iraq was trying to get rid of the Soviets, and manufacture its own arms.

MODWG would have met a week earlier, around 11 September. This was only a couple of days after 'Ford' had written the key Source Reports. There was some excuse, perhaps, for the information not catching up with the September IDC. But the licence application was then temporarily postponed 'for further assessment'. There were two months of delay during which an MI5 or MI6 warning could have been effective. What happened at the IDC in October? Or November? It was a bad Whitehall blunder: the documents did not reveal who or what was to blame for it.

Whatever past failures had occurred, MI6 were now moving purposefully. The Secret Intelligence Service, as they are officially known, work closely with the Foreign Office. They clearly regarded this belated intelligence as disturbing and important. They acted as soon as they received the copy drawings – further hard documentary corroboration from MI5's secret source that these were arms deals. An MI6 report was drawn up: 'TELEGRAM 894, 30 November 1987'. This four-paragraph report was short and unequivocal. The front page read as follows (with government 'security' deletions):

UK SECRETXXXXXXXXXXXXXXXXX
XXXXXXXXX
XXXXXXXXX
XXXXXXXXX
XXXXXXXXX

xxxxxxxxxxx30 November 1987

IRAQ: THE PROCUREMENT OF MACHINERY FOR ARMAMENTS PRODUCTION [AUGUST 1987]

. . . .

Department of Trade and Industry   xxxxxxxxxxxxxxxxx
FCO   xxxxxxxxxxxxxxxxxxxxxxxxxxxxxxxxxxxxxxxx
xxxxxxxxxxxxxxxxxxxxxxxxxxxxxxxxxxxxxxxx
xxxxxxxxxxxxxxxxxxxxxxxxxxxxxxxxxxxxxxxx
MOD   xxxxxxxxxxxxxxxxxxxxxxxxxxxxxxxxxxxxxx
xxxxxxxxxxxxxxxxxxxxxxxxxxxxxxxxxxxxxxxx
xxxxxxxxxxxxxxxxxxxxxxxxxxxxxxxxxxxxxxxx
xxx   xxxxxxxxxxxxxxxxxxxxxxxxxxxxxxxxxxxxxxxx
xxx   xxxxxxxxxxxxxxxxxxxxxxxxxxxxxxxxxxxxxxxx

. . . .

Beginning, 'According to a British businessman involved in some of the deals . . .', the report said bluntly that the Iraqi government was signing machine-tool deals 'for the production of armaments in Iraq'. There followed the salient points culled from the four MI5 Source Reports of 6 August, based in turn on an exhausting four-hour hotel session with Mark Gutteridge.

Paragraph 1 repeated the list of UK, German, Italian and Swiss machine-tool companies with arms contracts, headed by Matrix Churchill. Paragraph 2 was censored by MI6 and blacked out in the defence copy. Paragraph 3 quoted Anis Wadi's explanation of why it was cheaper for Iraq to build its own arms factories than buy from the USSR. Paragraph 4 laid out the shell production targets at Nassr and Huteen, and described how British businessmen had visited Nassr and seen its military purposes.

This report was written for circulation outside the intelligence community. Its distribution list on the front page shows it went to the Department of Trade and Industry. Copies also went to the Foreign Office and the Ministry of Defence. From 30 November, the date of the intelligence report, those departments should have been under no illusion as to what the machine-tool trade with Iraq was about. But once again, there was an unfortunate gap. The MI6 report went direct to the DTI, just two days before that department finally issued export licences to Matrix Churchill. It seemed from the files as though someone had not been reading his in-tray.

The Christmas holidays came and went in Whitehall. In the new year, panic broke out about the MI6 report. The first sign of it was at a meeting of the Restricted Enforcement Unit on Friday 8 January. Normally chaired by Eric Beston of the DTI – who said he was absent that day – the REU brought together Customs and intelligence people to police Iran-Iraq embargo breaches. The minutes record as Item 15:

SECRET UK EYES ONLY . . . MACHINE TOOLS FOR IRAQ. MOD and SIS reported that machine tools sent to Iraq were for use in the manufacture of munitions. The IDC would watch out for licence applications.

That Friday, the IDC went into emergency session: licences had, of course, already been issued, and the horse had bolted. There is no explanation of why it had taken nearly six weeks for the intelligence report to circulate. The emergency IDC agreed that this was too hot for officials – it was one for their Ministers. The head of the licensing unit, Tony Steadman, was deputed to find out what the contractual position was of the companies. The Whitehall weekend intervened.

On Monday 10 January, Tony Steadman started phoning round. He was warning the startled and furious companies that their licences might be revoked because they were making munitions. Commercial manager Trevor Abraham took the call at Matrix Churchill; when managing director Paul Henderson heard about it, he at once began to lobby the local Tory MP, John Butcher (who was himself a junior DTI Minister) and the trade association to demand a protest meeting with Ministers.

The DTI's first instinct was to hush the discovery up. The companies were painting a black picture of how they would suffer. On the Wednesday, Steadman wrote to his opposite number at the MOD, Alan Barrett, of defence

1 According to a British businessman involved in some of the deals, the Iraqi government has been signing contracts with British, West German, Italian and Swiss firms for the purchase of general purpose heavy machinery for the production of armaments in Iraq. Details of those contracts about which the businessman knows are as follows:

a TI [UK] 19 M worth of multispindle and Computer Numerical Control [CNC] lathes;

xxxxxxxxxxxxxxxxxxxxxxxxxxxxxxxxxxxxxxxxxxxxxxxxxxxxxxxxxxxxxxx
xxxxxxxxxxxxxxxxxxxxxxxxxxxxxxxxxxxxxxxxxxxxxxxxxxxxxxxxxxxxxxx
xxxxxxxxxxxxxxxxxxxxxxxxxxxxxxxxxxxxxxxxxxxxxxxxxxxxxxxxxxxxxxx

2 xxxxxxxxxxxxxxxxxxxxxxxxxxxxxxxxxxxxxxxxxxxxxxxxxxxxxxxxxxxxxxx
xxxxxxxxxxxxxxxxxxxxxxxxxxxxxxxxxxxxxxxxxxxxxxxxxxxxxxxxxxxxxxx
xxxxxxxxxxxxxxxxxxxxxxxxxxxxxxxxxxxxxxxxxxxxxxxxxxxxxxxxxxxxxxx
xxxxxxxxxxxxxxxxxxxxxxxxxxxxxxxxxxxxxxxxxxxxxxxxxxxxxxxxxxxxxxx

3 Iraq intends to use the machinery purchased to manufacture its own munitions. According to ANEES WADI of MEED INTERNATIONAL, Iraq has been paying inflated prices for finished products from the Soviet Union and now wishes to manufacture its own cartridges, shell-cases, mortars and projectile nose cases.

4 The armaments production is to take place in two main factories in Iraq: the Hutteen General Establishment for Mechanical Industries in Iskandria; and the Nassr General Establishment for Mechanical Industries in Taji, near Basra. Both factories are large by Western standards and the annual production targets for the Nassr factory (the smaller of the two) are as follows:

a 10,000 122mm missiles pa;

b 150,000 130mm shells pa;

c 100,000 mortar shells (60, 80 and 120 mm) pa;

d 300,000 fin-stabilised 155mm shells pa (similar to those produced by PRB in Belgium)

Most of the technical drawings used as blueprints for production at the Nassr factory are Russian. The one exception noted was a set of American drawings used for a large bomb. British businessmen visiting the factory were told that it was a 1000lb bomb. The businessmen were also told that all the Soviets had been expelled from the factory.

export sales, saying the consequences of cancellation were going to be 'catastrophic'. Matrix Churchill had shipped only 13 of 141 lathes and cancellation would be 'terminal' for the firm, costing 1,000 jobs (at the Coventry factory and at Matrix Churchill's subsidiaries). Paul Henderson was already getting up a protest campaign. Wickman Bennett said that cancellation would cause 'serious financial difficulties' and half the workforce would be sacked. Keith Bailey at BSA said that his company might cease to be solvent and there would be 'significant lay-offs'.

Steadman, who copied the letter to the Foreign Office and to his boss Eric Beston, suggested that the three Whitehall departments turn a blind eye to what had happened, but ban future contracts with Nassr and Huteen. This was, in his view, 'the balanced approach': 'Since the evidence was not available to us prior to the issue of licences, it should not be too difficult presentationally to do nothing about the existing contracts.'

His attitude was shared by the export marketing section of the 'Department for Enterprise'. Bill Morgan wrote to his head of department on the same day, saying 'the Iraqi representatives' had given assurances the tools were civilian. But now Steadman's intelligence report said the opposite. Perhaps it was wrong: 'There may be an element of mischief-making. The contracts were won in competition with other countries.' Injured companies might seek redress through the courts. And Ministers needed to be forewarned, because the news might leak. In any event: 'There seems to be considerable merit in keeping as quiet as possible about this politically sensitive issue.'

At 6 p.m. the next day, Thursday, 'Michael Ford' was ensconced in his Coventry hotel bedroom, ready for the monthly intelligence session. Gutteridge had been performing excellently lately: he had briefly gained entry to the Huteen plant on his Iraq visit, and had filed a vivid intelligence report on his return of its strict security; the anti-aircraft guns lined up on an earth redoubt all round the perimeter of the seven-kilometre site; the Swiss-built 130mm shell and mortar shop with fifty CNC lathes and conveyors working twenty-four hours a day; the workers having to maintain production by kicking through shell cases straight from the forges, still too hot to touch with bare hands. All this information had gone off to MI6.

The corpulent 'Ford' painted a picture afterwards of how he had settled down, relaxed in his chair with a cup of tea and the hotel fruitbowl to hand, ready for another congenial debriefing of 'Source 528'. But Gutteridge was not in a good mood: he was apparently very upset. The DTI had been ringing round threatening to cancel the export licences, he said, saying 'HMG did not wish to prolong the Gulf [Iran–Iraq] War'. If they were cancelled, Gutteridge might lose the money he had put into buying discount shares; and he might lose the chance of a new £100,000 a year sales job with Anis Wadi and the Iraqis. 'Source 528' was suspicious that his own information was to blame. 'Ford' recorded that he had tried to divert his suspicions: 'a very tricky period, with my nose growing ever longer'.

Back in London, first thing on the Friday morning, he sent off a sharp cypher telegram to MI6. '£50 million of contracts and 1,500 jobs are at risk . . . There is a witch-hunt to find out how the information was leaked . . . Is it possible the DTI has used the SIS report? . . . We would be grateful for your assurances. Presume you will now earmark your share (£30 million) of the damages if Source 528 goes wrong!' The same day, MI6 replied rapidly and soothingly. They would ask the DTI not to act until the next REU meeting, on 22 January. 'We will then state our preference for the licences being granted.'

This exchange of cypher telegrams between the two secret intelligence organisations marked the beginning of a bout of backstairs lobbying. The intelligence agencies had set up a channel through which they had successfully found out something secret, just in time for the discovery to change government policy. This was, presumably, the whole reason for their existence. It was rare for intelligence operations to be so obviously useful. Yet, at the moment when their intelligence had belatedly become effective, the secret channel turned to flow the other way: it became a conduit to put pressure on the government to change government policy back again.

Paul Henderson had no doubt complained bitterly to his export manager Mark Gutteridge about the moves by the DTI to destroy their profits. Gutteridge, an unpaid agent who had signalled more than once to his MI5 controller that he wanted this profitable business left alone, now had a chance to exert pressure back up the line. He did not complain that he was about to be exposed as an MI5 agent; still less that his life was at risk or that he would no longer work for MI5. But he was, in 'Ford's' words: 'very upset'. Was Her Majesty's Government 'running' Gutteridge; or was it the other way round? Which was the tail and which was the dog? The answer to this question turned out to be curiously irrelevant. For Whitehall did not need encouragement to hush up its apparent blunder, however many extra artillery shells Saddam Hussein acquired as a result.

The following Monday, there was the whisper in corridors of words being had in the right quarters. An MI6 officer quietly got hold of the head of the DTI export control department, Eric Beston. It was a twin-pronged lobbying operation; as he minuted: '[DELETED] had also mentioned it to him on my behalf, in the margins of another meeting'. The MI6 manager had another MI5 telex from 'Ford' in his pocket, saying the companies would be 'brought to their knees' by losing the licences. He had shaded down the original basis for action to a mere 'probably': 'Our information points to their probable use in an armaments factory.' 'Ford' stressed that his source was convinced the whole corporate purchasing operation was a covert front for the Iraqi government, but had no direct evidence. One could almost see the unwritten words: 'Therefore, further research is necessary . . .'

The MI6 officer was in for a surprise, once he accosted the senior official from the DTI. His lobbying mission to stop the licences being revoked was unnecessary. Of his discreet approach, he noted: 'This actually suited Beston, who was himself reluctant to implement any retrospective action. He was pleased to have our view in support of his own, and said he would raise it at the Enforcement Committee meeting.'

Beston now had the task of advising his Minister. The lobbying activity by the MTTA had produced the promise of an urgent meeting with Alan Clark, two days hence. Beston had to brief him. His starting point was a confidential draft by the licensing unit head, Tony Steadman. Beston adopted Steadman's suggestion that the companies' should avoid press attention if they wanted the licences restored, scribbling: 'The need for a low profile by MTTA/companies is important. We do not wish to leave the FCO with "presentational difficulties".'

But he removed from general circulation Steadman's paragraph quoting the basic facts from MI6 Telegram 894. He put it in a separate minute, classified SECRET, which was much less widely circulated. In this he alerted Clark that MI6 would be on his side against the Foreign Office: 'If we need their backing . . . they will weigh in with others in Whitehall . . . They, like the DTI, would favour allowing the present contracts to be completed, and export licences refused only for any future suspect business.' They did not want their source put at risk by reference to *detailed* information from intelligence in a meeting with the companies.

Thus, Alan Clark had in front of him at the meeting a brief telling him that the companies were supposed to keep their mouths shut. He had another brief, marked SECRET, giving him details of the munitions factories involved, and telling him that MI6 were going to back his own officials in seeking to keep the contracts in place. If he wanted to mount a cover-up, he knew he had the support – for reasons of their own – of his own department and of the secret intelligence agencies.

DIRTY WASHING

It was against this background – very different from the one the Customs QC had depicted to the jury – that Paul Henderson and the four-man delegation of machine-tool manufacturers filed into the Minister's room in Victoria Street that Wednesday, to be confronted by Alan Clark, Tony Steadman from the licensing unit, another official from export marketing and a Private Secretary.

The Private Secretary's official minute, circulated throughout the department afterwards, stressed how supportive of the companies Clark was, and how optimistic he seemed about the prospect that the licences would not be revoked. But nowhere did it mention the blunt phrase Henderson claimed had been used: 'Let's not waste time. You know what the machines are for. We know what they're for.' The minute said that Clark was 'fully aware' of the effect of 'this matter' on jobs and profits. Like the MTTA minute, the Whitehall minute was oddly silent as to what 'this matter' actually was.

The statement made by Clark which he had so disputed when 'interpreted' in the MTTA minutes was handled by the Whitehall official note-taker in a most unusual way. He wrote:

> Choosing his words carefully and noting that the Iraqis would be using the current orders for general engineering purposes, Mr Clark stressed it was important for the UK companies to agree a specification with the customer in advance, which highlighted the peaceful (i.e. non-military) use to which the machine-tools would be put.

This could certainly be interpreted as a 'nod and a wink' about future, follow-on orders of the same nature. Clark certainly knew that 'general engineering purposes' was a false description. Everything would depend on what Clark would admit his ambiguous statements were actually supposed to mean.

Whatever Clark was to say, one thing was already clear. If Whitehall had ever genuinely wanted to enforce the law in the way Customs at the Old Bailey later wanted to persuade the jury was right, their reaction would have been completely different. They would have been indignant at the intelligence reports; investigated the companies; immediately discovered from their paperwork that they had sold machines 'specifically tooled up for armaments' – and arrested the lot of them for deceiving the department by filling in forms with the words 'general engineering'. Instead, a Minister of the Crown was fawning on their managing directors and making promises to inconvenience them no further.

The companies had already been in touch with the *Daily Telegraph*, complaining about their treatment. Clark, according to Henderson, told the meeting he would ring up the editor, Max Hastings, and sort it out. Did he ever do so? On the morning of the Friday meeting of the enforcement committee, a *Telegraph* piece appeared: 'MINISTERS SPLIT ON £50M MACHINE-TOOLS FOR IRAQ'. It was vituperative against the Foreign Office: 'British manufacturers say they have no evidence that their exports are being used to produce arms . . . They argue that the Foreign Office line is short-sighted and against Britain's economic interests.' Sir Geoffrey Howe and his guidelines seemed to be the focus of attack.

Officials and intelligence officers read the *Telegraph* piece that morning, before going into the REU meeting. There, a typical Whitehall charade took place. As they discussed the problem, MI6 pretended they had not been meeting privately in advance with Eric Beston of the DTI. The representative from MI5, whose source they were all talking about, and who had also been meeting MI6, also pretended that he knew nothing about it. Everyone, recorded MI6 contentedly, 'fully understands the risks to our source and shares our view on the way ahead'. The only anxiety remaining was about the *Telegraph*-style publicity: 'the final decision is likely to have a high profile'.

In the end, that problem, too, was to be solved. After

Ministers had been manipulated into line, there was simply no announcement of the result. The Defence Procurement Minister, Lord Trefgarne, received a lengthy Civil Service submission from Alan Barrett. The *Telegraph* piece had not been too dangerous for quiet decision-making: 'It was on a financial page and has not attracted attention as far as we know.'

Had the intelligence information been available earlier, MOD's working group 'would have advised the IDC that the military assessment was that the use of the lathes for this purpose would have constituted a significant enhancement in Iraq's capability to prolong the conflict . . . Ministers would have been advised accordingly.' As it was, MODWG and IDC had managed at the time to 'satisfy themselves' the goods did not have a military end-user.

As things now had all gone wrong, Barrett at the Defence Ministry produced no less than seven ingenious reasons for Trefgarne, if he needed to justify a cover-up.

1 The intelligence had arrived too late;
2 The Iraqis were only substituting one source of shells for another;
3 The machines were not defence equipment, but for 'general engineering', so did not breach the guidelines;
4 The 1985 guidelines mentioned 'fulfilling existing contracts': and the companies faced ruin;
5 Britain's reputation would fall in Saudi Arabia as well as Iraq if the deals were cancelled, and the Germans would step in;
6 The intelligence community 'feared for the safety of their source' and needed to gather more information;
7 The shells 'could not be used against Western shipping in the Gulf'.

If his Defence Ministry submission to Trefgarne (with a copy to Defence Secretary Tom King), had contained one good reason, it perhaps would not have needed seven bad ones. Simultaneously, the Foreign Office civil service submission went off to David Mellor, then a junior Minister. Although the Foreign Office were supposedly the liberal 'enemy', there was universal agreement on this occasion that the blind eye should be turned. Bill Patey joined his colleagues Barrett from the MOD and Steadman from the DTI in recommending this. His submission contained, in different words, the first five reasons thought up by the MOD. Then it stopped. There was no mention of the intelligence issue, supposedly the main reason. Perhaps it was considered too secret to put in writing. He did address himself to the all-important issue of 'presentation':

> If it becomes known that UK companies have supplied equipment for manufacture of munitions, we could truthfully say that when the licences were issued we had no reason to believe that this civilian equipment was for other than general industrial purposes.

Patey was proposing, in the famous phrase, to be 'economical with the truth'. There is a hoary Whitehall joke about parliamentary questions and answers which captures the spirit of Patey's memo. A civil service Private Secretary is accompanying a new Labour Minister back from an official visit to the West Country. They are snug in the government car. Freezing night has fallen. A howling gale is blowing as they climb ever higher and further from habitation. Suddenly, an exhausted and snow-covered figure appears in the darkness and hammers on the car window. 'I'm lost!' cries the traveller. 'Please tell me, where I am.' 'You're on Dartmoor,' says the Private Secretary briskly, winds up the window and signals the chauffeur on. The Minister, aghast, asks him why he did such a heartless thing. 'But, Minister, I thought you'd be pleased. I was completely truthful but gave out the minimum information. Isn't that the ideal parliamentary answer?'

DIRTY WASHING

Patey's superiors approved. William Blackley handwrote at the bottom that a UN embargo might soon be imposed: 'If it becomes public knowledge that the tools are to be used to make munitions, deliveries would have to stop at once . . . The companies should be warned of the falling [UN] guillotine and urged to produce and ship as fast as they can. They must also be urged to renounce publicity and lobbying for their own good.' His boss in turn, Sir Henry Miers, head of the Middle Eastern department added in his tiny, neat hand: 'Another difficult case of dual-purpose equipment. I think we must let the contracts stand.'

But there was then an extraordinary development. In February, one of Paul Henderson's 600 employees at the Matrix Churchill factory in Coventry – perhaps concerned about alleged links with the Iraqis, perhaps morally distressed, or perhaps merely startled to read in the *Telegraph* that the Foreign Office had nothing to be suspicious about – wrote to the Foreign Office himself. He confirmed that, in the FO's words: 'Machine-tools for manufacturing shell cases are being supplied to Iraq.' (This dramatic letter was almost certainly the letter 'from a confidential source' which the FO succeeded in keeping from the Old Bailey.)

The letter caused some excitement at the next, 5 February, meeting of the secret enforcement committee, the REU. The Foreign Office were still waiting to hear from their Ministers. But the Foreign Office representative had news: the recommendations to let the licences stand 'had been made so as not to prejudice the information source. But in light of recent developments from a different, overt source, the recommendation could be altered.'

This announcement proved that the issue of 'protecting intelligence sources' became in the end a complete red herring. Once there was so-called 'collateral' from another direction, the Gutteridge intelligence could have been left aside. Any action could be explained as coming from a tip-off within the company. However, this was good news which, curiously, no one seemed to want to hear. David Mellor scrawled assent across the original memo waiting in his red box. At the next meeting of the REU it was noted, tersely: 'IRAQ – MACHINE TOOLS. It was understood that Ministers had agreed that the licences should *not* be revoked [author's emphasis].'

Two major munitions factories were therefore set up in Iraq with British help over the coming months, as the Iran-Iraq war continued. Up to a million people would eventually die in the conflict. This serious breach of the arms embargo had been described in exact detail to Ministers by intelligence reports. They had decided to hush it up. This guilty secret was only the first part of the government's 'dirty washing'.

8

THE FAT CONTROLLER

Testimony from MI5, 30 October 1992

> We parted good friends.
> *MI5 Contact Note, 20 January 1988*

The promise that Gutteridge would testify had brought forth into defence hands secret documents which told a bizarre and discreditable story. It was one that, if confirmed, ex-Trade Minister Alan Clark was going to have to answer for in the witness-box. But as yet, the jury at the Old Bailey were entirely unaware of that.

The jury were also unaware of Customs moves afoot to bring not one, but two intelligence officers to court. Having broken the intelligence taboo by promising to call 'Balsam' from MI6 to contradict Henderson, Alan Moses QC was now planning to call another intelligence officer beforehand. Gutteridge's own case officer, 'Michael Ford' from MI5, would be summoned to testify. Moses hoped the intelligence man would similarly contradict the threatened testimony of Gutteridge.

Little knowing the drama that would unfold, the jury were presented with Customs' opening witnesses. On 14 October, the first to come was Ron Ash, Matrix's former defence projects executive. He did not give Moses much comfort. Ash denied that there was any mystery about the Iraq contracts. He said that drawings for the ABA project were freely circulating around the company. 'There was nothing secret about the project, everyone knew [the drawings] were from Iraq.' The same applied to the Cardoen contracts.

Cross-examined by Robertson, Ash agreed Cardoen was a well-known arms company – as well known as Adnan Khashoggi, one of the world's most notorious arms dealers. Ash said there had never been any secret that the firm made machine-tools for defence use. He spoke of cut-throat competition at home and abroad, Coventry jobs at stake – arguments which were to become familiar in the days ahead. It was starting to become clear what tactics Robertson would pursue – tactics which the judge unsympathetically described as 'political'. 'Geo-political' might have been more apt. Ash agreed with Robertson that it was clear the machine-tools were being used by the Iraqis to make shells. He agreed that Iran, provided with arms by 'Oliver North and others', was pressing the Iraqis hard during the period before the August 1988 ceasefire.

Though it was only the third day of what was expected to be a long trial, Kevin Robinson, Henderson's solicitor, was puzzled by the lack of media attention. He had been preparing the case for two years and, unlike most of the media, knew what high-explosive munitions lay in store. Only the *Guardian*, the *Financial Times*, Channel 4 News and, intermittently, BBC Radio, had journalists in court.

America's Saddamgate had been hitting the headlines in the US, with an added political interest given the impending presidential elections. Bobby Lee Cook, the defence lawyer for Christopher Drogoul, former manager of the Atlanta branch of the BNL bank, indicted for alleged Iraq-related fraud, had been comparing notes with Robertson over the summer. Now he had arrived in person to sit in the Old Bailey court alongside the Robertson team, looking rather like Colonel Sanders. On his departure, he presented Robertson with a photograph of himself and Bill Clinton embracing.

'Did you know,' Robertson asked Ash quietly, 'that throughout 1987 and 1988 Mark Gutteridge was working as an agent for British intelligence?' There was a stunned silence. Ash's jaw dropped in amazement. 'No,' he finally stuttered in some bewilderment. It was a tribute to Gutteridge's ability to keep his cover, even from his closest business associate with whom he had spent long hours in the Bonn bars, waiting for the summons from Dr Safa al-Habobi. There were open mouths too, on the jury: it was their first inkling, after three days of machinery and legalisms, that there was more to this case than met Mr Moses' eye. The point was made, not only to the jury, but to the outside world. Whitehall's worst fears were beginning to be realised. Gutteridge was on a business trip in Czechoslovakia at the time, not expecting the spotlight to fall on him quite so early.

The prosecution witnesses from Matrix Churchill – there to identify drawings, describe the training of Iraqi engineers and the installation of the machines at Nassr – frequently seemed of more help to the defence than to Customs. After a few days, Moses' enthusiasm for questioning them seemed to be wearing thin. But Robertson continued to use the parade of company testimony to useful effect. John Adams, Matrix Churchill's former purchasing manager, eagerly emphasised the point – directed at the jury – that while Henderson was managing director, the firm and its subsidiaries employed nearly 1,000. Now there were fewer than 100. Did Adams hand over documents relating to the Iraqi ABA project to his managing director? Robertson asked. 'Yes.' And were those documents then handed by Henderson to MI6? Well, to 'a government department' Adams replied. The point about British intelligence had again been made. Greville Cooper, former engineer, was asked by Robertson how he rated Henderson as managing director. 'I wish he still was,' came the reply.

BETRAYED

Adrian Whickham, operations manager of FMT, a Matrix Churchill sub-contractor, visited the British embassy in Baghdad in 1989. He said the British embassy seemed to know that Matrix's exports were defence-related. He painted a picture of British companies doing a roaring trade: answering a question about when he met British embassy staff in Baghdad in early 1990, Whickham replied: 'There were so many cocktail parties at that stage . . .'

There was one thing about many of the Matrix Churchill witnesses that the jury were bound to recall as clearly as the details of their testimony. They were mostly now unemployed. One tall and imposing engineer, Barry Tomalin, a man in his late forties, confidently gave his name, address and past position at Matrix Churchill. 'And what is your present employment?' asked Moses jauntily. Tomalin's manner dissolved – he seemed physically hurt by the question. 'I have no employment,' he said, close to tears. 'I haven't been in work since this case was brought.' It was a sombre moment. The reality of skilled men in the Midlands, thrown on the scrapheap in their prime, was brought home to a roomful of barristers each of whose annual earnings were well into six figures. Moses apologised profusely. But the moment would have stayed in the memory for the defence to capitalise on.

Upstairs in the public gallery, sinister moves were afoot. People wanting to hear the trial were asked for identification and their names and addresses. Notices on the gallery door stated that the court was not sitting, when it was, and that it was full when it was more than half-empty. Indeed, there was rarely more than a handful of people in the gallery at any one time throughout the course of the trial. One of those who complained was Gerald James, former managing director of Astra, the British fireworks company and defence contractor which had helped bring to light the Supergun. He wrote to Lord Mackay, the Lord Chancellor, on 22 October. More than a month later, on 7 December, he received a reply from H. Zafar, of the Lord Chancellor's department's criminal operations branch. Zafar explained that: 'It was at the advice of the police that names and addresses of those people sitting in the public gallery were taken and that identification was asked for.' The measures were taken: 'because if a security problem arose, it would be possible to trace all of those people sitting in the public gallery'. He apologised for the misleading notices outside the court.

Another who complained was Tim Laxton, one of James's former accountants. Laxton had been approached by a police constable who replaced the normal attendants. Laxton was asked why he was interested in the trial. The following day, 23 October, he found that the notice on the door read: 'No Admittance by order of the Judge'. He nevertheless opened the door to the public gallery, where an attendant allowed him access after he had produced proof of his identity. On 12 November, he received a reply from Graham Addicott, the Old Bailey courts administrator. It would appear, wrote Addicott, that the signs had been 'misused'. Security arrangements were 'very much a matter for the police . . . in this particular case, it was considered necessary to take the names and addresses of those entering the public gallery and to ask for some form of identification.' The matters, he said, 'related to security'.

The witness from MI5 with the cover-name 'Michael Ford' had already supplied a two-page prosecution statement with name and signature left blank. The statement was based on no more than the contents of the disclosed secret documents. Where portions were blacked out, 'Ford' was silent. In his witness statement, he confirmed that Mark Gutteridge of Matrix Churchill was a 'contact', and that he had first talked about the firm's affairs with him on 6 May 1987. But he denied that Gutteridge had kept him briefed on the two 'criminal' contracts, Cardoen and ABA. On the contrary, he said, Gutteridge had refused to search company files for copies of contracts, saying it might get him into trouble. Gutteridge never reported Matrix Churchill tools were going to Iraq for fuses under the Cardoen contract, testified 'Ford'; he merely mentioned the company had exports to Chile, and there were contacts between Chile and Iraq. When 'Ford' asked him what 'ABA' meant, Gutteridge had said that he did not know, and did not say Matrix Churchill 'were directly involved'.

Most apparently damning of all, 'Ford' asserted in his statement: 'Gutteridge was adamant that Mr Henderson should *not* become aware he was passing information on Iraqi contracts.' In the poker-game of the trial, it was vital for Gutteridge to prove the opposite. The defence line was: 'HMG knew. Henderson knew that Gutteridge was telling HMG. Therefore, to all intents and purposes, Henderson himself was telling HMG from the beginning. Therefore there was no deceit.'

Henderson and his defence team were nonetheless happy to see 'Michael Ford' come from MI5 headquarters to appear at the Old Bailey and talk about Gutteridge: even if the evidence in his testimony was questionable. They thought he could not prove the negative – that Henderson did *not* know about the hotel meetings with Gutteridge. Whatever 'Ford' said in the witness-box about that would count merely as hearsay. What he would say in evidence was likely to be less important than that he would lay the ground for Gutteridge himself to testify. And Gutteridge was the highest card in the defence hand. He would be a most impressive witness, because he was not charged with any offence. He had plainly detected the nature of the covert Iraqi procurement network from the beginning: since the collapse of the Cold War, he may have been MI5's most genuinely useful spy.

Defence solicitor Kevin Robinson had interviewed Gutteridge – and loved him. He was convinced that Gutteridge was going to come across in the witness-box as warm, decent, straightforward and patriotic. He would say that he had told MI5 all about ABA and Cardoen, in the course of giving them extensive and detailed information on the company's business with Iraq. 'Michael Ford's' very presence in the witness-box would confirm the authenticity of Gutteridge's role, however grudging 'Ford' was about the details of their conversations.

So the Henderson camp welcomed MI5's appearance in the courtroom. To Judge Smedley, anxiously patriotic, 'Officer B', as he was to be known, was more of a headache. The premises were elaborately prepared for the appearance of serving intelligence officers in open court. It was something of a pantomime, with everybody enjoying the show in their different ways: the jury bemused and expectant; the original handful of journalists now swollen in numbers by colleagues confident that there would be a story which even the most tired and cynical of editors would appreciate; the judge, prosecution and defence lawyers, bossy ushers, self-important court attendants (mainly former policemen): all shared a certain *frisson*.

These last busily placed police tape in front of the public gallery to prevent the witnesses from being seen. Brown paper was stuck over the glass panels in the doors of the court. Screens were erected – even the narrow gaps between the hinged panels of the screens were papered over with household tape. The screens protected a specially-constructed witness box hidden from the journalists, who were ordered to leave the press bench next to the jury and sit at the back of the court. Henderson – who, the judge had to accept, needed to vouch that one officer was indeed his contact – and his two co-accused were allowed a line of sight. The plan was that, on the days of their testimony, the intelligence officers should enter the court early, emerging from a small room in the corner – little more than a cupboard – to go to the makeshift witness-box.

Henderson's QC was dissatisfied by the mumbo-jumbo. He protested that there were valid reasons why intelligence officers should give their true names and addresses. Parts of their written statements to the court were not accurate and suggestions of perjury might be put to them. Moreover,

Robertson said, MI6 was a 'lawless' organisation (in his evidence later from the witness box, 'Officer A' of MI6 said that 'questions of law' were not a matter of concern to his agency) and so the conventional argument that officials were subject to Ministerial accountability did not apply: 'Judges are best placed to know what the interests of justice require, though they are not the best judges of national security.'

Robertson questioned whether such special provisions were in the interests of justice. The evidence given by Officer B of MI5 and Officer A of MI6 was 'specially protected'. The body language of the special arrangements would give their evidence special weight. Open testimony might well mean, he said in reference to the wording of the Home Secretary's certificate, that the intelligence officers could not in future be employed in certain operational jobs. But there were many desk jobs to which they could be assigned.

This onslaught produced another split among the defence, James Hunt QC saying that he would not support Robertson's argument. For the Crown, Moses rehearsed the PII claims that the lives of security and intelligence officers were endangered by disclosure. There was a risk, he repeated, that innocent civilians could be killed. Judge Smedley refused Robertson's application. Quoting the Home Secretary's concerns, he said that by disclosing their physical appearance, the lives of the MI5 and MI6 officers could be put at risk and it 'would certainly limit their usefulness in the future'. The jury had been routinely ejected for these arguments. On their return, Judge Smedley addressed them:

This witness, and indeed the next one, are both serving members of the security and intelligence services. Obviously, it is vitally important in the course of their work that they are not readily recognised by members of the public because of the security nature of the work they do, and the risks they inevitably take. In these circumstances, arrangements have been made for the witness-box to be positioned under the public gallery . . . and the press removed from their normal seats. Counsel, the defendants and you and I are the only people that can see their faces.

'And their stomachs,' he might have added. Although 'Ford' was invisible to the public, he had already been dubbed the 'Fat Controller' by the defence team, because, from Gutteridge's account, he was a twenty-stone *bon viveur* who gorged himself on Gutteridge's brandy and his wife's Polish cooking. (The cost to the agent of keeping 'Ford' must have been considerable.) An expert in technology transfer, 'Ford' turned out to be qualified as an engineer. With his girth and a taciturn, policeman-like manner went a slight West Country accent. It was no wonder that the press – who were now facing the jury but could not see the judge – strained every muscle: they could see under the screen that Officer B wore brown shoes. This was a discovery that featured prominently in ITN's television report that evening.

A big man with a military bearing appeared in court to supervise 'Ford's' debut at the Old Bailey. This was David Bickford, MI5's legal officer. It may have been his coaching that was responsible for 'Ford's' demeanour: Officer B answered clearly, with a voice both confident yet deferential. There were many 'My Lords' and frequent use of 'sir' . . . 'Box 500, sir.' 'I found them [the Gutteridges] a very charming couple, sir.'

'Ford's' evidence about the internal workings of intelligence was nearly excluded from the outset. Barely had Moses begun the task of evoking the 1987 hotel-room meetings between controller and agent, than Judge Smedley became uneasy and tetchy. 'Ford' started off: 'It would seem from my report that Mr Gutteridge told me . . .', when Smedley broke in. 'Just pause there, please. Mr Moses, does this fall foul of hearsay evidence?' Moses said: 'It all does. This is the problem. I'm calling this evidence in anticipation of a particular line of defence.' Moses began to explain that he was not trying to prove that what Gutteridge said to 'Ford' was actually true – merely what information he had passed over and what he had not. Judge Smedley spoke to the jury: 'Normally what a witness told somebody in the absence of the accused is not admissible. Would you mind leaving us?'

Robertson explained the defence view to the judge. He had waived his right to object to the testimony: he wanted the jury to understand the full background of Gutteridge's relationship with the intelligence services. Gutteridge would give evidence himself; the defence could simply have presented his account, but they wanted part of it to be corroborated by Ford and his 'Contact Notes'. Robertson said that he also wanted the jury to understand just how much information was being passed up to the government, particularly the DTI, and just how vital it was.

Smedley took the point: 'The information which the secret service had,' he called back in the jury and told them, 'as you know was seen by people like Mr Beston and Mr Steadman and others, and they based their decisions perhaps on that information. So it is important you know . . . what information they were in possession of at any given time.' Or, as he might more succinctly have put it: what did they know, and when did they know it?

'Mr Ford', as Robertson referred to him throughout, was on balance good value for the defence, although he insisted that he was in no position to evaluate Gutteridge's material – a task for his 'line manager' and 'analyst' and 'sister service'.

GR: He gave you information right from May '87 that the Safa group were in his view a front for the Iraqi government?

'MF':   It was the general theme of his reporting, yes.

He gave you information about his company and the other companies sending machines especially tooled up to make munitions at Nassr and Huteen?

Yes, he reported that.

And he gave you valuable information . . . about the Iraqi procurement network?

He gave us information. I understand from the desk officer at the time that that information was valued.

'Ford' explained, stiffly but helpfully, how MI5 worked – the difference between a Contact Note and a Source Report; and how a Contact Note was divided into three parts: what the informant knew; the 'source comment' (which was what the informant thought); and the 'field comment' (which was what the case officer thought). He explained that if they communicated with MI6, they were trained always to send secret intelligence-style telegrams. Packets and enclosures went by 'Box 500' mail, which was slower. They always referred to themselves in the plural in telegrams: 'the Royal we', as Robertson put it.

There came a hint from 'Ford' of why the intelligence agencies had originally been so slow to act on Gutteridge's August disclosures. 'Ford' had no particular interest in the Iraq arms embargo. He had recruited Gutteridge to spy on Eastern Europeans. The raw material had gone to MI5 analysts first – and only when MI6 had got involved in November had any moves been made to stop the unlawful trade: 'These were very early days in talking with Mr Gutteridge, and we were unsure what we were dealing with. Was it a problem of technology transfer, or a matter that should be addressed by my sister company? You will probably find that it went to both . . .' And it had been the Secret Intelligence Service which had pursued the issue, once it came belatedly to their attention: 'I was asked by the desk officer in SIS who was dealing with this, whether we could sight some copies of the contracts.'

Why had MI6 suddenly woken up? Or why, come to that, had MI5 been asleep before? There may have been a clue in the sparse minutes released of the joint intelligence-sharing committee, the Restricted Enforcement Unit. From the numbering system, it was clear that the secret unit had not been set up until autumn 1987 to swap information on 'sensitive cases' of export licensing: just before the flurry of joint MI5–MI6 activity over trade with Iraq. Why the REU had been invented, the documents did not reveal: and the DTI did not tell a later parliamentary committee why the REU had had such a short history, merely boasting that it was the 'main forum for discussions'. It would be safe to assume such a body was set up because some grievous failure in the existing machinery had come to light.

There was one very important aspect of Gutteridge's story which 'Ford' did unexpectedly volunteer to confirm. Gutteridge had told the defence team that British intelligence had indeed compiled a report on the original 1987 machine-tool contracts for arms production and their importance for British companies. MI5 had been so excited, his case officer had told him Margaret Thatcher herself might see the report. The prosecution claimed at first there was no such report. Robertson had spotted that there was a missing Telegram 894 from comparing two sets of blacked-out documents, on one of which there was a reference to it inadequately obscured and a date still legible. The telegram had been disgorged by MI6 only the day before 'Ford' entered the specially-built witness-box.

GR: Was it your knowledge at the end of 1987 that your report, or at least information from that report, was going to Ministers?

'MF':   I was told, sir, on one occasion, that one of the

reports could be the sort of report that would end
up in Whitehall.

'Ford' was also asked:

Do you recall telling Mr Gutteridge that your report was
going to be seen by the Prime Minister?

I may well have done that, sir.

The episode of the cover-up made 'Ford' touchy. Robertson
amused the court by reading 'Ford's' Contact Note describing
the way he tried to reassure a suspicious Gutteridge that his
report had not been to blame for the danger of the licences
being withdrawn: 'with my nose growing ever longer'. 'That
being,' said Robertson, 'a reference to Pinocchio?' 'Correct,
sir . . . My Lord, some time ago at one juncture I was accused
of telling lies to Mr Gutteridge. This I have never done and
it would certainly not be in anyone's interest to do so . . .
It was my job as case officer to leave the situation as best I
could, so I could make urgent inquiries to find out exactly
what the position was.'

Robertson brought out the way the task of a British intelligence officer was to exploit and manipulate his sources, who
were all unpaid businessmen:

His dominant motivation for doing all this was a belief,
which you shared and encouraged, that his co-operation
would be in the national interest?

That is exactly so, yes, sir . . . no different from my service
relationships with any other British businessman. There is
always a conflict between asking their help for the very
best of reasons on the one side – and, on the other, the
commercial consequences should it go wrong . . . It is a
fine balance. One hopes one's contacts are robust enough
to cope with it, but it is not always so.

Robertson read out the brusque telegram 'Ford' had then sent to MI6, after the threat to revoke the company licences – saying MI6 would face damages claims of £30 million if the affair went wrong. 'Ford' felt obliged to try to mend the image of the intelligence agencies, depicted in spy stories as being constantly at one another's throats:

> My Lord, there are various reports in newspapers and books which indicate otherwise, but the two services do work closely together. This is just a little comment from me to a brother officer in another organisation.

> From brother to sister?

> That is correct.

Gutteridge, it was established, did not merely hand over detailed information about the original 1987 contracts. Later, in 1988 and 1989, even when he had moved jobs, to a sales firm acting for several machine-tool companies, he supplied intelligence of growing significance: 'One has to end up telling one's contact more than what would be read in the newspapers: we were very concerned that British companies were helping the Iraqis build nuclear weapons, right? Therefore I told Mr Gutteridge of our worries and concerns . . . Since he had never signed the Official Secrets Act, I asked him to do so then.'

As 'Ford's' cross-examination went on, Judge Smedley seemed not to comprehend at first Robertson's determination to put large chunks of the 'secret' documents to the MI5 man in the witness-box: 'Mr Robertson, I do not want to stop you – but I really do wonder what on earth is the relevance of Dr Safa's future with the Iraqi government . . . I really do think to go into this enormous amount of detail about every single document that this witness produced is only confusing, and certainly is not helping either the jury, your clients, or anybody.'

Robertson managed several times to work in the thought that intelligence – even information about the Supergun – would have been finding its way from Gutteridge – via British intelligence – to the CIA in the United States. By February 1989 at the latest, and much earlier according to Gutteridge, MI5 had pointers from him to schemes to manufacture 210mm projectiles, bigger than the largest conventional howitzer, through a company called SRC which had Belgian connections. This is a thread which, had it been followed, would have led direct to Dr Gerald Bull and his Space Research Corporation in Brussels: busy at that moment purchasing steel barrels and propellant for even bigger members of the gun family – the 350mm and the 1,000mm 'Babylon' Supergun.

On the front page of the *New York Times*, Dean Baquet wrote from the Old Bailey public gallery: 'As part of an intelligence-gathering effort, the British government helped Iraq build up its military forces in the years before the invasion of Kuwait, by allowing the illegal sale of arms-manufacturing equipment to Baghdad.' As the Foreign Office would have said, 'presentationally', the Matrix Churchill trial was fast deteriorating.

The exchanges also offered reporters illuminating pieces of 'raw' intelligence: for example, into the way Saddam Hussein's family was said by Gutteridge to do business:

GR: . . . In discussing details of a contract, Anis Wadi said in a private, off-guard moment, that a small percentage of each contract goes to a Swiss account in the name of the President of Iraq's son?

'MF':   That is correct – that is what I was told.

In the witness-box in Court 16, 'Ford's' denials that Cardoen had ever specifically been mentioned by name were weakened by the fact that a number of Source Reports and Contact Notes seemed to be missing from the disclosed bundle, or were too heavily blacked-out for him to recall their contents. As 'Ford' seemed unwilling to commit himself on any point that was missing from the documents, the defendants knew that they could always tell the jury later that 'undisclosed documents' held the key to Henderson's innocence.

Those files Robertson did bring before the jury's eyes were in themselves quite satisfactory. After a tussle with Moses, the defence succeeded in having some blacked-out portions restored: Robertson's argument was that it was unreasonable to hide on 'security' grounds items that the defence's own witness had told MI5 in the first place. So the jury saw, for example, a Source Report filed in July 1988, to MI5, on Matrix Churchill's US subsidiary, saying that they: 'had dealings with the Chileans through their office in Miami. An agreement has been signed for a large consignment of fuses to be sent to Iraq.'

Another blacked-out Source Report from six months later, after Robertson had persuaded the prosecution to 'de-redact' it, was seen to confirm the details. Gutteridge had left Matrix Churchill by this point for an outside sales job. His access to information was only scrappy. But he confided that the machine-tools being produced in the Coventry factory were formally known as the 'Chilean project'. He had been told privately that 'the Chilean project covered 210mm shells, missiles and a range of fuses'. And a month later, in February 1989, 'Ford' reported in a telegram direct to MI6: 'We [i.e. MI5] have variously reported on the 'Chilean project' which is a priority Iraqi activity setting up the manufacture of missiles.' It was connected with the mysterious company SRC, Gutteridge had said. He was asked about the ABA project and said that he had seen the initals on component drawings for the 'Chilean project'. This was garbled (they were two separate projects). But it was explicit intelligence that the ABA project was military in nature. And it was undoubted, detailed and repeated intelligence about the military nature of the Chilean project. The only thing missing was the name 'Cardoen'.

On balance, Officer B had served to set up Gutteridge nicely for the jury, so far as the defence were concerned. He clearly did not relish his role in the special witness-box – although it is a role MI5 officers may find increasingly forced on them, as they move out of the Cold War era into their new responsibility for anti-terrorist operations. Officer B had served to paint for the jury an intriguing picture of Mark Gutteridge, the main defence witness whom they were yet to see. The 'charming' secret agent's early perception of the Western arms-buying network's organisation as a 'front' for Saddam Hussein and the Iraqi government was an insight of major significance.

As the US presidential election loomed, it was hard to avoid the obvious relationship of the Matrix Churchill case to the broad political issues: thanks to Gutteridge, the White House could – should – must! – have known of Dr Safa and his Euro-American procurement plans as early as 1987. That was two years before the date they had given the Gonzalez committee as the point of their awareness of Iraqi malpractice. The American press were in court, drawn by such thoughts, and this link was being published in US newspapers a few days before the US went to vote. Did it benefit Clinton's campaign? It certainly could not have hurt it. Did it help Paul Henderson to be acquitted? The spectres of Iraqgate and the publicised notions of large foreign conspiracies at work were only going to strengthen the jury's perception of Paul Henderson as a pawn in someone else's game.

9

THE MIDDLE EAST EXPERT

Testimony from MI6, 3 November 1992

We believe an approach to Henderson is feasible.
MI6 telegram, 26 March 1989

The man from MI5 was a challenge that Geoffrey Robertson QC seemed able to handle: the man from MI6 was a more dangerous proposition. The Secret Intelligence Service came to testify for the first time in their secret life, on Tuesday 3 November. As before, the defendants were allowed to leave the Old Bailey dock at the back of the court and sit with their barristers, so that they could see Officer A along with the jury and the judge. Paul Henderson himself was amused to register his secret service controller's new appearance. His hair had been extensively rearranged and he was wearing a large pair of spectacles that seemed to be made of plain glass.

His evidence would be crucial for the defence. In his witness statement, 'Balsam' (named as 'Not Given') had done his best to minimise the managing director as a low-level contact who had attended a few meetings, passed a few useless documents and not talked about Matrix Churchill's active business with Iraq. Robertson would need to make him be

THE MIDDLE EAST EXPERT

a lot more forthcoming before Henderson's second defence
– that 'British intelligence knew' – could be made out for the
period of machinery sales after Gutteridge left the firm, in
1989 and 1990.

'Balsam' did not seem hostile to Henderson. In examination-
in-chief by Alan Moses for the prosecution, he admitted to the
Customs QC that Henderson had indeed spoken about Matrix
Churchill business.

> Yes, there was discussion of Matrix Churchill business. He
> was managing director so it was bound to come up in our
> meetings . . . The first time I met him, he took me on to the
> shop-floor. It seemed fairly successful, a very good example
> of British industry working – he employed 600 people so he
> had an enormous responsibility to preserve those jobs.

Henderson was 'very sociable', he said; the first time they
had met, he'd been taken to his brother's restaurant just down
the road. 'Balsam's' main interest was in finding out whether
the Iraqis were acquiring 'weapons of mass destruction', but
he had got a general grasp of the fact that Matrix Churchill
exported machine-tools and associated computer software.
'Balsam' also conceded that they had discussed export licence
applications: 'Export licences would all be bundled together
and he had to wait while they were considered by the DTI
at a certain level, and passed up through the system. Mr
Henderson, like a lot of British businessmen, was annoyed
by the delays.'

'Balsam' said he was handling 'a large number of operations'; he was receiving sensitive information from various
sources, and Henderson only took up a small portion of his
time. But, he admitted, helpfully: 'I felt my relationship with
Mr Henderson was a good one – and important.'

Robertson began to cross-examine the MI6 man. He started
at a complete tangent:

GR: Your last meeting face to face with Mr Henderson

took place at a Heathrow hotel on July 31st 1990 . . . the day before Iraq invaded Kuwait?

'B':   Two days before.

You discussed with him the reports of the build-up of Iraqi forces on the border, and the Matrix people still in Iraq?

I do not recall discussing it in such detail, but I think, yes.

. . . And you expressed the opinion that no invasion would take place!

I can't recollect what my opinion was.

This off-beat opening must have been a deliberate cross-examination tactic. It was an anxious day for the defence. Henderson felt betrayed, he said, by MI6: he seemed to have no doubt in his own mind that he had told them about Cardoen, and they had not been particularly interested. He also maintained that he had told them all about ABA – 'Project 144', as it had been known. He had discussed repeatedly the delays in export licensing. Alan Moses QC for Customs had conceded that if he passed information to British intelligence, it was the same as passing it to the government. Henderson maintained that MI6 should have told Customs the truth: and stopped the case. Their original statement, in his view, was so parsimonious with the truth that it made him inclined to believe they were out to 'get' him – a belief strengthened by the documentary evidence that in the early stages of the prosecution, MI6 had been so closely involved with Customs.

So the defence expectation was that 'Balsam' would be a hostile witness, and a dangerous one, given the special protection and importance accorded to his evidence. 'Balsam' was likely to have been extensively rehearsed. The number of unfamiliar suited men in the public gallery suggested that MI6, too, had been following the trial with care, and would be able to predict the nature of the defence's approach. All the more reason for it to be changed, perhaps: instead of proceeding chronologically, as was his usual practice, Robertson unexpectedly focused on the last meeting of all, at Heathrow, and 'Balsam's' failure to predict the invasion.

He then zoomed in on the most potentially embarrassing aspect of the case – the involvement of MI6 in the preparation of the defence. Where 'Ford' had received kid-glove treatment, 'Balsam's' experience was going to be confrontational. He was challenged over his contacts with Customs while they were preparing the case against his agent.

GR: You had been in touch with a man called Peter Wiltshire who had been leading the Customs investigation?

'B': Yes, it had become clear there might be some connection the intelligence services in general had with people connected with Matrix Churchill . . . Mr Henderson had given me some blueprints . . . I was told by others in authority that, because of this connection – because Customs realised – because of the K1000 blueprint problem, it would be worthwhile for me to meet Mr Wiltshire.

After the Customs visit, he agreed he had told Henderson, the way the evidence was looking: 'they would not have anything to worry about'. 'It was not the feeling I gave – it was the feeling I got from two people [Henderson and Wiltshire] who knew far more about the export licensing procedure than I did.'

Henderson told his MI6 case officer that he was going to make an emergency trip to Baghdad, and tell Dr Safa, the Iraqi boss, that for the company to have 'continuing contact with

Cardoen and Space Research would be dangerous'. The memo 'Balsam' wrote then recorded: 'I advised him on the line to take with [the Iraqis] and told him not to exaggerate the threat of prosecution, as this might lead the authorities in Baghdad to cut off contact completely – and more importantly not to pay the letter of credit.'

Robertson adopted a critical tone:

> Here you were, advising the managing director of Matrix Churchill how he should conduct himself with his Iraqi principals . . . He wants to make sure Safa realises their pressure for continuing contact with Cardoen is not going to be to the company's benefit?

> Cardoen is a well-known arms manufacturer. Space Research had been involved in the supergun . . . I did not know before this came up in June 1990 that there was Cardoen contact with Matrix Churchill.

It was awkward territory for MI6: their officer had effectively been a go-between for a potential defendant and his prosecutors in a 'difficult and sensitive' political case. 'Balsam', the MI6 intermediary, was himself a potential witness in that case. Procedurally, it was very murky: the defence planned to condemn these back-door dealings at a later stage of the trial, when the Customs officers were due to give their evidence. At the Old Bailey, it would appear as an unprecedented legal situation; and 'Balsam' was clearly unhappy at the role he played.

What was even more curious was the fact that he was forced to admit giving Henderson advice on how Matrix Churchill should relate the Customs visit to their Iraqi bosses. At this point, MI6 appeared to be actually using Henderson to warn the Iraqis off contact with Cardoen and the Space Research Corporation. It was, on any view, striking confirmation of how closely, and valuably, Henderson was serving intelligence purposes.

The tone of 'Balsam's' cross-examination soon changed, however – and changed dramatically. Where 'Ford' had been stodgy and taciturn, 'Balsam' was of a different type. He was intense, concerned, intellectual: capable of being voluble. He was to electrify the court with his account of Henderson the secret agent, and the nature of his role.

'Ford' from MI5 had already explained how Henderson had been signed up. 'Ford', together with Henderson's friend, agent Mark Gutteridge, had advised on the covert recruitment of the managing director as a replacement agent after Gutteridge left the firm: 'The analyst desk officer [from MI6] wanted to improve coverage of Iraqi matters, and I was asked if I saw any objections if Mr Henderson was approached . . . I discussed it with Gutteridge.'

Information had been filtering in since the end of 1988 that Dr Safa al-Habobi and his companies were trying to obtain magnet rings in the UK – components of gas centrifuges, which are one of the few methods available of enriching uranium to make nuclear weapons. Saddam had long had a passion for acquiring atomic bombs. Margaret Thatcher had expressed concern in April 1989, and authorised steps to uncover and disrupt Saddam's procurement network. Military intelligence were working on a study of the Iraqi armaments industry: and MI6 appeared to have been urged to increase their flow of Iraqi intelligence.

In this atmosphere, Matrix Churchill had already, astonishingly, been awarded a second batch of licences for 'general engineering' – machines which were to make fuses and missiles. Foreign Secretary Geoffrey Howe himself had approved the licence award in February 1989 along with his junior Minister, William Waldegrave, and the Defence Procurement Minister, Lord Trefgarne. David Gore-Booth, head of the Middle East and Africa department, was the only senior official who went on record as disapproving:

I am distinctly sceptical about the wisdom of approving

exports of potentially lethal equipment on the grounds that to deny it will deprive us of intelligence – particularly when the availability of such intelligence – *even if we can use it without compromising its source* [sic] – is on past form not guaranteed to prevent other countries doing the business.

The key question was whether the machinery would contribute to Iraq's nuclear programme, the most recent cause of alarm. The information available, said Gore-Booth, 'makes me distinctly uncomfortable'. One Labour MP, George Robertson, 'is on the warpath about Iraqi weapons'. He added, to emphasise the kind of warning he was giving: 'There has already been one leak from a Matrix employee.' (This was presumably a reference to the 1988 letter from a Matrix worker confirming that the company's machines were for making shells.)

Military intelligence had also originally told the Defence Ministry that they wanted to block the licences. They said that MI6 ('Box 850') fears about their source's security were now unnecessary. A licence application from another firm had come in, stating that the Nassr plant was the end-user. The firm said that it wanted to sell the Iraqis a moulding machine to produce plastic parts at Nassr for missiles. This development, officially revealing that Nassr was making arms: '. . . gives us the collateral we have sought. I think we can now present a case against these tools being shipped to either establishment without compromising the Box 850 source.'

However, the consensus Foreign Office line was the opposite. A new 'intelligence' reason for granting the licences was produced. 'The refusal of these export licences could force Matrix Churchill to close down. If this happens, we would lose our intelligence access to Habobi's network. By keeping access open, we could obtain more important information, in particular on the procurement of some item which is far more important than magnet rings.' Waldegrave scribbled: 'I agree. Screwdrivers are also required to make H-bombs.' There may have been a clue to his original Ministerial anxiety in Gore-Booth's rueful note, that refusal could also cause 'damage to Anglo–Iraqi relations, especially since the Iraqi ambassador has raised the issue to the inter-governmental level'.

In March 1989, the moves began to recruit Henderson to 'Balsam's' MI6 stable of agents. The nature of 'Balsam's' preoccupations briefly, but illuminatingly, shone through at the end of quite a passionate speech to Robertson shortly before the coffee break:

> Our obsession almost, was with three things. It is our job to collect strategic intelligence which is vital to threats to Britain. Concerning Iraq, we were most worried about nuclear capability; long-range missile capability; biological/chemical. Trying to find out about efforts to obtain such technology had nothing to do, in our understanding, with Matrix Churchill, but involved [its Iraqi holding companies] in London . . . If Mr Henderson came along with something about conventional arms, I would pass it on to the experts . . . I am not sure whether it was an issue to customers, as our jargon has it. Our obsession was with these other areas, rather than conventional fuses. Given the intelligence services had, through 1987 and 1988, passed, in my understanding, quite considerable bits of information about Matrix Churchill . . . This was a matter for the decision-making people in processing export licences. It was not for my service, but the DTI primarily . . . You have to concentrate on the strategically important things. That is what we were doing, and going for.

You were not so interested in conventional weapons?

Not in terms of strategic intelligence to Britain, frankly . . . conventional weapons were less a strategic intelligence priority, because it would obviously be a great threat to stability in the Middle East, even to Europe itself, if Saddam Hussein developed these weapons of mass destruction. And thank God he didn't, as far as we know.

That 'Thank God he didn't' was an intriguing personal comment, indicating a certain obsession of 'Balsam's' own with the evil of Saddam Hussein. It may have been the cue for a remarkable change in atmosphere after the break. It altered from confrontation to what seemed almost like a meeting of Amnesty International, between a human rights lawyer and an Amnesty case officer. Suddenly and dramatically, the nature of Saddam Hussein's regime was brought home to the court: the one reality quite absent from the policy documents and the arid testimony that had gone before.

A paperback book with a red cover called *Republic of Fear* can be bought for £7.99 in London, in the new 1990 edition. Written under the name Samir al-Khalil, it is an exile dissident's lengthy analysis of Saddam's regime. Telling stories of children's eyes being gouged out and bodies tipped into huge vats of acid, he says: 'The chamber of horrors that is Saddam Hussein's Iraq has mushroomed into something that not even the most morbid imagination could have foreseen.' The author makes the point that, towards the 'Number one human rights violator in the world', both Arabs and the West have ambiguous attitudes: 'Western governments looking towards lucrative markets in the near future – for oil prices are expected to rise – are not doing enough. They turn a blind eye to the worst excesses when these do not involve them directly.' The hanging of *Observer* journalist Farzad Bazoft for so-called spying was a case he mentioned: after a temporary recalling of ambassadors, many in the British government wished to return quickly to business as usual.

'Balsam' presented an edition of *Republic of Fear* to Henderson, as the managing director had told the defence team.

GR: And you remember giving him this book . . . ?

'B':   Yes.

. . . And inviting him to read it to understand just how dangerous the characters and personalities he was dealing with were?

Yes – and also because I think that it is a superb description of the appalling regime in Iraq.

. . . Its message is that there has been a ruthless and relentless build-up in Iraq of terror; and that Iraq was a dictatorship based on terror?

Yes. I agree.

And it describes Saddam Hussein himself as the only genuinely free man in Iraq, as a megalomaniac whose secret police and courts system had been devised to torture and execute those who were disloyal to the state?

Yes.

And it particularly stressed that disloyalty was regarded as acts of spying, or hostility to the state?

Yes.

In particular that the targets of state terror were spies, saboteurs and foreign agents?

Yes, that is the sort of brutal regime it is.

Your warnings to him were re-emphasised after the arrest and execution of the journalist, Mr Bazoft?

They were – because obviously that was an appalling crime Saddam Hussein carried out against an innocent journalist.

It was as if 'Balsam' were unburdening himself of a horror he had been secretly amassing for years in his job of collecting evidence and advising his superiors about the *Republic of*

Fear. Few in court were likely to forget the chill of these exchanges – and how they were transmuted into a tribute to the extraordinary courage of Paul Henderson himself, who had secretly and repeatedly met 'Balsam' at the factory the Iraqis controlled; and had travelled into Iraq eight times in the period, while spying for MI6. He had reported back on troop and tank movements after his visit during the period of high friction after the Bazoft hanging.

> 'B': Mr Henderson was a very brave man. Together with all the problems, the pressures on his business from media coverage, financial pressures – to take this extra risk, he was extremely brave. There are very few people I have met who would take such risks and take them so much in their stride, with all the pressures on him.

According to Henderson, one of 'Balsam's' interests had been to identify top-rank Iraqis in the procurement network who could be 'turned' to work for MI6, either through inducements or pressure. They were interested in both Anis Wadi and Dr Safa: 'Balsam' pressed his agent to find out what personal weaknesses they might have that could be exploited. How much did they gamble, for example, or chase women? Safa had been approached once already by the intelligence services, 'Balsam' told him, but nothing had been achieved:

> GR: He was telling you not only about their commercial dealings, but about their personal lives?
>
> 'B': Yes. That is true
>
> GR: And personal weaknesses they might have – was that a matter you asked him about?

Moses sprang to his feet on behalf of the Crown. Questions of this kind were clearly regarded as a breach of security: 'I do not see what that has got to do with it – and you have got to be very careful.' Robertson glided around the topic:

> We will leave that. The things he saw and the people he met on his trips to Iraq –
>
> Yes . . .
>
> In doing that, you accept he was running personal risks?
>
> Absolutely . . . I mean, our relationship was voluntary, but as I say, he was a very, very brave man who, on top of all the other pressures on top of him – took these extra risks.

Balsam had deliberately praised the defendant's courage in strong terms for the second time. The defence team were awestruck by the implications of his change of tone. To observers, indeed to the jury, the prosecution must, they thought, be looking crazy. Henderson was now, if anything, a national hero who deserved a medal, not a scoundrel who should be put in jail. It was difficult to conceive that a jury would convict him, whatever the details of the evidence. Not a word that Henderson had behaved with courage was to be seen in the prosecution papers. Cynics might say that MI6 had realised which way the trial was going and changed their testimony to place themselves on the winning side. Cynics, too, might think that MI6 were publicly distancing themselves from government actions in selling arms to Iraq. The message of the evidence was: 'We told you all along that this was a brutal and megalomaniac regime.' If this message had ever been received in Whitehall, it had certainly not been a factor in any of the decisions.

Paul Henderson, sitting beside counsel and observing 'Balsam's' new hairstyle and spectacles as he praised him, felt that he understood the MI6 man's testimony: 'I believe that what he was doing was trying to help me,' he said afterwards. 'I think it was his way of trying to help me, with regard to the situation I was in with the prosecution.' If he is asked why 'Balsam' should help him in that way, Henderson answers, a touch grimly: 'Because I'd spent a number of years helping *them*.'

At any event, 'Balsam' and his cross-examiner had become a lot more friendly. They went on to talk of all the meetings between Henderson and the agent-runner – many more than MI6 had originally conceded. There was evidence that 'Balsam' had often spoken to him about licence applications. And there were revelations in court that Henderson's material had caused excitement at a high level.

The whole story of Iraqgate had started to break on both sides of the Atlantic in August 1989. When the FBI raided the BNL bank in Atlanta, they uncovered not only the billion-dollar loans to Iraq, but the identities of the companies in Iraq's covert procurement network. Matrix Churchill's Iraqi links were exposed – links of which British intelligence had been aware for nearly two years. At the time, 'Balsam' went to see Henderson for a four-hour meeting, carrying a copy of the day's *Financial Times*.

The effect was electric. Henderson faxed it to Safa and called his bankers. 'Balsam' recorded: 'Henderson had always been mystified as to why the Iraqis channelled their business through Atlanta. They always undercut terms that Matrix Churchill could get from other banks.' The firm had recently taken on a contract to equip a forging plant, which BNL had financed, and three BNL bankers had been in Coventry to finalise the deal.

'Balsam' said MI6 were not interested in past history, only in predicting the future: 'We do not think there is any mileage in us getting involved in the detail of these problems,' he wrote, 'which are not integral to illegal Iraqi high technology procurement.' However, he was sensible enough to recommend that his desk officer 'get details from the Americans' of all the companies involved in Iraqi procurement. 'And this session lasted for four hours?' demanded Robertson in court. '. . . We went to an Italian restaurant afterwards . . He talked about his family, me about mine,' 'Balsam' replied. He was flying to California shortly to get married. Henderson had a son in the Coldstream Guards.

The glare of publicity on Henderson grew worse. In early September 1989, the story was 'leaked' that the Foreign Office was blocking attempts by an Iraqi procurement group, in league with the Space Research Corporation, to buy the high-tech Belfast firm Learfan. The company possessed carbon-fibre technology with missile potential. The procurement group was named TDG. And the fact that they controlled Matrix Churchill was trumpeted in the Sunday papers. Within a week, Henderson had admitted in the *Financial Times* (to the confidential consternation of the DTI) that Matrix Churchill had previously sold machines to Baghdad to make components for artillery shells – complete with DTI licences.

> 'Even if some machines had gone into defence areas, I don't see anything wrong with that,' said Mr Henderson. 'They cannot produce anything but that which will contribute to the making of conventional type weapons. We have hidden nothing.'

Against this background of controversy, MI6 continued to milk Henderson. 'Balsam' made arrangements the following month for 'a long session with Henderson in London' after a visit to him from Iraq of the director-generals of the weapons plants there.

> We would get much more [DELETED] information out of him if we had at this meeting a map of where we suspect sensitive research establishments are, and an organogram of the establishments so that he can fill in the gaps from his own personal knowledge.

BETRAYED

The day before the planned meeting, there was again a commotion in Whitehall over that morning's *Financial Times*. An article had tied in Matrix Churchill with the BNL Iraqi finance scandal in Atlanta, as well as with the Learfan scandal in Britain. There was an elaborate diagram showing where Matrix Churchill fitted into a covert military procurement network involving Dr Safa al-Habobi of the Nassr plant. It ranged from the Space Research Corporation in Brussels through to a pair of British 'front' companies called TMG and TDG.

Before the trial, Henderson had described to his lawyers how he was met by 'Balsam' in a chauffeur-driven big black car when he arrived at Euston for an unusual day in town. 'The house, I recall, was Georgian with a large bay window, high ceilings, a large central mahogany table, sofas and chairs – extremely drab wall-coverings. On one of the walls was a map of Iraq and a satellite photograph of Baghdad.' Henderson had been taken down for the morning to the impressive MI6 house at 3 Carlton Gardens, just off the Mall, which they commonly use for meetings with outsiders. There he had been drained of all his geographical knowledge. Robertson cross-examined at the trial:

GR: That took place on September 22nd 1989, when you met him at the station and in a chauffeur-driven car you took him to what you describe as a 'safe house'?

'B': That is correct, yes . . . various of our experts who had been involved in a long line of reporting on things to do with Matrix Churchill, to see whether Mr Henderson's knowledge of – particularly – plants inside Iraq, added to the knowledge we had . . . People take in very, very few things at enormous risk. One wants to find out how much their knowledge adds . . . a number of technical experts had various maps . . . They were from Head Office taking notes in some form . . . We had experts in nuclear, chemical and long-range missiles.

Henderson had claimed he pointed out the location of the Nassr plant; the Huteen factory; a highly secret building where work was occurring on 'Project 1728' (a Scud missile improvement programme, using Matrix Churchill machines); and the 'April 7th' factory south of Baghdad where Matrix Churchill were equipping the Cardoen fuse plant. (He also said he was asked if he knew anything about 'Project Babylon' at this particular meeting, and handed over a set of six blueprints of parts for the ABA contract. 'Balsam' did not accept these last two claims. The dates turned out to be impossible to prove or disprove; as there was no formal record of the meeting.)

GR: He recalls being asked about SRC, the Space Research Corporation?

'B': Yes, that would have been very likely . . .

Project 144?

Project 144 we thought was a cover-name, possibly for parts of a long-range missile – quite likely.

. . . And Cardoen?

Cardoen – perhaps in the general sense we had discussed with him as being involved – as being a major arms firm who had all sorts of dealings with Iraq.

Henderson claimed he had then been taken to lunch in a gentleman's club, with 'Balsam's' boss – a man called 'Peter'. 'We talked about licences . . . during the lunch he used the phrase "dual technology", saying it was difficult to categorise the products made on a machine tool.'

In the witness-box, Balsam confirmed all this. '. . . Lunch at the club?' 'Yes.' '. . . Your boss . . . known only by Christian name, and you discussed export licence problems?' 'I think we may well have done in a general sense because it was a major problem for Matrix Churchill.'

Henderson maintained in his own statement that the group had then returned to the big room in Carlton Gardens. 'I was introduced to a lady called Louisa Symondson . . . another female with her remained anonymous.' Henderson was spending much time in the Soviet Union: 'She wanted to know what was happening there in the light of *perestroika* . . . I had toured factories there with the MTTA.'

In the witness-box, the MI6 officer confirmed this meeting too: 'You then introduced him to a Soviet expert?' . . . 'I think they had dealings thereafter.'

And finally, to round off this momentous day, Henderson had asserted to his lawyers that his MI6 case officer had arranged an appointment with the head of the Middle East department at the Foreign Office, to help sort out his current problem with the export licences for the Cardoen fuse factory. 'Balsam' had explained: 'The problem creating the hold-up in the Cardoen licences was the Foreign Office. Everything was then arranged . . . He gave me the name Rob Young.' After the Soviet debriefing session, said Henderson, his MI6 officer walked him down to Horse Guards Parade and showed him in at the grandiose entrance to the Foreign Office. There he had duly been granted a meeting with Rob Young (four days in advance of an official lobbying meeting scheduled at the Department of Trade between Henderson and the current Trade Minister, Lord Trefgarne.)

Was this extraordinary picture, too, to be confirmed by MI6 in the witness box? It was correct, said 'Balsam'. He had arranged the meeting at the Foreign Office, and walked Henderson down Whitehall to the door, saying, 'Just ask for the Head of the Middle East department':

Far better to go to the department concerned and pass your opinions and views up to the people who make decisions, the Ministers. To try and pass such things on to the Secret Intelligence Service channels would complicate the matter enormously.

For those few members of the public who got into the court-room or who read about the trial in an occasional newspaper report, a glamorous picture reminiscent of imperial days of espionage had now come into focus. A high-ceilinged room off the Mall – satellite photographs and maps – the respectful circle of 'boffins' – the chauffeur-driven black Granada – and lunch at the club in Pall Mall, followed by a stroll down Whitehall for an appointment with the head of the Middle East department at the Foreign Office. The images evoked were of Bulldog Drummond; brandy and soda at the 'Travellers': *The Empire Fights Back*. This man Paul Henderson, giving his time, his mind – and possibly his life – to the service of his country: what was he doing, the jury must have been asking, in the dock at the Old Bailey?

The head of the Middle East department, Rob Young, did not mention MI6 when he wrote a careful minute of that meeting afterwards to go up to William Waldegrave. Attitudes at the Foreign Office had recently hardened. The Minister had very recently written a strong, confidential letter saying that he would refuse the new licences. The FO minute said that Henderson, as part of his lobbying campaign, had 'called on me at his request', and told Young that the licences were for equipment 'of a type previously approved [he claimed] for the same end-user as before . . . But he had been frank in admitting that he could not guarantee the lathes would not be used for military manufacturing purposes.'

On paper, Young was mildly unsympathetic to this piece of lobbying: although there would be a danger to the company's viability if Iraq financiers backed out: 'I see no reason to alter the view expressed in [Waldegrave's] letter.' His boss, Gore-Booth, was even less sympathetic: 'Claims that the future of the company is at stake seem undermined by their own publicity material.' The Minister scrawled: 'I agree', and pressed down on to the front page his little inked rubber stamp reading 'WILLIAM WALDEGRAVE'.

Yet, within a month, their apparently unsympathetic determination would give way to a much weaker stance. The evidence shows that the FO stand was fatally weakened thanks to a 'fix' put in by the intelligence agency. On 31 October, a Third Secretary at the Middle East department, Simon Sherrington, stamped the classification SECRET on a Ministerial briefing. It was circulated to PUSD, the department that maintains liaison with SIS. This note said the whole issue was now much more 'finely balanced':

> [DELETED] have since said they believe the lathes, at any rate initially, may *not* be used for the direct manufacture of munitions or for nuclear applications. They are inclined to believe statements by Dr Safa al-Habobi, head of Nassr and Huteen, that his organisation is now dedicated solely to the post-war reconstruction of Iraq. [author's emphasis]

This was one of the 'intelligence-related' documents that the Foreign Office originally tried to withhold from the court. There is no doubt that the deleted reference was to MI6 – and indeed to the information that was being put into the system by 'Balsam' and his superiors. Someone in the secret world had decided to give Paul Henderson a further helping hand.

For the secret service, it was to prove worth keeping Paul Henderson in play. Did they try to help solve his problem in order to promote their own ambitions? The evidence that now came out in court certainly seemed to suggest it. For during this period, Henderson was persuaded into supplying blueprints which helped provide MI6 with a coup over a major subject of espionage concern that autumn – the Supergun.

The MI6 records showed him handing over the material

by 27 October – a month after the meeting in Carlton Gardens, and only a few days before the Foreign Office finally dropped its objections and let Henderson have his licences. When Geoffrey Robertson pursued this subject in cross-examination, he dug up treasure for the defence. The blueprints were of the ABA project. The letter Balsam sent with them to MI6 headquarters said in the disclosed version:

> The Iraqis, probably NASSR establishment, have asked his company to 'machine' [provide the machine-tools] to make the circular part detailed in most of the drawings. Henderson says that the part is for the projectile shown in some of the subsidiary drawings. Matrix Churchill engineers have been told that the interior of this projectile – with retractable fins – must be able to withstand 3000 degrees C for 10 minutes. They have calculated that this could give it a range of 1200km: it could be connected with Space Research Corporation's long-range artillery research [DELETED DELETED DELETED]. We will get further details from Henderson. Please could you get the blueprints copied [DELETED]. We will go over the blueprints with you the next time we visit Head Office.

Some of the drawings were marked: 'cassette warhead bottom/B ABA 200-000-03/B'.

The drawings appeared to be of a four-foot-long projectile, 262mm across, with fins at the base. Neither Robertson nor his client Henderson knew what had become of the blueprints after the hand-over, or the significance of the transaction. No documents had been disclosed by MI6. But as soon as 'Balsam' began to co-operate in the cross-examination, it was clear to Robertson that a vitally important report must exist.

'B': We were trying to technically analyse what all this meant . . . In fact it was the technical expert present at that [Carlton Gardens] meeting . . .

GR: Who presumably kept his own notes and generated his own report?

Yes, he was bringing things together from a number of sources, and seeing how relevant it was to other work he was doing . . . My understanding was that that drawing was included in a report – together with information from many other sources – which was issued to interested parties in Whitehall.

. . . Parties in government who had a need to know technical details of the kind of weaponry that was being canvassed by Iraq at that time?

Yes. I mean, that's right –

Judge Smedley intervened, full of interest: 'Do you know which department?' 'Balsam' replied: 'A wide and high-level readership, which would include the DTI, the FCO and the MOD.' By now, his courtroom audience were all paying hushed attention. 'Balsam' went forthcomingly on:

It was an important report – of which this particular information provided by Mr Henderson was a very, very small part, but at this stage also very useful . . . I think it was dated early November. It was an item potentially of great interest . . .

Do you know whether a report, or at least a summary of it, would have got to Ministerial level or not?

I understand a summary of that went to a very high level . . . Obviously nothing at all of the blueprints. A summary of that went to a very high Ministerial level.

'Yes', said Robertson, halting while his luck still held: 'I am obliged.'

For the defence this seemed like the equivalent of the Crown Jewels: incontrovertible evidence about detailed plans of the ABA project that Henderson had actually produced from Matrix Churchill offices. These plans had been immediately assessed by experts to relate to a long-range gun, details of which had been sent to the highest Ministerial level. Where was the report?

Efforts were made by the prosecution immediately to locate this whole document – a copy was brought to court and it was identified by Balsam at the end of the day. Pages of it were blacked out before the defence were allowed to have it, but the underlying nature of the report was not concealed by the censor's pencil. It was the missing key to the Supergun affair – the intelligence report that MPs on the Supergun committee had failed to find.

At the time that this report was compiled, in autumn 1989, the intelligence services were also collecting information from the British company Astra. The firm had taken over a Belgian explosives company, PRB, based in Brussels close by Gerald Bull's mysterious Space Research Corporation. Former managing director Gerald James was intrigued by what they found: 'The [Belgians] produced a lot of contracts and pointed to a contract with Jordan – and made it quite clear that contract was for Iraq, and was for a very large gun.' This was Project Babylon.

One Astra board member, Stephan Kock, who had a military intelligence background, told the committee that he had first telephoned 'the security services' direct about the Supergun, as early as 22 September. The day before Henderson handed over his ABA blueprints, 26 October, Astra had similarly handed over to the MOD in London the Babylon contracts. They were for explosive propellant apparently to go in the barrels of two enormous guns – the first of 350mm, more than twice the size of a conventional howitzer; and the second a truly gigantic 1,000mm. As the MI6 technical experts played detective, they would quickly have divined one startling fact: the ABA missile, for which Henderson's Coventry factory had the contract, would, if it was surrounded with some form of shielding, fit snugly into a gun-barrel of 350mm.

The Supergun report, which first went on 10 November to the Customs–intelligence enforcement committee, the REU, was headed:

SECRET

IRAQ:

PROJECT 'BABYLON' TO DEVELOP THE TECHNOLOGY FOR HYPER-VELOCITY GUN WITH EXTREME RANGE CAPABILITY (OCTOBER–NOVEMBER 1989)

On the second page, there was a distribution list. It had indeed gone to the DTI in Victoria Street (two copies). One copy had gone to Customs and Excise. Five recipients, whose names were blacked out, had had it in the Foreign Office. Eight secret addressees were to see it in the Defence Ministry. There were at least twenty other departmental recipients whose organisations were kept secret. Some will have been in MI6 itself and MI5. Others might have been in the Cabinet Office – or even Number 10.

The opening page classed the date of the information as October-November '89, and classed the source as 'Multiple'. Other source details were deleted.

Two pages of drawings were inked out. The third said: 'Fig.3 Possible Operational Projectile'. There, reproduced, was Henderson's ABA blueprint, with a few more dotted lines sketched in where the artist had made assumptions about the missing parts – the fuse projecting at the front, a rocket motor behind the war-head, and a nozzle at the back. It showed that Henderson's information was regarded as absolutely vital. Cabinet Ministers were being supplied with analysis of a

1 The Iraqi Ministry of Industry is, under Project BABYLON, endeavouring to acquire the technology for a hyper-velocity gun capable of delivering substantial payloads to extreme ranges. There is no indication of the intended operational role of such a weapon, but it would seem most suited for long-range strategic bombardment of wide area targets such as cities.

2 xxxxxxxxxxxxxxxxxxxxxxxxxxxxxxxxxxxxxxxxxxxxxxxxxxxxxxxxxxxxxx
xxxxxxxxxxxxxxxxxxxxxxxxxxxxxxxxxxxxxxxxxxxxxxxxxxxxxxxxxxxxxx
xxxxxxxxxxxxxxxxxxxxxxxxxxxxxxxxxxxxxxxxxxxxxxxxxxxxxxxxxxxxxx
xxxxxxxxxxxxxxxxxxxxxxxxxxxxxxxxxxxxxxxxxxxxxxxxxxxxxxxxxxxxxx
xxxxxxxxxxxxxxxxxxxxxxxxxxxxxxxxxxxxxxxxxxxxxxxxxxxxxxxxxxxxxx

3 At a later stage in the project, a larger operational version of the gun will fire 262mm projectiles with flip-out fins. This will be a rocket-assisted projectile (RAP) and carry a warhead section of 1.28m length. This is unlikely to be a simple high explosive (HE) device and is most likely a carrier arrangement for Cluster Munitions, although Fuel-Air Explosive (FAE) or Chemical Warfare payloads cannot be ruled out. The project specification calls for it to be able to withstand a considerable amount of kinetic heating (3000 degrees C for 10 minutes). While it would be unwise to use this to read back to a velocity and ultimately a range requirement (safety factors being unknown), it is clear that ranges of several hundred km are contemplated. A figure of 600km has been mentioned.

4 xxxxxxxxxxxxxxxxxxxxxxxxxxxxxxxxxxxxxxxxxxxxxxxxxxxxxxxxxxxxxx
xxxxxxxxxxxxxxxxxxxxxxxxxxxxxxxxxxxxxxxxxxxxxxxxxxxxxxxxxxxxxx
xxxxxxxxxxxxxxxxxxxxxxxxxxxxxxxxxxxxxxxxxxxxxxxxxxxxxxxxxxxxxx
xxxxxxxxxxxxxxxxxxxxxxxxxxxxxxxxxxxxxxxxxxxxxxxxxxxxxxxxxxxxxx

5 Drawings are attached showing:

a xxxxxxxxxxxxxxxxxxxxxxxxxxxxxxxxxxxxxxxxxxxxxxxxxxxxxxxxxxx
b xxxxxxxxxxxxxxxxxxxxxxxxxxxxxxxxxxxxxxxxxxxxxxxxxxxxxxxxxxx
c elements of the larger operational projectile.

Desk Comment

1 We do not underestimate the difficulties of developing such a weapon to the point where it gives a meaningful operational capability. However, the Iraqis would appear to have adopted a proper systematic approach xxxxxxxxxxxxxxxxxxxxxxxxxx which could lead to a successful outcome given continued access to the necessary resources and West European technology.

2 The weapon is not dissimilar in concept to the V3 developed by the Germans towards the end of WWII. Similar concepts have been described by Dr BULL in some of his published works for a range of applications, including that of a Space Launch Vehicle.

3 The technology required to achieve this project would not appear to be constrained by the terms of the Missile Technology Control Regime (MTCR) which may be part of the motivation for the project given the difficulties of acquiring ballistic missile technology.

Supergun nearly six months before any action was taken by Customs against the British barrel manufacturers. Surely for the jury it would make nonsense of the claim that Henderson had 'held back' on the ABA project. On the contrary, he was giving MI6 the most vital drawings, with ABA written all over them.

This evidence, if it was ever pursued, was not only likely to acquit Henderson; it was also likely to plunge Ministers into fresh controversy. Trade Secretary Nicholas Ridley had excused himself to the Commons in April 1990, when the Supergun tubes were discovered on the dockside, by saying: 'The government *recently* became aware in general terms of an Iraqi project to develop a long-range gun [author's emphasis].' Civil servants had also given the impression, in evidence to the Supergun committee, that Ministers had never been told the autumn 1989 information. Alan Clark had testified that, as junior Trade Minister, he had not received intelligence about the Supergun. He could not speak, he had added, for Ridley.

Clearly, what Ridley said to the Commons had not been correct. 'The government', in the sense of Whitehall, had known six months earlier. 'Balsam', in his evidence, was contradicting the evidence given to the Commons committee. He had testified on oath that Ministers themselves also knew. 'A summary of that went to a very high Ministerial level.' If Ministers knew about the Supergun, why on earth had they not done anything to stop it?

'Balsam' continued, during his time in the witness-box, to be helpful to Henderson (or perhaps, though it seems implausible, artlessly truthful). He confirmed Henderson's interest in getting civilian as well as military contracts: 'That sort of project, particularly, Mr Henderson used to talk a lot about – the General Motors project; the tyres project; Perkins engines and Perkins diesel project . . .'

GR: The various automobile projects did seem to indicate

some sort of shift after the Gulf [Iran–Iraq] War to an industrial base?

'B': Yes, one hoped so. It was not something I reported, but one lived in hope.

Other examples were given of information Henderson was 'very kindly' providing. He had mentioned that a company, Leigh, was exporting surface-coating technology which was more relevant to missiles than machine-tools were: 'I think it was the comment of a technical specialist who had a lot of industrial dealings, who was very kindly advising us what to look out for.' In December, 'Balsam' recalled, they had had 'a very rushed Christmas drink':

In fact Mr Henderson tried to cancel because he was also very busy with the Korean delegation. And he was still nice enough to come out for a quick drink, even though he had all these preoccupations . . . He was very kind.

It seemed as though MI6 were almost pathetically grateful for the assistance and indulgence that Henderson had shown to them over a period when he had, on his visits to Iraq, risked his life for their sake. It would have been hard for anyone in court on 3 November to believe that MI6 had assisted in the preparation of the prosecution – or would want anything so much as to take tea with kind and nice and brave Mr Henderson.

There was a hint of scepticism in the judge's intervention before Officer A stepped down. When he was in Coventry seeing Henderson, the judge asked, was not anything said about how Henderson got hold of Iraqi weapons drawings and whether Matrix Churchill was making the machine-tools for the weapons? 'It was never discussed,' answered 'Balsam'. MI6 maintained to the end that Henderson had not told them all the details of Cardoen or ABA: but it was difficult to believe he had held anything back intentionally.

It was also difficult not to believe that MI6 had decided by now that this extraordinary prosecution had served its original purpose and that it was doomed to failure since the disclosure of the documents. The best thing that could happen would be for it to end as decently as possible – so that 'Balsam' and his colleagues could be present for the celebrations after Henderson received, if not the Queen's award for exports – at the very least the Victoria Cross.

This startling testimony by MI6 had its effect, on two levels. Beyond the immediate level of the trial was the political significance of the world it revealed. Never before had the public seen in this authentic and detailed way just how secret intelligence worked – how the government set tasks for the intelligence agencies and how their behaviour in turn influenced government policy. Mark Gutteridge and Paul Henderson both believed that the immediate, practical result was going to be ruinous for British intelligence – no British businessman would want to sign up for intelligence work in future, now it had been revealed that sales managers who worked abroad were – as often as not – amateur James Bonds.

But the material that came out in court was likely to discredit the workings of ordinary government in Whitehall as well. Not once, but three times in three years, export licences were issued to Matrix Churchill. Each time, machines for making armaments were permitted to be exported, destroying the Foreign Secretary's published policy; and each time, the involvement of the intelligence agencies merely served to muddy the waters.

In 1987, MI6 discovered too late that armaments were involved – and then allowed themselves to be used by Whitehall as an excuse for continuing the shipments. In February 1989, the Foreign Office were able to use 'intelligence access' as an excuse for capitulating to pressure from the DTI. In November 1989, MI6 helped Henderson to get more licences, against Foreign Office resistance, because he was functioning as their agent. The only apparent government achievement to set against these massive exports of weapons machinery to Iraq was a contribution to an MI6 report identifying the Supergun – a report which was then ignored by Ministers.

The state of one half of Henderson's defence looked reasonably healthy after the intelligence evidence. British intelligence clearly did know a lot about the exported machine-tools without minding very much what became of them. But what about the other half of the defence? To show that 'HMG knew' and deliberately turned a blind eye was going to depend on the artful cross-examination of the Department of Trade and Industry's Ministers. A small squadron of civil servants stood between Geoffrey Robertson QC and his final Ministerial target.

10

DTI IN THE DOCK

Testimony from civil servants, 26 October 1992

I called Eric BESTON about this.
MI6 minutes, 26 January 1988

It was the inevitable fate of Assistant Secretary Eric Beston that he would be compared in the witness-box to the Whitehall mandarin in the TV comedy series *Yes, Minister*: a top civil servant who was both pompous and devious. Gilbert Gray QC was not the man to flinch from the cliché: 'You were the sort of Sir Humphrey of the situation in your little sphere of activity, were you not?' But the head of the DTI's export control division had by then brought the joke on himself.

Beston had some problems. The newly-discovered documents showed he had been keen on a cover-up in 1987, when MI6 revealed that his own organisation had mistakenly issued the first licences for machines to equip Iraqi arms factories. Beston had later gone on record pooh-poohing the significance of the Iraqi shareholding in Matrix Churchill. And he had composed parliamentary answers to put off and bamboozle MPs who were suspicious of the company's dealings with Iraq.

The Ministers to whom he was answerable were fanatical Thatcherites who admired 'enterprise' and spent their time trying to water down or abolish the Howe embargos; and the intelligence officers from MI6 were whispering in his ear about their 'sources'. In this governmental atmosphere of the late '80s – a blend of incompetence, secrecy and deference to greed – Beston backed Matrix Churchill and its bogus licence applications through thick and thin.

The first senior Whitehall official to appear, he had been waiting outside the courtroom, disguising his nervousness by burying his head in a book – Beston had read English at St Peter's College, Oxford, and had been in the department since leaving an advertising agency seventeen years before.

In the witness-box he found it hard to admit the plain fact that his Ministry had allowed munitions equipment to go to Iraq in 1987 and 1988 in the knowledge that it would be used to make artillery shells. Beston's degree seemed to have equipped him to make the English language as meaningless or meaningful as he chose it to be: he found dozens of evasive phrases when he was in a corner. 'That is what it appears to say . . . It could well be . . . apparently . . . It would seem so . . . I am not in a position to answer . . . I am afraid you will have to ask them . . . It is a long time ago . . . I don't know how accurate a record of the meeting this is, I wasn't there . . . You say it's a political judgement so you will have to ask a politician . . . There is a danger in assuming that civil servants draft everything so carefully they are not capable of ambiguity.'

Over the two further licence applications granted to Matrix Churchill in 1989, this high-ranking and intelligent civil servant depicted himself as a soul who knew little about the world and would believe what he was told about machine-tools:

I, to my regret, accepted the assurances of the company, and I actually believed they were going into rebuilding the civil manufacturing capacity in Iraq . . . I regret to say, I believed the company's assurances.

His cross-examination by Geoffrey Robertson was designed to strengthen the defence that 'HMG knew'. It also revealed the way in which the Howe guidelines had been secretly watered down by Ministers as the years went by. The revelation in the Whitehall papers of secret manipulation of the Howe guidelines provided Robertson with yet a third potential line of defence for his client. According to the documents so suddenly disclosed, it probably would not have mattered even if Henderson had specifically declared that his machine-tools were 'specially designed' to make munitions – some Ministers were so enthusiastic for trade with Iraq after the August 1988 ceasefire that they were trying to abolish, or at any rate 'relax', the guidelines. In February and November 1989, even if Henderson's application forms had not been ambiguously filled in, would not the *political* decision have been secretly the same – 'sell, sell, sell'?

Beston first made a statement just before the Matrix Churchill directors were charged in February 1991. He implied then that he had been wholly unaware that any of their machines had ever been sent to make armaments.

I had not received any information indicating that . . . any . . . licence applications submitted by Matrix Churchill during my time as head of Branch, were for equipment specially designed for the production of controlled military goods.

When he made this statement, neither the Whitehall documents nor the intelligence reports had been disclosed. In November 1991, before the committal proceedings, Beston retired to a slightly new position: 'I can say I was aware of suspicions and allegations at various times that machine-tools which Matrix Churchill had supplied or were seeking to supply to Iraq were for the production of military equipment. For example, there were stories in the press in 1988.' The committal depositions record Beston in the witness-box: 'I was certainly aware of the suspicion that machine-tools supplied by Matrix Churchill may in fact have been used for military production in Iraq. The earliest I can recall of such suspicions was at the end of 1987. They were press reports.'

These statements were travesties of the truth. Robertson began his cross-examination on the real position, by now exposed in the documents.

GR: Mr Beston, when were you first informed that Nassr was an establishment that was making munitions?

EB: Erm – early January 1988, I think.

And who informed you?

I think it was an intelligence report.

But Beston had to be dragged into accepting the accuracy of the contents of Telegram 894, the intelligence report that Iraq was planning to make munitions. (The civil servant was greatly helped by the fact that, at this stage of the trial, the government was still refusing to hand over the exact text of the telegram. It was acquired by Robertson only on 29 October, three days later.)

EB: That is the suggestion in the intelligence report, for which there is no collateral.

GR: It was not a suggestion, it was information from a reliable source?

Which is a term the intelligence services use to describe people that they had used before, I think.

But you believed it?

Indeed . . .

. . . The dramatic news for you was that you had licensed UK machine-tool makers to send their equipment to factories in Iraq which would use them for making munitions?

I don't accept that we knew that they would use them to make munitions.

Beston persisted until the end of his testimony – when even the judge found it hard to credit – that the knowledge that machines were going to munitions factories was not reason to suspect they might be used to make munitions. This assertion seemed to belong in a conceptual fairyland, because the 'defence bundle' contained detailed accounts of a Matrix worker leaking the truth, and of an MI5 agent describing his visit to Iraq to sort out technical snags on the artillery-shell production-line. There were simply no two ways about it. A moment's serious investigation by the DTI would have revealed that the machines were never 'diverted' by the Iraqis – the companies signed explicit contracts in advance to deliver shell-making machines, complete with successfully machined samples.

Robertson probably felt frustrated when he finally obtained the text of Telegram 894. For it could have been used to nail Beston down. The MI6 report quoted a 'UK businessman involved in the deal' actually visiting the plants and inspecting the drawings for the shells and bombs that Matrix Churchill machines were to make.

It was Beston who urged upon his Minister the need to tell the companies to keep their mouths shut, if they wanted to hold on to their 1987 licences for exports to munitions factories. What did he mean by 'presentational difficulties'?

EB: The situation in which the decision that has to be taken . . . risks becoming unbalanced by some sort of press campaign which may not take into account all of the factors . . .'

GR: Doesn't presentational difficulties mean political embarrassment?

That is certainly one.

. . . It was a reference, I suggest to your determination that the British public should not find out that this country was contributing to Iraq's armaments.

That was your interpretation, but not my intention . . . There could well have been stories from others about suspicions about Iraq or dislike of Iraq or whatever, which would have formed a rather difficult background to a decision that needed to be made by a Minister.

The general feeling among officials after the 1987 crisis seemed to be in favour of what Tony Steadman from the licensing unit called the 'balanced approach'. Matrix Churchill and the others would be allowed to benefit from the crime – so long as there was no publicity. But 'follow-on' orders would have to stop. That was not what happened. On the two future occasions when Matrix Churchill applied for suspect licences, both of them witnessed by Beston, a variety of excuses ensured that the company continued to export munitions machines to Iraq. Never once was any substantial future order for Iraq from Matrix Churchill turned down by the 'Department for Enterprise'.

The key event which strengthened the hand of DTI Ministers against the Foreign Office was the Iran–Iraq ceasefire. This offered the prospect of a sales bonanza to both sides. There are recurring words and phrases in the Whitehall documentation as British companies and their governmental sponsors positioned themselves at the trough. The DTI speaks the language of 'international competitors' and 'valuable orders';

the Foreign Office more anxiously of 'the moral high ground' and media opinion. The MOD recorded in a Defence Exports Services memo:

> As expected, UK companies are keen . . . to start promoting weapons systems to Iran and Iraq to ensure a share in the lucrative market which will develop as both sides start to re-equip their forces.

'A gradual relaxation of Ministerial guidelines' was the most offered by the Foreign Office in August, as a ceasefire loomed. They envisaged perhaps letting through the outstanding Matrix Churchill lathes as soon as the ceasefire took hold – along with a Ferranti aircraft training simulator, 'dual-purpose aircraft spares' and possibly, for the Iranian navy, Westland hovercraft spares, Marconi radars, Kelvin marine engines and GEC ship propulsion gear spares.

There was a long three-way debate at the August Inter-Departmental Committee. Howe was not apparently prepared to ditch his guidelines. The FO said: 'Ministers would not wish to change our policy in the short term and would seek to maintain the moral high ground.' They outlined Geoffrey Howe's 'proposed approach', warning anxiously of 'the presentational problems of too precipitate a relaxation of export controls. Parliament in particular had shown a strong interest in this issue and would look for a restrained approach.' The guidelines might be relaxed somewhat, they said. At some point in the future they might be more thoroughly reconsidered. The DTI put in a bid for freeing alleged 'dual-use' equipment which could be used in civilian reconstruction. The FO countered that they would have to be certain it genuinely was civilian: 'We could not afford to appear precipitate or irresponsible.'

This meeting was interesting for one remark. William Blackley of the Foreign Office gave the assembled company a warning which appears sensible with hindsight: 'Significant defence sales to Iraq might . . . cause Gulf states some concern. They would be wary of a battle-hardened Iraq, free from the conflict with Iran, to indulge its pretentions to regional dominance.' Apart from this one remark, none of the disclosed papers showed any awareness at all that a re-armed Iraq might be a dangerous neighbour.

At the end of August, Geoffrey Howe circulated a scheme which the DTI and its eagerly snuffling companies found too timid. But it was a beginning. His officials said: 'We can . . . use discretion within the Ministerial guidelines to adopt a phased approach to borderline cases.' Higher authority was sought to rein the DTI in somewhat. A letter issued from Prime Minister Thatcher's office two days afterwards said that no military sales initiatives were to be taken without her approval.

Beston and his licensing unit colleague Tony Steadman could have given startling evidence to the parliamentary Supergun committee about the kind of military material which now started to go through from Britain, thanks to the unannounced 'relaxation'. But they had been forbidden 'on Ministerial instruction' to testify. Beston was nervous and uncomfortable on this subject in the witness-box:

EB: No, I didn't give evidence.

GR: You did not give evidence because – why did you not give evidence?

I assume that my department said that I should not.

You *know* that your department said that you should not; and you *know* that the committee wanted to ask you questions about the Supergun affair?

Yes.

In September, the DTI celebrated the ceasefire by handing out to Matrix Churchill a licence to take £400,000 worth of machines 'temporarily' to the Baghdad trade fair, without consulting the Foreign Office in advance. The FO bowed to this *fait accompli*. (The machines never came home as promised, but were installed in the secret 1728 Factory outside Baghdad, where they ended up making parts for an improved Scud missile, of the kind which later killed Israelis and Americans during the Gulf War.)

Other Iraq equipment approved more conventionally by the IDC that month included Thorn-EMI's Cymbeline mortar-locating radar ('old technology'). A licence for the supply of 35 litres of hydrofluoric acid was refused to BDH Ltd, however. The acid had legitimate industrial uses but was also 'an essential precursor for the manufacture of chemical weapons'.

The next month, the IDC approved a bid from the government-owned IMS (International Military Services) to sell spare parts for armoured recovery vehicles – identical to Chieftain tanks – on the grounds that they were 'automotive parts only'. But it refused an application from Plessey to sell encryption units for faxes and secure telephones, after consulting the government's codebreaking agency, GCHQ. Matrix Churchill's lathes were still held up, along with a pile of other bids, because the Foreign Office had failed to issue its promised new 'relaxed' guidelines on dual use.

The DTI decided that it was time to put on heavy pressure. The department told the December 1988 meeting of the IDC that Alan Clark, the Trade Minister, was going to confront the Foreign Office head on. He was writing to William Waldegrave, 'calling for radical relaxation of the existing export regulations'.

Beston's role in the witness-box was a relatively passive one while these policy documents were read to him.

GR: And this is a letter headed 'End of the Gulf [Iran–Iraq] War: Defence Sales Guidelines?

EB: Yes.

  He writes: 'I am concerned about the large number of licence applications for export of dual-use equipment

176

. . . deferred by Ministers . . . spare parts for civil air-craft and helicopters, communications and transport equipment and machine-tools?

That is right.

Clark, who was copying his letter to Mrs Thatcher, said £8 million worth of orders had piled up, and all of them ought to be issued forthwith. The case for 'a wide-ranging unilateral UK embargo on defence sales is well-nigh impossible to justify to British firms'. A familiar refrain flowed from his pen: 'Our international competitors . . . marginal relaxation . . . important new orders to be won.' He held out the prospect that the troubled defence firm Westland (former focus of Thatcher's 'Westland scandal', when she and Michael Heseltine had quarrelled over the best way to rescue it) might win the £14 million contract, in a new atmosphere, to renovate a pair of Iranian hovercraft. Continued vetos on the grounds of preserving the strategic balance in the Gulf 'would strain credulity'.

Clark said that no public announcement need be made of the issue of outstanding licences, but 'appropriate defensive briefing would need to be available to meet possible criticism'. At the bottom of the letter, he wrote in his spiky hand: 'This is important!' Beston had been working for the Minister who wanted to sweep away the embargos like this. Would he admit anything about Clark's real attitude? With Robertson, before the documents were read, he dodged:

GR: Ministers made those decisions according to their political philosophy?

EB: I am afraid you will have to ask them.

. . . Some Ministers, Mr Clark in particular, were in favour of military trade with Iraq?

I think you will have to ask Mr Clark.

You know, from the time you were at the DTI under Clark, that he was firmly in favour of trade of a military nature with Iraq?

I'm afraid you will have to ask Mr Clark.

. . . Do you not know what your own Minister's attitude was?

. . . What was in his mind is for Mr Clark to say.

. . . Did Mr Alan Clark never speak his mind to you whilst he was your Minister about his attitude to trade and military-related goods?

He spoke his mind about trade and goods generally.

Are you saying he never indicated to you he was in favour of military-related trade with Iraq?

I do not recall his words. It is a long time ago.

Later, Gilbert Gray QC picked up these cudgels and successfully confirmed one small nugget:

GG: He used to say, 'I am the Minister for Trade and it is my job to help British trade?'

EB: Oh, yes.

Repeatedly?

Yes, indeed.

To appease Clark, a new 'relaxed' set of guidelines were drafted by 20 December. Where the original Howe embargos prohibited anything likely to 'significantly enhance' military capability, the new form of words merely banned military equipment which 'in our view, would be of direct and significant assistance to either country in the conduct of offensive operations in breach of the ceasefire'.

Beston agreed with Robertson: 'It was a very much more relaxed guideline than the original third guideline, was it not?' 'Yes.' 'It is a considerable change.' 'Yes.' The remarkable fact was that these new guidelines, under which Matrix Churchill could probably have equipped whole factories, were kept secret from Parliament and the public. The Whitehall code for 'secret change' was – in Tony Steadman's phrase – 'internal re-interpretation'. Officially, the original guidelines still held good. This was in line with Clark's original suggestion, to make no announcement. It certainly avoided, as Beston would have put it, 'presentational difficulties'.

Politically, the pressure was all to grant Matrix Churchill its outstanding licences [they were, in fact, for the ABA rocket missile]. The Foreign Office told MI6 that they were going to approve the grant of machine-tool licences, in the name of, once again, protecting their intelligence source. MI6 passed on this message to MI5, who consulted Gutteridge, their source, now a sales manager considering taking a full-time job with the Iraqis in Baghdad. Gutteridge's handler, 'Michael Ford', reported back: 'It might be best to go along with the FCO view . . . There seem to be so many uncertainties that granting this particular set of export licences will at least give time for [DELETED] to discover more about Iraqi intentions.'

As the political input came from above, so a chiming intelligence message came from the subterranean depths. It was in November that MI6 heard that Dr Safa al-Habobi and the procurement network were trying to buy nuclear components. 'Michael Ford' rushed off to Coventry to re-activate Gutteridge:

We were keen to see 528 after his holiday because of the new SIS interest in the Iraqis. 528 arrived promptly in the hotel . . . He is no fool. He is an experienced businessman and well appreciates the effect this could have on Matrix Churchill and other machine-tool operations. [DELETED DELETED DELETED] He promised to help us all he can.'

This was the chain of events that was to culminate in the recruitment of Paul Henderson himself by 'Balsam' of MI6. Beston of the DTI chaired the Restricted Enforcement Unit meetings which had debated the ominous information that Christmas. He told the Old Bailey:

> Certainly the procurement network was quite widely active in this country, and other countries, in trying to obtain a lot of nuclear equipment, which is one reason why we wanted to keep a careful eye on Matrix Churchill.

At the next IDC, Matrix Churchill's licence bids were taken off the agenda and left for Ministers because of their 'sensitive nature'. The IDC refused an application from Miriad International to sell an 'Explosives Detector' because it could be of use to terrorist organisations. But the new relaxed regime enabled Marconi to gain approval for an S711 military radar system: 'state-of-the-art highly-mobile tactical radar . . . Possible to argue (if stretching a point) that its supply could enhance the purchaser's offensive capability for example by installing the radar at a newly-captured airstrip. However, the IDC agreed to recommend approval in view of the more flexible approach agreed between Ministers.' This was an £11 million system, to be sold to the Iraqi air force, which the MOD technical group said was 'a very significant enhancement of Iraqi capability', and would have been refused under the wording of the original guidelines. The Foreign Office accepted: 'These should not be regarded as offensive under the revised guidelines.'

And Rob Young, head of the Middle East department, accepted that Paul Henderson's lathes could now go, whatever their military nature: 'The Matrix Churchill lathes for which licences have been sought may be destined for munitions manufacture. But in the circumstances of the ceasefire this is not a sufficient reason to withhold licences.'

At the Old Bailey, Geoffrey Robertson had ploughed

through a verbatim reading of four pages of a Foreign Office submission – before an increasingly tetchy judge – to reach this one cross-examination point:

GR: . . . Now, 'not a problem in view of the relaxation or flexible interpretation of the guidelines after the ceasefire'?

EB: Yes, the emphasis is on 'even if' – and the assumption they were dual-use, industrial list lathes.

But it was quite clear that these may be used for munitions manufacture. And they were saying even if they were, now the Gulf War has ended, no reason not to allow them to go – under the relaxed guidelines?

Not a sufficient reason in the absence of certainty that that was what they were for.

I suggest it is read the other way. That the view taken is, even if they are used or destined for use in a munitions factory – now that Iraq is no longer at war, it does not now matter. They can go through under the relaxed guidelines?

I read it my way, you read it your way.

. . . If it does happen, it doesn't matter?

It is much less of concern than it would have been.

In February 1989, rubber-stamped by Geoffrey Howe, the Foreign Secretary, the second batch of Matrix Churchill machines were approved for export, although everyone knew they might go to make munitions.

It was not long before the guidelines, having been stretched, were also twisted. In February, Iran had called for the murder of British writer Salman Rushdie for publishing a novel, *The Satanic Verses*, which it claimed was disrespectful to Islam.

The death threats caused a considerable international incident, and another freeze in relations with Iran. 'In the present uncertain circumstances, the more flexible interpretation of the guidelines . . . would be no longer appropriate for Iran,' agreed the IDC. Any large-scale defence sales to Iran were going to cause 'major presentational difficulties'. But there was no reason to penalise Iraq. Waldegrave should propose to his fellow-Ministers that the 'flexible guidelines' would still apply to Saddam Hussein.

There was henceforth to be a secret 'tilt' towards Iraq. Clark, Waldegrave and Trefgarne had a meeting in April at which Clark pressed for the abolition of the guidelines entirely. Waldegrave accepted that they 'could not be maintained indefinitely'. But, he said, the ceasefire was fragile and neither side should be induced to resume hostilities. Therefore: 'it was not right for the present to withdraw the guidelines; and . . . it was preferable not to have to announce publicly any change in them.' Only if pressed in Parliament would the government say something – and the agreed form of words was mendacious to a degree:

> The guidelines . . . are kept under constant review, and are applied in the light of prevailing circumstances, including the ceasefire and developments in the peace negotiations.

Matrix Churchill was given consent to exhibit machining centres and lathes at the Baghdad arms fair, along with scores of military manufacturers ranging from BMARC ('60mm mortar bomb') to British Aerospace (the Hawk trainer). It is difficult to reconcile this decision with the protestations of civil servants that they had no idea Matrix Churchill was making military sales.

Other military contracts with Iraq also found their passage eased: at the April IDC, a Racal radio system which had been refused because it could be used to jam radio signals was approved. And a Plessey 'Datalok' system which 'allowed secure communication with a large number of people . . . would allow a command unit to co-ordinate a major attack' was returned to the MOD for them to reconsider their refusal. In May, Martin Baker ejection seat equipment was approved for Iraq ('on humanitarian grounds'), but it was simultaneously refused for Iran.

Sinisterly, a 'highly advanced' IBM XT286 computer was being purchased by Dr Safa al-Habobi's Nassr plant – the destination of so many munitions-related shipments from Matrix Churchill. The MOD working group wanted to refuse, saying it could potentially assist with quality assurance in missile production. It was not the first missile-related purchase proposal from Nassr. The IDC decided 'it could equally be used for legitimate industrial purposes'. The committee approved the sale, under the new relaxed regulations, although 'there was inevitably some risk attached'.

While these 'relaxations' were the order of the day, Iraq's underground procurement network was going extremely well. In March, a tube for the first Supergun barrel was flown out of Manchester airport in an Iraqi air force Ilyushin, re-painted in civilian colours. Nobody noticed, except for one puzzled plane-spotter.

Four days before Bonfire Night, when the air was cold in England, three government Ministers gathered under Big Ben in an office in the House of Lords. This meeting, at 4 p.m. on 1 November 1989, was designed to be a showdown. Each contestant had a little group of 'seconds' – officials and secretaries to take notes, offer advice and hold the towels.

From the Foreign Office, there was William Waldegrave, who with the support of his officials had been campaigning strenuously since the summer to stop the repeated issue of export licences to Matrix Churchill. The chorus of newspaper publicity had increased about the Iraqi procurement network. This was no longer the same man as the one who, in deference to MI6's wish to keep an agent active, had languidly scrawled on a memo back in February: 'Screwdrivers are also required to make H-bombs'.

For by April 1989, Number 10 had been supplied with so much material about Saddam's nuclear ambitions, that they had taken fright and backed a series of moves against the Iraqis. MI6 was to recruit more agents; military intelligence was to compile a survey of suspicious company sales from Britain; the DTI was to organise a 'Working Group on Iraqi Procurement' to analyse export licence applications. And a series of stories began to appear in the newspapers: Matrix Churchill was prominently mentioned in an *Observer* article on 3 September by the well-informed Alan George. In it, he disclosed that Iraq had been blocked by the Foreign Office from attempts to buy the Learfan company in Belfast, in an effort 'to acquire technology for its ballistic missile programme'. On 6 September, Waldegrave wrote sternly to his colleagues ('softened up' as they were by such publicity): 'I should like to draw your attention to four applications from Matrix Churchill . . . and to recommend that these applications be refused.'

These were bids to sell machines from the Baghdad trade fair to 'Project 1728'. MI6 knew this was a missile programme. Other applications were for the ABA project, which MI6 had recorded their belief was for the manufacture of 'artillery rockets'. (Information about both these matters was, of course, coming from Matrix Churchill's own managing director, Paul Henderson – but no one outside the intelligence agency was aware of that.) Stephen Lillie of the Middle East department had advised refusal on 24 August, saying: 'In addition to strengthening Iraq's indigenous arms industry . . . approval of the licences would be inconsistent with our current policy towards the procurement network.'

Waldegrave's letter was uncompromising in tone.

Matrix Churchill was taken over as part of a procurement network for the Iraqi nuclear, CBW [chemical or bacteriological warfare] and missile programmes. We know, originally from secret sources, that contrary to the assurances of the manufacturer, its high-technology machine-tools have been shipped to the major Iraqi munitions establishments.

MI6 had withdrawn its original veto, imposed to protect their sources. The Iraqis would go to great lengths to obtain sensitive technology and it was necessary to undermine their procurement network, even if it led to bad publicity about lost jobs in the Midlands. The FCO did not any more think the company would go bankrupt: 'The Iraqis are likely to sell it as a going concern or maintain it as a money-spinner, rather than simply allow it to collapse.' The company might demand a meeting with DTI Ministers to protest. If they did: 'You would no doubt wish to justify the refusal of the licences by saying we have firm evidence that equipment has previously been shipped to Iraqi munitions factories.'

Eric Beston was in the witness-box for three days, while his cross-examination marched on, document by document, to the final account of this confrontation between three Ministers. Among the Old Bailey audience for this Whitehall comedy, a daily pattern had emerged. At about 9 a.m., Paul Henderson, who, for the duration, had rented a flat in Docklands with a fine view of the river, would arrive. He would have breakfast in a snack bar across the road from the Old Bailey. Sometimes, he would be joined by Peter Allen and his partner, Karen, who travelled up and down each day by train from their home in the Midlands. Henderson used to say whenever he was asked that deep down he was confident that the Customs case would collapse. But he seemed to be not entirely sure. Allen, who joined Matrix Churchill late in the day as far as the indictments were concerned, was more confident. At lunch, Henderson and Allen usually had a beer in Harry's Bar, also opposite the Old Bailey. Trevor Abraham took a stroll.

Henderson's lawyers, Robertson, Macdonald, Robinson and Weatherby, never joined them, but ate a hurried sandwich as they trawled through the 400 pages of documents for incriminating material. The other members of the defence team were in a position to adopt a much lower profile. Some – from the Northern Bar – would place bets on horses. Gray was at times occupied in other cases.

Their opponents from Customs formed a little gang. Each morning, and during the breaks, the team – Alan Moses, his junior Gibson Grenfell, Peter Wiltshire, the leading Customs investigator in the case, his colleague Chris Constantine and the Customs lawyer Annabel Bolt – would huddle in a tense group, puffing at their cigarettes.

Back in the courtroom, hour after hour, Robertson's cross-examination of Beston exposed the story.

Waldegrave's 1989 opponent at the DTI was now Lord Trefgarne, who had swapped jobs with Clark. The top officials who advised at the department had not changed, however; and Eric Beston, head of export control, had been briefing his Minister frantically to oppose the Foreign Office. He was undeterred by Henderson's public admission in the *Financial Times* that he had indeed sold past machines for shells and guns. Beston had in his in-tray a memo from Tony Steadman about that piece of 'dirty washing':

> Urgent . . . Further press comment over the weekend is likely . . . The possibility has always existed [of] the production of military equipment, which the company has hitherto denied, in contravention of our policy . . . [In 1987] intelligence sources reported that the factories . . . had substantial munitions manufacturing programmes as well as general engineering activities. Even so, *there was no evidence that the British-made machine-tools would be used other than for the purpose originally stated*' [author's emphasis].

This was a ridiculous rewriting of history. Had Steadman been aware of the actual contents of the 1987 intelligence report? His memo did not read as if he had. But Beston found the 'line' acceptable. Instead of calling for Paul Henderson's arrest for deceit, he urged his new Minister to meet the manager of Matrix Churchill and listen sympathetically to his representations. 'Far too much is being made of Iraqi majority [80 per cent] ownership in the firm . . . there are strong arguments in favour of granting the licences.' (His percentage figure was actually too low.) Iraq was already in a sulky mood, Beston felt, over Alan Clark's summer failure (before leaving the Trade Ministry) to push through the sale of Hawk trainer war-planes.

Beston's main point was that, since the DTI had forced through a relaxation: 'We do not believe that these exports would breach the Iran/Iraq guidelines in the more relaxed form.' In effect, the DTI did not care if the machines were to make munitions, because that would not be 'direct . . . assistance in the conduct of offensive operations'.

Henderson posted off a suitable position paper for Beston to put in front of his Minister ('Machine-tools, like many other products, can be used for both civil and military applications'). On the same day, the *Financial Times* published their large diagram of Matrix Churchill's place in the Iraqi procurement ring. It was much admired in the Foreign Office. While Henderson was in London holding MI6 seminars before a satellite map of Baghdad, the DTI needed no further encouragement to promote his commercial interests.

Beston briefed his Minister to lob certain questions at the managing director: how much Iraqi influence was there on management? What did Henderson know of the uses of previously supplied machines? Henderson was, it turned out, to answer these easy questions in the spirit of the advice the previous Trade Minister had personally given him. The 'Alan Clark' answers would be ones which 'highlighted the peaceful purposes to which the machines would be put'. Henderson sent a deceptive letter as well to the Minister:

Machines supplied from the British machine-tool industry

were not supplied until mid-1988 and even if the machines had been tooled up to produce arms, it is unlikely any contribution to the war effort could have been made.

Henderson had, of course, tooled the machines up himself specifically to produce arms. Did he tell the Minister the *Financial Times* had misquoted him? Or was it an elaborate charade? The official minute of the meeting was also to record Henderson stating to the Minister that the licences he wanted were for 'civil production' for 'automotive parts'.

At the Old Bailey, a theatrically incredulous Robertson demanded of Beston whether the DTI had ever asked to see the firm's contract with Iraq:

EB: Well, I certainly never saw the contract.

GR: You never called, as you could have done, for the contract for the ABA project, which was a £16 million project for the production of metal components in what you knew to be a munitions factory?

I think one has to recognise, if a company sets out to conceal its intentions, it is perfectly possible to produce false paperwork.

Did you ever call, as you could, for the drawings of these 'metal components' . . . ?

I did not, no.

. . . You or your staff never sought any technical information about the ABA project by way of drawings, part [computer] programs, or tooling?

Not that I am aware of.

The Export Credits Guarantee Department had all this time, in 1989, been plucking at Beston's sleeve. They had been suspicious about Matrix Churchill's attempts to obtain trade finance for the Cardoen deal with Chile. Their records show concern that Cardoen was an arms manufacturer; that the shipments might be diverted to Iraq; and that the machines might be used to make munitions. Both the Foreign Office and Customs had been alerted. Steadman himself of the DTI had been in correspondence with Customs about it. ECGD were unnecessarily suspicious about one thing: there was no secret that the end destination was Iraq. And although Cardoen was a well-known arms manufacturer, it was theoretically possible that they, too, were diversifying into civilian work in Iraq. ECGD information at the time, however, was that Cardoen was a 'major weapons supplier'.

D. R. Coombe of the ECGD – on the same day that, unbeknown to him, Henderson was in London briefing MI6 – recorded his attempts to interest Beston in his information:

> I have given him the outline, orally, of the Matrix Churchill Chile/Iraq business and if Mr Henderson does not include this item in his account to the Minister, Mr Beston will ask him about it following the meeting.

After the bland and successful meeting between Minister and manufacturer, Beston did not keep his promise. The ECGD man recorded: 'I spoke again today to Mr Beston . . . to ask him about the meeting . . . although Mr Beston did not get an opportunity to raise the sales through a Chilean middleman, nothing gave rise to any suspicion that Matrix Churchill were doing anything against the rules.'

A month after Waldegrave's stern letter from the Foreign Office, Beston felt in a position to offer his own Minister a draft reply. Trefgarne sent it off word for word. In it, it seemed, he disagreed strongly with the FO. Matrix Churchill, he said, should get their licences.

Signs of history being rewritten peeped through Trefgarne's ready-drafted prose. It was 'no secret' that the Iraqis owned a 'majority stake' in Matrix Churchill. (This was a more pleasant turn of phrase than the truth, which was that the Iraqi government had surreptitiously been in total control of the company since 1987.)

Back in 1987, the original argument against allowing exports, said the letter, had been that 'the general purpose lathes might well be put to use in the production of munitions'. (The new nuance of phrase made it sound like an airy whim. The lathes 'might well' have been used for anything. What the phrase concealed was the truth; MI6 Telegram 894 had revealed in detail exactly what the machines were for.) Trefgarne's ready-to-send letter was a testament to the 'drafting skills' which senior civil servants cultivate.

There was one solid point. Since the guidelines had been relaxed, who cared what the machines were going to make? Beston's draft, adopted by Trefgarne, said:

> The continuing ceasefire has necessitated reconsideration of the Ministerial guidelines and weakened to the point of extinction any case for prohibiting exports of general purpose industrial equipment for fear it might be put to military use.

There was a third Minister present at the House of Lords when the showdown meeting took place four days before Bonfire Night – the Defence Ministry's representative. There was little danger that the new Minister for Defence Procurement would make trouble for the Trade Secretary. As the former Trade Minister, Alan Clark had been loudly in favour of sending Matrix Churchill munitions equipment to Iraq since 1988. He therefore decided to oppose the Foreign Office, contradict his own official advice and back the DTI 'line' once again.

The relevant Defence Ministry department, Defence Exports Services, seemed aware enough that they were going against the Ministerial grain. Alan Barrett minuted: 'I think we have no option but to recommend the Minister accepts the refusal of these applications.' He drafted a letter for Clark to send to Waldegrave saying, in tortured terms: 'I must admit that it is with great reluctance that I have to accept that in the circumstances I have no alternative but to support your recommendation that the licences be refused.'

Barrett was as blunt as he could bring himself to be: 'Ministers are left with the question of whether or not to allow the lathes to be exported, knowing that they are going to a munitions factory.' He disputed the claim that the guidelines had now been relaxed to the point where this did not matter: a ban on artillery rockets for Saddam 'would still apply even using the more relaxed interpretation of the guidelines'. But he did back down to the point of saying that 'the arguments are finely balanced' and the evidence for munitions use was only 'circumstantial'. This may have been because Clark was on the rampage in several directions. He had sent another memo repeating that he wanted to scrap the guidelines entirely.

Clark rejected his officials' view. He sent a letter to Waldegrave stating bluntly: 'I have much sympathy with what [Trefgarne] says, and feel unable to agree to stop the exports.' Clark added that he wanted to abolish the guidelines. The three men agreed to meet and thrash it out.

The odds at the House of Lords meeting looked as if they were going to be two against one, with Waldegrave outnumbered. In fact, the odds worsened further – for MI6 now proceeded to undermine the original Foreign Office submission. As they obtained important details of the Supergun from Henderson, and as he complained to them about his export licence problems, the MI6 secret input to the FO altered to say that there might not be much current evidence that the lathes were going for a military use. Their agent would have been pleased and grateful if he had known what was being said.

On the international stage, the odds against a military shipment to Iraq being stopped would also have looked slim to any outside observer early in that November. Important people wanted to be nice to Iraq. It was true that a young *Observer* journalist, Farzad Bazoft, had been arrested after getting too close to a munitions plant where an explosion had occurred. Waldegrave's new superior as Foreign Secretary was John Major. He had the job of speaking to Iraq's Foreign Minister, Tariq Aziz, about Bazoft at the UN in New York. Extraordinarily, Major later said – yet again – that he had not been briefed about Matrix Churchill before lobbying Aziz. Perhaps the Farzad Bazoft question was not regarded as important.

In Washington, President Bush had issued to his colleagues National Security Directive 26 on 'US Policy towards the Persian Gulf'. Despite Saddam's reprehensible record of slaughter, torture and pursuit of chemical and nuclear weapons, the policy was to tilt towards Iraq, allegedly to lead the regime towards behaving better:

> Normal relations between the US and Iraq would serve our longer-term interests and promote stability in both the Gulf and the Middle East. The US Government should propose economic and political incentives for Iraq . . . We should pursue . . . opportunities for US firms to participate in the construction of the Iraqi economy . . . Also, as a means of developing access to and influence with the Iraqi defense establishment, the US should consider sales of non-lethal forms of military assistance.

In the streets of Baghdad, it was sometimes difficult to move for the crowds of British Ministers following in the footsteps of Alan Clark himself and banging the drum for British products. John Wakeham, the Energy Secretary, was there on 13 October; as the hand-out said, 'Today [he] underlined Iraq's increasing importance to the UK as a trading partner.' Wakeham was warm: 'Beyond question . . . having maintained strong commercial links with Iraq throughout the years of conflict, Britain is now ready and anxious to help with the peacetime reconstruction.'

In this Iraq-friendly atmosphere, and subverted by Whitehall intrigue, the Waldegrave proposals stood no chance. David Gore-Booth at the Foreign Office minuted ruefully: 'I agree that Mr Waldegrave may have to concede. But I hope he will keep his colleagues dangling for a while.' The best they could hope would be that the DTI would agree to answer the embarrassing parliamentary questions that would probably follow, and not, as was traditional, the Foreign Office itself.

There were two versions of the minutes of the House of Lords meeting on 1 November, both given the high security classification SECRET. The Foreign Office minutes were less dreary to read than those compiled by the rival note-taker from the DTI. They were also much more candid about Alan Clark:

LORD TREFGARNE: said he thought the licences should be authorised . . . concerns for the future of the company . . . Dual-use equipment which may not have a military application.

WALDEGRAVE: . . . Incorrect to claim as Trefgarne had done that the Iraqis had no say in the management of the company: Matrix Churchill was 95% Iraqi-owned . . . Defence Intelligence Staff were conducting a survey of Iraqi procurement activities in the UK. Would this have a bearing on Matrix Churchill?

CLARK: . . . Only just been told about the DIS survey, and would make sure it was stopped. It was outrageous that DIS should spend their time seeking to damage our trade surplus . . .

WALDEGRAVE: . . . We had strategic interests at stake . . . strong hope the DIS survey would not be abandoned . . .

CLARK: . . . Time to dismantle the guidelines . . . not

linked to the security of the UK, but had been set up in response to pressure from lobbies in the House – and in the media . . . Little likelihood of ceasefire being broken.

LORD TREFGARNE: supported Mr Clark . . .

WALDEGRAVE: . . . Guidelines were government policy and could not be lifted at the level of this meeting . . . Very much in British interests for hostilities not to resume . . .

LORD TREFGARNE: . . . Questioned whether Matrix Churchill lathes were of serious importance . . .

WALDEGRAVE: . . . Less concerned than by the company's involvement in the procurement network. Given the recent indications that the equipment would be unlikely to be used in the military field, Mr Waldegrave agreed to withdraw his objections to the issue of licences, provided:

a the DIS survey on Iraqi procurement continued
b the guidelines on defence sales remained in place
c any Parliamentary Questions or public condemnation arising from the issue of licences should be dealt with by the DTI.

Thus, submerged in a pile of Whitehall paper, the final heap of 'dirty washing' disappeared. Once again Matrix Churchill was supplied with licences to export machines which were going to make rockets, missiles and fuses.

The existence of the grey 'defence bundle' full of secret files succeeded in switching the emphasis of the case so much that it sometimes seemed as if it was the DTI on trial. Paul Henderson and his colleagues were accused of deceit and covertly arming Iraq. But surely, on that charge there were turning out to be so many guilty men that a dock could not be constructed at the Old Bailey big enough to hold them?

Several civil servants had been discomfited at length by Robertson. When Peter Gall, deputy at the licensing unit, said his understanding of official policy was that no military-related items would be authorised for Iraq, Robertson took the print-out of hundreds of export licences approved by the DTI in the period. He proceeded to read out, one by one, all the military items, of which there were a fair number. Gall was made to squirm. 'It was not up to me to determine what was lethal or not.'

Similarly, when David Bryars of the ECGD took the stand, Robertson dumbfounded him by producing ECGD correspondence which had been freely supplied by the Crown in bundles of 'unused material'. Its significance must have been overlooked, for one of the letters was a complaint from the ECGD to the Ministry of Defence about definitions. It seemed that the trade credits for Iraq – negotiated by UK Ministers – included an allocation of 20 per cent for defence items. There was a clear policy to sell some military equipment to Iraq. The only questions were: how much? and of what, politically tolerable, kind?

Eric Beston was now followed into the witness-box by his less senior colleague, Tony Steadman. Steadman's was the name on scores of the Whitehall documents. He was head of the Export Licences Unit at the time, and he was thus the person whom the defendants were alleged to have deceived. He was, as it were, the 'victim' of the crime and the man who knew how the export licences machine actually worked, down at desk level, in the unregarded, overworked, uncomputerised world of Whitehall.

He, like Beston, had been refused consent to appear before the Supergun committee, allegedly because he was due to testify in this trial. Now he was here, with the reputation on his shoulders of a whole Ministry and a notoriously peppery new Minister, Michael Heseltine, who had unsuccessfully applied to suppress the pile of documents upon which he was about to be cross-examined. It could not have been comfortable. Gilbert Gray QC said cruelly, in cross-examination: 'I made thirty-seven ticks during the whole of your evidence before

I stopped counting the occasions when you said: "I can't remember".'

Steadman had actually been present at the notorious 'nod and wink' meeting between the manufacturers and Alan Clark, which was turning out to be the focus of the trial. And it was Steadman who had first heard the alarming news, at the turn of 1987, that he had personally managed to issue licences to machines for two Iraqi armament plants. Robertson's cross-examination recalled how Steadman then rang up the companies to freeze their licences and allegedly said, 'Her Majesty's Government doesn't want to prolong the War.'

TS: I don't think I said that.

GR: What did you say when they hit the roof . . . ?

      I think I would say there was some concern over the end use to which the machines might be put.

      . . . concern over the military use of these machines?

      Yes.

At the time he also warned Trevor Abraham, one of the three defendants, not to seek publicity:

GR: These machines were going to make munitions and it would be better for the company if the public didn't know about that?

TS: Yes, it would make it difficult for Ministers . . .

      Because there would be a possibility of questions in Parliament by MPs opposed to selling arms to countries at war?

      Yes.

      And editorials perhaps, and critical articles about

whether we should sell arms-making capacity at all to countries at war?

Yes.

Steadman underwent an ordeal with Robertson, trying to protect his Minister, Alan Clark, over the notorious 'nod and wink' meeting (his emotions after Alan Clark's own testimony on the subject the following week must have been tumultuous):

GR: Mr Clark, I suggest, began the meeting with a statement. He came in and explained he was very busy and he didn't want to waste time?

TS: I don't recall that.

That's his style, is it not?

I don't know. I had not met him on many occasions.

'Let's not waste time. You know what they are for; we know what they are for . . .'

I don't think he said that.

Don't you? I suggest to you that was how the meeting started.

I do not recall that, I'm sorry . . . I do not recall him congratulating the companies . . . I can't remember unless it is in the minute recording the meeting.

He said to couch those [future] applications in a manner so as to emphasise the peaceful use to which the machines would be put?

I don't remember the word 'couch' but he told them future application should be for civil purposes, he told them to go and search for such projects.

. . . No, this meeting was not about peaceful projects! It was about munitions factories, as everyone knew?

But for future exports they would have to be for peaceful projects. That was my understanding of what he is getting across to the companies. I am quite sure about that.

. . . Mr Steadman, I have to suggest that was not said at all . . .

I am quite certain he said it in the context of meaning peaceful projects . . . no Minister would go against the guidelines.

These exchanges did not do Clark any good in the long run, but they whetted the court's appetite for the Minister himself. The defence team had noticed a puzzling gap in the documents. Although Whitehall records everything on paper, there was no document recording the eventual 1988 decision that the licences would be unfrozen for the munitions machines. The companies were apparently never notified. The secretary of the MTTA, John Nosworthy, turned out to have the key to this: he had been phoned discreetly to pass on the message – leaving no paper trail:

GR: You called Mr Nosworthy to tell him the existing licences would be unfrozen?

TS: I could well have done. I can't remember.

Can you explain why there is no letter?

No, I can't. It would presumably have been done on the telephone . . . for speed, basically.

The reason, I suggest, was the reason you told Mr Nosworthy . . . namely the determination to keep the whole thing secret.

On the morning of 29 October, the defence team at last received the text of Telegram 894 – the secret intelligence report (from Mark Gutteridge) revealing in 1987 that the machine-tool exports were all going to munitions factories. One of the great mysteries of the case was why nothing was done about this dramatic intelligence report for six weeks. It was issued on 30 November, but the DTI took no action on it until 12 January when they rang the companies to revoke their licences.

Steadman provided an explanation – and it was one which left the jury members unable to keep straight faces:

TS: It went to a central document section which I would have visited once every fortnight, three weeks, that sort of thing –

GR: But Mr Steadman, this is headed 'UK SECRET'. It was very secret and very urgent and very important information, was it not?

Yes.

Of enormous importance to your decision in relation to these export licences?

Yes.

Are you really saying that secret intelligence of this urgency and importance goes to a central document section which you collect every two to three weeks?

Which at that time I went to visit on that sort of basis – every three weeks it would have been . . . it would have gone to the central documents section and it would remain there until picked up by the officials who were authorised to see this sort of information.

Steadman went on to say that he perhaps remembered being eventually alerted by the Foreign Office to the document's existence. An emergency meeting of the IDC then took place on 8 January. There might have been an explanation for the mystery here: if the MI6 report had lingered until approaching the end of December, and its discovery was then followed immediately by the civil service Christmas holidays, it was no wonder action took so long.

This was going to be a major question for any subsequent inquiry into arms for Iraq: why did the government machine function so badly? It took more than five months in all to circulate a completely accurate intelligence report, which those involved then merely decided to suppress.

The ambiguous atmosphere at the IDC meetings subsequently attended by Steadman while the Iran–Iraq war was raging emerged from the 'grey bundle'. In February, immediately after the authorising of the 'dirty washing' munitions contracts, Steadman was present for the debate about a pair of pistols. The Browning 9mm pistols which the London firm of May wanted to ship to Iraq were, according to the Foreign Office, 'clearly lethal and therefore prohibited by the Ministerial guidelines'. However, the Defence Ministry intervened: they were going to bring in their Minister, because the pistols were for Saddam's son.

Saddam Hussein's eldest son, Uday, figured prominently in *Republic of Fear*, the book about Saddam's regime that 'Balsam' of MI6 insisted his agent Paul Henderson should read. Uday was, according to the author, a notorious psychopath, 'who in full public view stomped and clubbed to death his father's official food-taster . . . Uday was packed off to Switzerland as ambassador. There . . . he beat up a Swiss policeman.' Steadman and the DTI chimed in to bend the rules, saying that a refusal to send off the pistols as demanded might have 'unfortunate diplomatic consequences'.

Steadman's account of the IDC meetings which thrashed out licence decisions brought out one thing very clearly. The process was not law – it was politics. The licences were secretly awarded on all kinds of fluctuating policy grounds, often by Ministers themselves. The guidelines were, said Steadman, 'very widely interpreted'; and Judge Smedley twice intervened to clarify this point, which clearly was beginning to trouble him. The rationale behind the prosecution seemed to those in court to be slipping away. The Howe guidelines were not administered as a matter of law. The secret subversion of them, similarly, was a political matter. This put the accusations of deception and deceit laid against Matrix Churchill in a different light. In politics, if not in law, doublespeak was apparently the normal language.

11

ECONOMICAL

Alan Clark in the witness-box,
4 November 1992

Their Minister (Alan Clark) was briefed . . .
MI6 minute 26 January 1988

On Wednesday 4 November, Alan Clark attended the Old Bailey to give evidence for the prosecution. It was the day after the US presidential election, and he looked hung-over. It did not look as though he had been celebrating the result. George Bush was out. Clinton was in. Richard Norton-Taylor, by now one of an enormous contingent of journalists, had been asked by Geoffrey Robertson a few days before for the clippings file on Clark. It had been full of hagiographic portraits of this cultivated, brilliant Thatcherite, who had run rings around his MP interrogators at the Supergun committee hearings, giving nothing away except a stream of *bons mots*. Norton-Taylor noticed, when the barrister returned it to him that morning, that occasional references to Clark's vanity had been underlined. This may have been the key to what was to be both the most devastating, and the most friendly, cross-examination heard at the Old Bailey.

202

Nothing of what was to come could be predicted from Clark's insouciance on that morning. He had already played one clever trick on the defence. On reading of his much-touted and soon-to-be-published political diaries, they had subpoenaed the papers. Clark had insisted (as was his legal right) that they should pay him 'conduct money': his fares for coming to court with the volumes. He arrived at the Old Bailey in a limousine, and then revealed that his diaries contained no reference at all to Matrix Churchill. But they soon would. While waiting to testify, during adjournments, he ostentatiously wrote his entries for 4 November.

Clark gave his full name, and announced his address as 'Saltwood Castle, Kent'. Alan Moses began his examination-in-chief by asking him 'to look, please, at that bundle which we call the defence bundle'. Court observers noted how the trial spotlight had by now swung, even in the prosecutor's mind, round to the defence case, contained in the grey bundle of documents which government ministers had fought so hard to keep secret.

To Moses, Clark played a perfectly straight bat. He recalled seeing the briefings from Eric Beston and Tony Steadman (which had informed him that the machine-tools were going to equip munitions factories) shortly before his meeting with MTTA on 20 January 1988. He described the official minutes of that meeting as 'completely accurate'. Asked what his attitude was to the purpose for which machine-tools should be put in relation to future exports to Iraq, he replied: 'Well, it was important that the specification should be of a nature that the peaceful use of tooling was the principal element in considering their eligibility [for licences].'

So far as a reference of his in the minutes to 'inflammatory press comment' was concerned, he said that Whitehall was afraid of reading headlines saying: 'Whitehall bureaucrats block British exports. Ministers' jobs put at risk.' They were not concerned about headlines saying: 'Whitehall poised to sell death-dealing weapons to Iraq'. He added, somewhat bitterly: 'That somersault had yet to take place.'

Moses took Clark through his communications with William Waldegrave and Lord Trefgarne in late 1988 and 1989 about the relaxation of the guidelines. Then Moses got from him the answer that the prosecution desperately needed to keep its case afloat:

AM: Can I ask you, Mr Clark – we are now in the autumn of 1989 leading up to the meeting you had with the other two ministers on 1st November. If you had known that machine-tools were going to be exported with tooling, fixtures and part programs to machine parts of fuses for military ordnance, what would your attitude have been then in relation to granting of licences?

AC: My attitude would have been that they would have fallen irredeemably within the guidelines, even though the guidelines had been relaxed.

Judge: You mean their export would be a breach of the guidelines?

AC: Yes, exactly. They would have been in a category likely to enhance or exacerbate the conflict.

So far as the Cardoen contract was concerned (the export licences for which had been granted after the 1 November Ministerial meeting), this answer suggested that the Ministers had been deceived as to the purpose of the application. Curiously, Clark had applied the test of 'enhancing or exacerbating the conflict', which the documents showed was a test no longer applicable by that time.

Clark's examination took only an hour, and the judge called a ten-minute morning adjournment. The prosecution team looked relieved – his evidence had been entirely consistent with their case. Their fears, which had risen after an apparently indiscreet *Sunday Telegraph* profile in August, had been put to rest. So concerned were they at the published suggestion in that newspaper that he had helped the machine-tool manufacturers to give false descriptions, that Cedric Andrew, the senior Customs lawyer, had telephoned him about it, and served a further statement on the defence. 'Mr Clark said that the journalist may have transposed what was said during the interview, and [Clark] said: "It is balls I would have said that".' The defence had been warned of the robust reply they would receive from this unimpeachable prosecution witness if they pursued *that* false trail.

Alan Clark's momentous cross-examination began quietly and politely. Clark was plainly on guard, cautiously giving nothing away.

GR: Mr Clark, can I ask you some questions firstly about these guidelines that you have spoken of? Throughout your period as Minister in 1987, 1988 and in the first part of 1989 at the DTI, and then at the Ministry of Defence, you are working to guidelines that had first been promulgated in 1985 by Sir Geoffrey Howe?

AC: Right.

In relation to sales to Iraq. And those guidelines became more flexible as the ceasefire held, the ceasefire that began on 20th August 1988?

Yes. Very slowly they did.

And they were not legal rules, so much as statements which allowed you to exercise a political judgement?

They didn't have the force of law.

They were not legalistic, they could be interpreted

in different ways, and there were a number of cases which were borderline cases?

I think every case was a borderline case that we considered. Plainly, otherwise it would not have come before us.

They were time-consuming and somewhat irksome, were they not, to apply?

They were not necessarily more time-consuming and irksome than many of my other duties.

But certainly so far as our competitors were concerned, particularly our European allies, they seemed to either not have guidelines or not implement them. They were selling equipment, lethal equipment, to Iraq during the war?

That was my impression.

And they were selling equipment like machine-tools, without any let or hindrance from their governments?

I am not in a position to say that is completely true. I do not know.

You know, of course, that France was selling Mirage fighters to Iraq?

Yes.

Throughout the '80s. Italy sold a navy to Iraq at some stage.

Yes, you mentioned two countries. I would not wish to categorize every country in that group.

But certainly our competitors, those two countries, and West Germany and Switzerland, were selling defence-related equipment in this period?

Yes.

As far as you were concerned, or we were concerned, in 1988 and 1989 we were prepared to sell items like battlefield radar, and encryption units, and ejection seats for fighters and that kind of material, which was defence-related?

I didn't know about any of those sales at the time it took place, the three items you mentioned.

You didn't know about them at the time. You learned about them subsequently?

Yes.

Robertson read Clark the Howe guidelines, and the changes to them that were secretly agreed at the beginning of 1989.

GR: At the beginning of 1989 those more flexible guidelines came into effect?

AC: That is right.

And the test is not whether it is going to 'significantly prolong' the Gulf War. It is whether it is going to be of 'direct assistance' in an offensive operation in breach of the ceasefire?

That is right.

And the longer the ceasefire held, the more flexible you were able to be under that guideline?

I think that is a matter of interpretation.

Yes, but clearly these, as we have said, are not legal rules. They allow the Ministers concerned to apply their political judgement?

Yes.

. . . It would be a decision as to whether making equipment for fuses would have been of 'direct assistance' to that country in the conduct of an offensive operation in breach of the ceasefire.

Yes. Fuses are very highly technical things, and the extent to which you can make fuse components, in the event – where you overstep the mark or where you were just simply making fuses – is a matter for expert testimony, not for me.

I accept that.

Then the cross-examination turned to Clark's own role in relaxing the guidelines after the Iran–Iraq war ended:

GR: The first note that we have of your position on the guidelines and, indeed, suggestion that you took the initiative in getting those revised guidelines in place, is at page 97, you see it, a letter from you to Mr Waldegrave in November of 1988 . . . You comment in your hand that 'This is important!'?

That is right.

And clearly that was a matter that concerned you in your position as an encourager of British trade, and with your concern for British jobs that you had at the time as DTI Minister?

Exactly.

. . . You say that you are concerned about the large number of licence applications for export of what you term as 'dual-use equipment'. You see that in the first paragraph?

Yes.

'Agreed at official level, but deferred by Ministers'.

You referred to some goods: including civil aircraft and helicopter parts, communication, transport equipment and machine-tools?

Yes.

In other words, machine-tools that could be used, of course, to make munitions or could be used for civil uses?

Yes.

You refer there to the official note enclosed with Geoffrey Howe's of 31st August suggesting, 'We can use discretion in the Ministerial guidelines to adopt a phased approach to borderline cases, relaxing control on a growing number of categories as peace takes hold . . .'

Yes.

In November 1988 you are calling consistently – with the discretion you had as Minister – to *interpret* these guidelines, to *interpret* them so as to allow defence sales in the communication, transport and machine-tool area?

Yes. It was a discretion that had to be exercised by three Ministers jointly. I didn't have exclusive discretion on this.

Of course. And if we look over the page and see: 'There are important new orders to be won' . . . and you say at the bottom of that paragraph: 'The continued denial of licences on these grounds' – namely the grounds that it would upset the strategic balance in the Gulf – 'would strain credulity'.

Yes.

You go on to say that you hope Mr Waldegrave and

Lord Trefgarne can agree to these proposals: and, of course, they would require the Prime Minister's approval?

Yes, but you note I copied that letter to her.

You 'would not propose an announcement of any decision.' But you would be prepared to explain it if necessary, and to meet any possible criticism.

Yes.

Is that you taking the initiative with the two other Ministers concerned, and seeking the support of the Prime Minister?

I think I wanted the Prime Minister to give it a shove, to shake the thing a little, and have the guidelines relaxed more, at a faster pace than was occurring at that time.

Robertson then showed Clark the FCO Lillie memorandum of 1 February 1989, which had supported the decision made by Ministers in that month to approve licences for the ABA rocket:

GR: Does it assist you to recall the basis for this decision? Although they 'may be used for munitions manufacture', the ceasefire had held for long enough to make that not of sufficient reason under the new guidelines to stop them?

AC: Yes.

The third reason you see is the attraction of allowing them to be sent, 'rather than lose an intelligence access' to the Iraqi procurement network that was in Matrix Churchill?

Yes. I think the anxiety by now had started to shift

towards Iraq's nuclear and chemical capability, and this rather pedestrian technology was no longer a matter of very great concern to us.

Clark's concession that machine-tools for making conventional weaponry was 'pedestrian technology', of little concern by February 1989, was obviously significant. Robertson moved swiftly on to the Waldegrave letter of April 1989, which confirmed the relaxation of the guidelines but urged that there should be no public or parliamentary announcement of any change:

GR: Can you recall why it was preferable not to have to announce publicly any changes in the guidelines?

AC: The Foreign Office was always very apprehensive of questions on the floor of the House, from people who viewed this kind of trade with disapproval. And for some reason, Foreign Office Ministers tended to find themselves answering them. They are steered by the table office towards the Foreign Office. If they were put to me or the Ministry of Defence, they may be given shorter shrift.

So the Foreign Office was apprehensive of getting criticism in Parliament, and preferred not to announce the guidelines publicly?

You would have to ask the Foreign Office about that. I cannot answer for them. There may be a policy element in not wanting to offend foreign missions.

And then Mr Waldegrave goes on: 'There are political factors which we have to take into account in deciding what arms we should and should not supply to each country.' He is there accepting that some arms under the new guidelines would be suppliable and some would not, and that really the decision now is 'which arms do we supply and which arms don't we supply'?

Yes. Yes, true enough.

And then he accepts the position that 'We can be more flexible in supplying arms to Iraq, as we have in practice been,' he says, 'since the end of last year.' But he goes on to make the point – no doubt in the light of the Rushdie and other matters – that we have got to keep tight guidelines for Iran?

That is right.

He then at page 170 suggests a form of words, 'if you are pressed in Parliament', which do not actually give away the fact that the guidelines are going to be interpreted flexibly to Iraq. But again, it is one of these formulas which use a great deal of Ministerial discretion?

Yes, but the discretion is apparent in that answer.

Yes, you may be able to read between the lines, but he suggests a formula which is going to give you, the three Ministers involved, a good deal of discretion?

Yes.

So Clark accepted that Waldegrave had opted for a public formula which gave nothing away but which could allow almost complete Ministerial discretion in deciding what arms to sell to Iraq. It was, as the defence had always contended, government policy to sell *some* arms to Saddam Hussein. By selling sophisticated machine-tools, of course, they were going one better: they were selling him the equipment to make arms for himself.

Robertson then turned to Clark's change of office in July 1989, when he left the DTI and swapped jobs with Lord Trefgarne, who had been at the MOD:

GR: Then in July, you became what is called the Minister for Defence Procurement?

AC: Yes.

We have heard about the Iraqi procurement network. You were head of the British procurement network.

Yes.

It includes not only buying weapons but selling them?

Yes. It does, yes.

And you have a big defence sales branch under your control?

Yes.

You were active at the DTI just before you left it in getting licences for exhibits at the Baghdad military fair. You recall that?

I do not recall it, but it would not be inconsistent with my attitude.

If we see at page 156, the next few pages indicate the military equipment that was approved to be sent to Baghdad for display?

Yes.

With the object of encouraging Iraqi interest in ordering these goods from British companies?

Not necessarily. It was a fair that was attended by a number of rich potential customers.

Customers in the Middle East, Saudi Arabia and other countries as well?

Yes.

With the object of attracting orders from those quarters?

Yes.

You say 'consistent with your attitude'. Your attitude was one that we should, in the British national interest, be prepared to sell as much as we could of defence-related equipment to these countries?

It was, yes.

I say 'attitude': it could be described as a philosophy that you brought with you to your Ministerial office.

Yes.

A political view or a philosophy that held that it is not weapons that kill, it is the people who use them?

Well, that sounds rather trite for me.

I am sorry. Put it in your own way?

Yes. I mean, I would regard our industrial performance and our balance of payments as overriding considerations: unless a particular policy issue was proposed.

. . . We had a list of proscribed countries where special concern was taken. They were at that stage basically enemy countries?

Yes.

Iraq in that period, could be regarded as a friend?

Um, I think that is stretching it a bit.

If not a friend, at least a good acquaintance?

A potential customer.

With whom we very much wanted to acquaint ourselves, very much in terms of trade, including defence-related trade?

We certainly wanted to maximise our trade where it was not proscribed.

. . . At the Ministry of Defence you have defence sales and British jobs as an important consideration?

Yes, I think it is true to say that Iraq was a very strong potential customer for defence sales.

By this stage, only an hour into the cross-examination, Clark was much more relaxed and forthcoming. He seemed to be under the impression he had struck up a rapport with his cross-examiner, and was giving him the answers he wanted. What the defence wanted – and was now getting, for the first time with any honesty at the trial – was an accurate reflection of the philosophy which had guided British policy towards arming Saddam. Clark at this point seemed conscious that he might have given away too much, and limited his support for defence sales to conventional weaponry. It was a limitation gratefully accepted by the defence, which needed to show Ministerial approval only for conventional shell fuses (Cardoen) and rockets (ABA). The rapport re-established, Robertson went on to extract from Clark some criticisms of the Foreign Office for its sudden cold feet over Matrix Churchill after the Learfan affair in August, a nervousness shared by the MOD until their new Minister reversed their policy:

AC: I should make it clear, My Lord and Members of

the Jury, in this case I have in my mind a very clear distinction between sales of arms and conventional equipment, and sales of anything which might enhance their nuclear or chemical capability. And there is a very clear dividing line for that category – and some countries were selling them. The Germans were selling them stuff to enhance their chemical capability – and so all the personal expressions you have drawn from me, I must emphasise, relate to conventional arms trade.

GR: Of course, and we heard yesterday in evidence from MI6 certainly, their intelligence was concentrating in this period on chemical weapon procurement, nuclear-related procurement and ballistic missiles, not conventional weaponry . . . Look at page 223, the Waldegrave letter of 6 September 1989. 'We have approved the company's application in the past but only because of the need to protect these secret sources.' Did that come as news to you?

No, because I had seen Mr Beston's notes to me when I was there much earlier, three years before.

That was certainly not the only reason, in February of 1989?

No, certainly not. That makes reference to it, but no, it's historic.

Robertson pointed out the Foreign Office assertions that the effect on jobs would be limited.

Did that seem to you to be a satisfactory way of considering the impact on jobs in the Midlands?

Well, the Foreign Office is at its least reliable when discussing the effects on local employment levels.

It was a rather cavalier approach, was it not, to what is a very real and important problem?

Yes, it was over-written, I think.

And then it goes on to make a suggestion to Lord Trefgarne, who has just stepped into your shoes at the DTI, telling him: 'If the company requests a meeting, you would no doubt wish to justify the refusal of the licences by saying we have firm evidence that equipment has previously been shipped to Iraqi munitions factories.' Did that seem to you to be a satisfactory way of disposing of the matter, to just tell the companies: 'Well, we know they have gone to munitions factories'?

It seemed odd. There is a note from Mr Young, the senior official, he says they *may* be used for making munitions. It seems they were slightly chasing their tails on this.

In the event, your officials at the MOD we see were rather taken by this new Foreign Office approach because they urge you to go along with it. At page 256 there is a note from Mr Barrett telling you that the Ministry of Defence working group has consistently recommended against the supply of Matrix Churchill lathes to Iraqi destinations known to be munitions factories . . . And then at paragraph 3: 'We have no option but to recommend that you accept the refusal of these applications.' . . . We see the reply they have drafted for you to send to Mr Waldegrave . . . saying that 'I must admit that it is with great reluctance that I have to accept that in the circumstances I have no alternative but to support your recommendation that the licences be refused'?

I do not think it was sent.

It certainly was not. If we look at the letter you *did* send at page 283: instead of saying you have no alternative but to reluctantly go along with the Foreign Office, you tell Mr Waldegrave a few weeks later, you have seen Lord Trefgarne's letter. 'I have much sympathy with what he says and feel unable to stop the exports'?

A good example of Ministers not taking official advice.

So you rewrite, and in fact completely change the position that is advised to you by your civil servants?

Yes.

. . . Lord Trefgarne's letter of 5 October to you and Waldegrave: 'Even if the lathes had been intended for the manufacture of munitions, and this was not established, there are no longer such reasons under the guidelines to prevent export.' This argument remains relevant?

Yes.

That argument, that had been accepted by the same three Ministers (albeit in different positions), in February of 1989?

Yes.

And that echoes your view?

His concluding paragraph does, broadly. I didn't want to offend them, as I thought, needlessly, and they are potential customers for the defence export sales side.

And even if the lathes had been intended for the manufacture of conventional munitions, there was no longer sufficient reasons under the guidelines to prevent export?

At this time I didn't see any, no.

Clark had just made another crucial concession. If there was no basis under the secret guidelines for stopping sales of conventional weapons and weapon-making equipment to Iraq in October 1989, the prosecution could hardly argue that Ministers were misled into granting the licences. Under Clark's interpretation of the secret guidelines, the machine-tools would have been approved whether it was known they were 'specially designed' to make conventional weapons or not. His answer to Moses – a little over an hour before – had been completely revised.

Robertson then showed Clark a briefing of October 1989, from his civil servants at the MOD working group, which had urged him to oppose the licences because they would create a significant enhancement of Iraq's arms-making capacity. That was, of course, the very argument that Ministers had rejected when they had granted the licences in February 1989.

GR: Can I just ask you this: were you aware that the indigenous conventional arms industry that was being built up by Iraq was a substitute for Soviet Union supplies?

AC: Yes, that was a factor that had been mentioned to us some years before.

And it was an important factor, wasn't it, in the 1987–1988 considerations, that Iraq had been in, in a sense, the pocket of the Soviet Union politically previously, because it had been so dependent for its ordinary ordnance on the Soviets?

That was a factor, yes.

And obviously a country, particularly a country at war, that is dependent upon a Superpower for arms supplies is going to be under the thumb of that

Superpower in international policy – in voting at the United Nations and so forth?

They are very broad policy considerations, yes, but I would not dissent.

And I am suggesting that in fact what the Ministry of Defence is overlooking here is that strengthening Iraq's arms industry, allowing it to make its own conventional shells, in fact was *helpful* in terms of Western policy because it diminished Iraq's dependence on the Soviet Union? It is true that the writer of this minute was ignoring that, but it was a factor that was taken into consideration by the Ministry of Defence. . . . Nothing in that briefing alters your judgement that it is right to allow this export to go ahead?

No. The briefing is very equivocal, there in the last few paragraphs.

It puts the case against and the case for?

Yes.

And you take the line in favour.

The court adjourned for lunch. Robertson's tactic, once he had overcome Clark's initial resistance, had been to flatter the truth out of him, alternating the hard facts in the documents with the exposure of Clark's Thatcherite philosophy and world geo-political view. He had not so far touched on the vexed question of Clark's meeting with the MTTA. After lunch, he turned to the DTI's own minutes of the meeting between Ministers in the House of Lords on 1 November 1989:

GR: The guidelines 'needed to be reviewed' or even scrapped because they had political origins, and in the politics of 1985 they were no longer relevant to a ceasefire that had held for over a year?

AC: That is entirely true.

But Mr Waldegrave . . . says, apparently in answer to you, that the guidelines are not just a response to political pressure and 'to remove them would give a green light to arms suppliers' and a review of the guidelines 'would have to take place in a different forum.' What does he mean by that?

In Cabinet.

And Lord Trefgarne says that Matrix Churchill lathes are not state of the art and would not affect the conflict. And this is attributed to you: 'Previous applications for licences have been granted and to refuse licences now, when the danger of conflict had arguably receded, would be difficult to justify'?

Yes.

Again, another comment you can remember making. Then Mr Waldegrave accepts that the lathes would not exacerbate the situation and that he is prepared for the licences to be granted. Of course you are discussing the guidelines – as we have seen, that indicates that you are looking for something that has a direct and significant bearing on the breaking of the ceasefire, offensive operations?

Yes.

And Mr Waldegrave gives in.

Yes.

Because that is a change in his position . . . Lord Trefgarne agrees to handle any parliamentary business. So, as it were, the political problems will be his if there was any parliamentary criticism.

Yes.

Do you recall making any comment about the DIS surveillance?

No.

We have got, if you look at the page 306, this is the *Foreign Office* minute . . .

Yes.

Their account of the same meeting . . . notes that the Defence Intelligence Staff at your Ministry, the Ministry of Defence, were conducting a survey of Iraqi procurement activities. 'Would this have a bearing on Matrix Churchill?' Then, to you is attributed this comment: that you had only just been told about the DIS survey and would make sure that it was stopped. 'It was outrageous that the DIS should spend its time seeking ways to damage our trade surplus in this way.' Is that a comment that accords with your recollection?

Not with my recollection. It cannot be invented, so I must accept responsibility for making it.

For feeling that intelligence activity monitoring Matrix Churchill was 'outrageous', because it was using the security service that way, in a way which would be to obtain information which could damage British trade?

Yes, we are talking about intelligence activity inside the United Kingdom. We are not, of course, talking about the paramilitary activity relating to Matrix Churchill's activities in Iraq, which was entirely valid and justifiable.

. . . Are you not saying, in effect, that it is outrageous that intelligence activity should be directed to obtaining information in this country about a British firm like Matrix Churchill and the use to which its machinery will be put, in the way that Mr Waldegrave has apparently used intelligence to resist the licences, partly because they were probably going to go to munitions factories?

Yes. I mean, one sometimes is more intemperate in a closed room than on the floor, for example, of the House of Commons – and perhaps I regret the word 'outrageous'. I still think it was a waste of resources.

For garnering information about the use to which Matrix Churchill machines were to be put?

Yes.

. . . Mr Waldegrave agrees to withdraw his objection to the issue of the licences on three terms. As far as you are concerned at the Ministry of Defence, you allow the DIS survey to continue. The guidelines remain in place. And any public condemnation or PQs – parliamentary questions – will be fielded by the DTI. They are his terms of surrender?

Exactly.

So far as his surrender is concerned, had he told you of any recent indications that the equipment would be unlikely to be used in the military field?

No.

I showed you the DTI minute of this meeting with Mr Waldegrave with him saying Matrix Churchill's exports 'probably went into the Iraqi armament industry?'

I do not think there is any dispute about that. From the very outset it was apparent from Mr Beston's original minute.

That they are going to these factories?

Yes.

So would it be fair to say the meeting of November 1st between you and Mr Waldegrave and Lord Trefgarne decided, as a matter of policy, that with the guidelines, insofar as they were still relevant – which in your mind they were not – but insofar as they were still relevant, that this equipment, even though it may go to a munitions factory to make components for conventional munitions, was not a problem.

No, there was unanimity about the equipment.

JUDGE SMEDLEY: I am afraid I do not follow that answer.

AC: All three Ministers, My Lord, were agreed that the equipment, namely the machine-tools – I take it that is what you mean by 'equipment'?

GR: Yes, I do.

That the machine-tools should go without hindrance. But we didn't get our way, Lord Trefgarne and I didn't get our way in dismantling the guidelines: although they were still further loosened, I would say, as a result of this.

They were further loosened but they remained at least publicly in place?

That is right.

And that then, was the position in November.

These answers hammered the last nails into the prosecution coffin in relation to the Cardoen contract charges. Clark was making it crystal clear that the export licences agreed by Ministers on 1 November were agreed irrespective of the prospect of the machine-tools going to make munitions. Robertson then turned to the ABA contract, and the correspondence relating to the revalidation of these licences (first approved in February 1989) in April and May 1990. He directed Clark's attention to a memorandum referring to the 'deeply charged atmosphere' after the Supergun parts had been intercepted in April 1990:

GR: Was it a factor that did affect you, the 'deeply charged atmosphere', after the Supergun?

AC: Yes.

How did that bear on your policy – or political judgement – in applying what remained of the guidelines by that stage?

Well, personally, I thought that it was probably appropriate to have an interval of reflection on this whole position – because the Supergun and other developments were indicating that Iraq, far from resuming war against Iran, which was no concern of mine (I disagreed with the Foreign Office, or their opinion), was actually assuming a more menacing posture generally. And we are only four months away from an invasion of Kuwait.

And you had by that stage had the Bazoft hanging, the Supergun, and you also had some nuclear triggers allegedly discovered?

Yes. That is right.

And these were all 'charging the atmosphere' and causing concern?

I don't think Bazoft mattered much. But the other two things were definite factors.

. . . So it had clearly reached a Cabinet Office committee to deal with the press over the Supergun. And you are suggesting that the committee should be at least appraised of the potential political embarrassment in granting further licences at this time?

Yes. I think that it became general practice to refer things, where there was any element of doubt, to this committee.

This reference to the Cabinet Office 'Iraq Gun Group' continues to fascinate. Documents from this mysterious committee were called for by the defence, but Judge Smedley, falling back on the PII certificates, had refused to order their disclosure. Quite plainly it was this committee, under the direct control of the Prime Minister, which co-ordinated the government's plans to keep the lid on 'Iraqgate'. It dealt with Matrix Churchill, as well as with the Supergun. It was a committee which would have been centrally involved in the next stage, the meeting of Ministers chaired by Douglas Hurd, and reporting directly to the Prime Minister, which took place on 19 July and which decided to lift all controls on machine-tools to Iraq. Robertson established Clark's position: he must surely have spoken for the PM at that meeting:

GR: Apparently a meeting was going to consider this matter, chaired by the Foreign Secretary himself?

AC: Yes.

. . . Can you recall what led to this top-level meeting on July 19th about defence-related exports?

Yes. Well, the principal factor at that time agitating me and parts of the Defence Export Sales in the Ministry of Defence was the potential sale of Hawk trainers, which was a very, very large order, very important for British Aerospace. And it would have been very – I can't remember the date, you may have it recorded, the date of Cabinet Committee at which this was considered, it was only a week or so away – and it was important to show a bit of muscle, I think, in a preliminary meeting at the Foreign Office on the whole subject.

It goes on to say that the Foreign Secretary will report the outcome to the Prime Minister . . . and machine-tools were considered here as 'defence-related exports'?

Yes.

'The Minister will remember that this' – the review of policy – 'was sparked off by the consideration of the export of some machine-tools.' [The MOD proposed arguing for removal of all guidelines, Robertson recalled.] Is that a recommendation you had sympathy with?

Yes.

And it would have cut the Gordian knot for the future?

Yes.

And save you all the agonising over machine-tools you had had in the past two years?

Yes.

Then there is a reference to the Foreign Office's new test, which apparently was 'destabilisation'. And over the page, in there, was the speaking brief for you, and on Iran and Iraq the Ministry of Defence preferred option is to have no special export controls on either country?

Yes.

And again the argument here, in July 1990, that the guidelines anchored to the Iran–Iraq war had no relevance whatsoever?

Yes.

And that they are penalising our exports and our competitors are cashing in?

Yes.

Is that, after all these years – or three years or so, that we have seen – is that getting to the position that you really had taken, all along?

Yes.

And that was the position you were recommended to argue, and did in fact argue at that meeting?

Yes.

The MOD brief proposed scrapping an embargo for all but 'lethal equipment' . . .

Then it goes on to define what is meant by 'lethal equipment' and it refers to an answer given in Parliament as 'equipment designed to kill'?

Yes, that is right.

And clearly a lathe – of whatever specifications – is not designed to kill?

Quite.

Then it considered some borderline cases, weapons platforms, unarmed patrol boats and aircraft, ancillary equipment for weapons platforms such as radios and radars and their spares, e.g. tank automative spares. And it invites you to press for those categories to be excluded from the definition?

That's right.

And again, I think it follows logically that CNC lathes would be excluded from that definition because they are not in the same – they don't have that direct relationship to lethal weapons as weapons platforms and . . . ?

No, they are miles off that.

So that is the position that you had reached shortly before the invasion of Kuwait brought UN sanctions?

Yes.

By 19 July – only two weeks before the invasion of Kuwait, and one month after Customs had raided Matrix Churchill – the position seemed to have been reached that machine-tools would in future go to Iraq and to Iran. That was the only way, as Robertson had put it, of 'cutting the Gordian knot' – a knot which Ministers had tied themselves up in by saying one thing and doing another. It was the only way that the state of play regarding Matrix Churchill could be regularised, consistent with stopping its prosecution (or proceeding only on the basis of a 'technical' offence: there would be no point in prosecuting, because munitions-making lathes were now to be freely exportable to Iraq).

Robertson, his witness now pliant and extraordinarily helpful, consolidated his day's gains. He received complete assent for his theory, which had produced the policy documents in the first place, that the government's secret political judgement had sent the arms-making machines to Iraq in full knowledge of their likely use:

GR: In all these matters that we have seen and you have been shown by Mr Moses and by myself, it is clear that there was a vast amount of discussion within three departments of state and at Minister level in relation to the export guidelines as applied to machine-tools?

AC: Yes.

And the discussion as far as you were concerned, was at a level of policy?

Yes.

And in February of 1989, and November of 1989, the position that was arrived at, as it were, as the basis to those policy discussions was: even if these machine-tools were going to munitions factories, that didn't stop them from being exported under the guidelines?

I don't think it was quite 'going to munitions factories,' to exclusively munitions factories, but certainly was 'even though they were capable of making munitions' it certainly didn't exclude them.

And even if they had made munitions in the past and might make munitions in the future, that would not exclude them, as the flexible guidelines were being interpreted in 1989?

No, not then, certainly not.

And of course I suppose it's trite, as you say, to realise that a country that goes to war will use whatever equipment it has available in the war effort?

Quite true.

Even if a machine-tool is sent off to Iraq at a time when it's at peace with the world, if it goes to war the likelihood is the machine-tool will go into the war effort?

Yes.

And even if these machine-tools were intended to make munitions at Nassr factory in 1989, the fact that they would make conventional munitions was not a matter for concern, given that you were assured that they would not make nuclear weapons or ballistic missiles?

Yes, 'not capable of making', I should say. I think you said 'not make', did you not?

So long as they were not capable of making. I am obliged, I accept that. A ballistic missile or nuclear weapon or chemical component for poison gas?

Yes.

And it was your political judgement, which at the time was shared by your fellow Ministers, in the end?

Yes.

Having established the political reality of Thatcher government policy towards the sale of defence equipment to Iraq, Robertson turned – at about 3 p.m. – to the first fateful decision to allow the machine-tool exports to go to set up an indigenous Iraqi arms industry. That decision had been taken by Ministers on 8 February 1988, after all had received intelligence information (originating from Mark Gutteridge) about the uses to which they would be put. The total order, Robertson reminded Clark, was worth £37 million:

GR: At that time enormously valuable to the struggling British machine-tool industry?

AC: Yes.

And another attraction of it was that, given that Iraq had been sold machine-tools in the recent past by West German and Italian and Swiss companies, in fact an order of this size would hopefully have the result of follow-on orders?

Yes.

Having established British tools in those factories, we could expect follow-on orders for them?

We could not expect it, but we would be better placed to look for it.

We could hope for them. So that the decision that you had to make in February 1988 was made, knowing that these machine-tools were going to munitions factories, to make munitions?

Yes.

At the time of the Gulf War with Iran?

Yes, some of them were, some were passive, simple machines.

You knew very well that, as a result of this Steadman memorandum, the vast majority of them had not yet been shipped?

Yes.

And you knew that your department had taken the action of freezing the licences, when they heard the news. Had that been done with reference to you?

No.

So that had been done in December without reference

to you. And here we are, in February, having to decide whether you were in favour. Was it your view in deciding in favour, in February 1988, that those machine-tools should go to those munitions factories to make munitions, that it was in our national interest they should do so?

I do not think you can put it quite as clear cut as that.

. . . What I am inviting you to indicate is whether it was your view in February – notwithstanding that they were going to munitions factories, to make munitions – that, nonetheless, that the export of almost £37 million worth of machine-tools was in our national interest?

I didn't think that they all were going to munitions factories to make munitions. We knew that there was a quota within that total, and Mr Beston had drawn that to my attention with his preliminary note. But the kind of beating on the surface, as it were, which I had no reason to question, was that the bulk of them were for peaceful purposes.

You see if you look at page 30, Mr Beston's briefing is pretty clear, is it not – that they were going to Nassr and Huteen 'engaged in a substantial munitions manufacturing programme' to enable Iraq to become less dependent on Soviet supplies?

Yes.

Among other things, the note lists production targets for shells and missiles. Over the page, you see your briefing for a meeting on 20th January. 'The export licences for CNC machine-tools to Iraq have been reviewed following an intelligence report that UK companies are supplying machines for munitions manufacture.' If we look back to page 21, the basic document, the Steadman memorandum, it refers at the very top of page 21, to a report that: 'the Nassr establishment and Huteen establishments are heavily engaged in this munitions production programme'. And it goes on —

But you see —

ALAN MOSES: Please let him finish, he was going to say something.

GR: All right.

AC: I am trying to say that you, Mr Robertson, have illustrated a perfect Whitehall muddle, which is exemplified by two consecutive pages in this folder. Mr Steadman says, and cites intelligence sources saying, that 'this is very important to us. We must allow these orders to go through.' The following minute says that intelligence sources are saying that the United Kingdom companies are supplying machine-tools for munitions manufacture, and for that reason it must be stopped. So you have got a conflict between the advice you are getting from intelligence sources. And in the light of that, it is very wise to apply some common sense.

The common-sense position that you applied was that the intelligence sources were unanimous that these machines were going to munitions factories, were they not, to make munitions?

Yes.

There was one report which indicated that that is why they should be stopped. There is another report to indicate . . .

They should continue, exactly.

And you had on February 8th to apply a political judgement, a common-sense political judgement. No legal guidelines to assist, but a common-sense political judgement based on your —

Preferences.

In what you regarded to be the national interest?

Yes.

And what was that?

My preference was they should be allowed to export this machinery.

It was a preference that you held – and indeed in the following year, consistently articulated – in these meetings. Namely, we should not have guidelines for Iran and Iraq over and above our normal controls?

Well, we had the guidelines. They were government policy and we had to live with them: but in so far as it was possible within them, and by stretching and bending them, we would try and get the best result.

By stretching and bending them, you could get a result which would serve certainly the interests of the workforce in the Midlands?

They were in their very nature elastic, because they were not – the definition, the wording was itself a matter for interpretation and argument. But there had to be unanimity on this in the Ministerial committee.

Your preference was, for those reasons, for those machine-tools to go to munitions factories to make munitions, given that that would be in the best interests of British trade – for all the reasons that you were concerned about?

Well, it's not really relevant to attach to my preference the purpose for which they were going to be used. My preference was that they should be sold: and that the customer would use them as he thought appropriate.

Including using them to make munitions?

We know from Mr Beston's note, that there was that element.

That that, was what they were going to do. And you saw no difficulty, no problem, in allowing that very large order to go for that purpose at that time?

The advice I received was that it was desirable, regardless of what my own views might be.

That part of the advice – that it was desirable for intelligence reasons – coincided with your preference?

Yes, it did.

And as a result of common-sense application of your political judgement to the guidelines in February – you allowed them to go?

Yes.

Michael Heseltine and other Ministers were later to claim that the trial did not collapse because of the documents, but because Clark changed his story. The fatuity of this distinction is demonstrated by the preceding passage. As soon as Clark's memory strays from the *actualité* (to use Clark's own favoured word), he is confronted with the documents and forced to give the answer that the questioner expects. Without the documents, the forensic *coup de grâce* – which happened next – could not have been administered. Robertson finally turned to the meeting of 20 January 1988:

GR: You knew by that stage, the 20th January, that the exports had been frozen because of the discovery they were going to munitions factories?

AC: Yes.

And it was, of course, the machine-tool manufacturers for their part —

JUDGE SMEDLEY: I am not sure, Mr Robertson, that is quite right. The evidence was that they were frozen because by that time it was discovered that they were going to munitions factories – and the intelligence was that they were being used in the manufacture of munitions.

GR: And intelligence was that they were being used in the manufacture of munitions.

JUDGE SMEDLEY: In the manufacture of munitions rather than the destination itself, which resulted in the freezing of applications.

GR: Correct. It was not simply that they were going to munitions factories. It was the fact that they were being used in the manufacture of munitions, that was the reason for the action. And it was the reason why the manufacturers had come to see you?

AC: The reason they had come was because they had been frozen.

They knew the reason why they had been frozen. There is no other reason that could be given?

Yes.

Was the purpose of that meeting to consider whether they could be unfrozen?

Yes.

And do you recall congratulating them on getting the order?

I expect, I hope I would have done. It would be uncivil if I did not.

. . . At the beginning you congratulate them on getting the orders?

Yes.

You used words to the effect: 'We know what the machines are for and you know what they are for. What is gone is gone'?

I think it very unlikely.

No?

One does not – these meetings are fairly – the courtesies are one thing, but the atmosphere at these meetings is very much more formal than that.

You think it unlikely you would have used *those* words. But, in fact, the position was, you *did* know what they were going to be used for, and the machine-tool manufacturers did?

Yes. But one has to maintain a decorum in these matters.

And you turned, as the first paragraph indicates, to indicate to them at the beginning, in your opening remarks, that you were sympathetic and would do everything possible to ensure that the orders went through?

Yes.

And you mentioned Mr Butcher having lobbied you? And your knowledge that £37 million worth of orders were at stake for this year alone? And there was a strong possibility of 'follow-on orders' in the future?

Yes.

And those 'follow-on orders', of course, would have been, could have been, to the same factories, for the same use?

Yes.

So long as the Gulf [Iran–Iraq] War lasted, and I think at this stage, in January 1988, Iraq was starting to get the upper hand because the previous year Iran had, with the help of the weapons that Oliver North and others had supplied to Iran, done rather well in the fighting.

Yes.

It was still not clear that an end was in sight?

I don't want to bring Oliver North into this. I do not know that what he provided had any effect on the outcome whatsoever.

You would accept that there is the strong possibility that orders would include 'follow-on orders' for the same factories for the same use?

Yes.

And then you stress that you will do everything in your power to ensure there is no interference with existing contracts. And the consignment that had already been shipped did not present a problem. You knew, of course, only a small number of the machines had left this country at this stage?

Yes.

That was in Mr Steadman's note?

Yes.

And you recognize that the deliveries were phased over the coming six months. 'We needed to consider consignments that had received a licence, but which had not been shipped, and consignments which had not yet been the subject of a licence application'?

That's right.

So, in this meeting, you are saying at this point, that you as Minister, and they, as the leaders of this particular part of British industry, had to consider the future of – not only the present orders, but the follow-on orders, the consignments which had not yet been the subject –

It does not need a gloss on it. I simply said what is down here.

You were then proceeding to give them some advice about future orders. About their future consignments, which had not yet been the subject of the licence applications which would be later in the year, or the following year?

I certainly summarised the position.

The minute then goes on to say 'Choosing his words carefully'?

Yes.

Would you have said 'now I am choosing my words carefully' or is that an interpolation of your –

I think it will be an interpolation. You see, you gave a very good example a minute ago, Mr Robertson, of not choosing one's words carefully.

I have given many.

No, you put it quite rightly. Not *your* words, of course: where you said – you attributed to me, or suggested I said, 'Oh come on, we all know what's going on. Let's try and sort it out.' Or something like that. Those are simply – and I said it was most unlikely – when one is dealing with a situation as sensitive as this, it is necessary to choose one's words very carefully.

And were the words that you 'chose to use' to say to them that the Iraqis would be using the current orders for 'general engineering purposes'?

They had – I mean, I do not see that we can really get any further with departing from this text. Because it actually sums up – this is exactly what we *did* say, *did* agree. Where something is capable of dual use and the guidelines are in position, plainly, it is appropriate that that element of the dual use which conforms to the guidelines should be emphasised.

JUDGE SMEDLEY: (Writing) Just a moment.

AC: I would have thought that was advice they hardly needed from me. It was a relatively harmless contribution.

GR: You knew that the Iraqis would *not* be using the current orders for general engineering purposes, but would be using them to make munitions?

The current orders, yes.

And they –

But the current orders have already received a licence, have they not?

Yes, and that licence had been frozen, and that was the reason for the meeting, and –

But paragraph 5 refers to *future* applications.

It refers to you 'choosing your words carefully' and noting that the Iraqis would be using the 'current orders'?

Yes, the current order.

For general engineering purposes?

Yes.

When you *knew* they would be using them to make munitions? And the delegates *knew* that they would be used for making munitions?

ALAN MOSES: I do not know how the witness can answer that, nor had it been established.

JUDGE SMEDLEY: Let him say what he knew.

GR: If you had said, 'Of course, the Iraqis will be using the current order for general engineering purposes', that could not be the case, to your knowledge?

AC: I do not see that the fact that they *are* using them, were they using them for munitions, excludes them using them for general engineering purposes, more than the other way round.

But here the writer of this minute is attributing to you a statement: 'The Iraqis will be using the current order for general engineering purposes' – *which cannot be correct to your knowledge.*

Well, it's our old friend 'being economical', isn't it?

With the truth?

With the *actualité*. There was nothing misleading or dishonest to make a formal, or introductory comment that the Iraqis would be using the current orders for 'general engineering purposes'. All I didn't say was 'and for making munitions'. If I thought that they were going to be doing that. It simply would not have been appropriate, at a meeting of this kind, to widen it any further than the rather stilted and formal language which I used.

But the meeting had been called because these Iraqis were *not* using the current orders for 'general engineering purposes' – and the licences had been frozen.

No, the meeting had been called because the licences had been frozen.

You go on to say, in the same breath, at least in the minute-taker's breath, 'Mr Clark stressed that it was important for the UK companies to agree a specification in advance which highlighted the peaceful, i.e. non-military, use to which the machine-tools would be put'?

Exactly.

In saying that, of course you knew that the machine-tools would be put to, were currently being put to, a munitions use. And that the follow-on orders, so long as the war lasted, would also be likely to be put to a munitions use?

Could be put, yes.

Yes. In this context, knowing that, you invited the companies to agree a specification, i.e. get something in writing. 'The customer to highlight the peaceful use to which the machine-tools would be put.' Even though to your knowledge, it was, at least so long as the war lasted, very unlikely they *would* be put to a peaceful use.

Yes. I would agree with that.

And so, you want to receive at the DTI in future, the 'follow-on' applications to some sort of written specification or indication – that these consignments for the future, the 'follow-on orders', are going to a peaceful use, a 'general engineering use'?

Yes.

A specification which highlights a peaceful use?

I doubt if I used 'highlighted'; I think I would have said 'emphasise'.

Emphasising, or stressing, the peaceful use that they would have?

Yes.

In the future. Even though, so long as the war lasted, they were going to the same factory – 'follow-on orders' for munitions use?

That is right.

And that indication was given, in order that, that is the way the applications would come into the DTI – would be presented to the DTI?

I do not think I said that. I simply said: 'You must agree a specification which highlights a peaceful use.' It is not for me to tell them what to do with that.

One thing they obviously had to do – under the procedures – was make application to the DTI for those follow-on orders for the munitions factories?

Yes, they did.

They would, in those follow-on orders, as a result of

your emphasis, be concerned to highlight a peaceful use?

That's right. We employ – the DTI employs – a very large number of highly expert scrutineers who will look at every export application, and will take very little before they could come to a conclusion as to what the specification actually covers.

Of course. But there would be a 'peaceful use' and a stress on 'general engineering'?

Yes.

That is the way the applications would come in and would be obviously then examined by the boffins?

Yes . . . They were fussing. They claimed that the situation was urgent and I say no more than –

You were a sympathetic Minister?

I was a sympathetic Minister.

And you would be there – if not for the foreseeable future – for at least some time?

Yes, I was there for another eighteen months.

And the other advice you gave them was that there should be no publicity?

Yes . . . The publicity about which we were apprehensive at that time, which was, as I said to Mr Moses, I think, 'WHITEHALL RED TAPE THREATENS JOBS' type publicity.

That would not be 'inflammatory press comment', would it, that would be conventional press comment?

It is very inflammatory. In the eyes of civil servants it is very inflammatory, because it brings them into the public eye, and MPs raise questions, and even leading articles are maybe written.

Yes. It would not be inflammatory press comment such as: 'DTI HELPS MERCHANTS OF DEATH', and that sort of thing?

That comes later.

It was still coming, at this time: because Iraq's use of poison gas had been pretty much established by this stage, hadn't it?

I do not remember that.

But in the event, that is your recollection . . . When you talk about press comment [in the minutes Mr Carter, of the manufacturers' delegation] says that Mr Gribben of the *Daily Telegraph* seems to be very well informed?

Yes.

And I think you said, or the recollection of one of those attending is that you said, 'Well, I will get on to the editor of the *Daily Telegraph*, he is a friend of mine'?

Yes.

. . . Did you in fact get on to the editor?

Yes.

And we see Mr Gribben's article is at page 32. So you were not able to stop the article appearing. But you were able perhaps to give it a definite anti-Foreign Office slant?

That is not difficult.

And it is an article that is largely concerned with describing the Foreign Office as 'short sighted' and 'acting against Britain's economic interests' if their moves to place machine-tools on the strategic embargo lists were successful?

Yes.

And I think also, do you recall speaking to the Labour MP Mr Ted Garrett after the meeting, within a couple of days of it?

Yes.

And he was a supporter, of course, of their case?

Yes.

And you told him that you would support their case up to Cabinet if need be?

Yes.

And you sent a message through him that the companies should maintain confidentiality, and try and avoid even this sort of article appearing in future?

Yes.

. . . Mr Mellor. Do you remember him? [Laughter.]

Well, I do not remember him [more laughter]. Not in that role, no.

At page 50, we see that he has had an enquiry from a trade union whose employees are affected by the story. There might be an embargo on machine-tools. And his PS says: 'On reflection it seems better for Mr Mellor to reply.' . . . You see the 'standard policy' being sent to an MP who has raised the question on behalf of them, assuring them that there is 'no blanket embargo on such goods'?

Yes. That is right.

That is the public position being taken at the time?

Yes, that is after we got the existing contracts through.

For which there was no publicity at all?

No, but they were unfrozen.

And that is the only indication that was given to the public at that time, in relation to government policy?

Yes. That is right.

And I think that there was an article – to take you fast forward now to December 1990 – an article appeared in the *Sunday Times* suggesting that you had helped break an arms embargo in 1988?

Well, it went a good deal further than that.

But you recall that there was the headline. Which was incorrect, because there was in fact no arms embargo, as Mr Mellor's letter pointed out in early 1988?

Quite so.

And as you say, it went a great deal further than that: and led to calls for your resignation? And to Statements made in the House?

Yes.

And it was an article which you said, at that time, was defamatory. Did you sue?

I was not allowed to.

Very well. And you then, of course, were aware of the importance being attached publicly to the meeting you had on January 20th 1988?

Yes.

And having had all that embarrassment and difficulty over it just before Operation 'Desert Storm' in December – it was a matter about which you would choose your words carefully, if asked in the future?

What was?

The meeting of 20th January 1988?

Well, depending in what context I was invited to express an opinion, whether I chose my words carefully or not.

You were invited to express an opinion by Mr Graham Turner in July, I think, of this year. He visited you twice at Saltwood Castle, in the course of doing a major *Sunday Telegraph* profile on you?

Yes.

And he asked you questions – which you answered – about the January meeting, didn't he?

Well, after the article came out I spoke to Mr Turner on the telephone and asked him if he had taken a note, and he told me he had not taken a note. Let me explain why there was a certain compression, of what was quite a long conversation.

Can I ask you to look, please, at what he said. Can we hand up a copy to His Lordship. The paragraph in this article, in relation to this matter, reads: 'Was it true that he' (that is, you) 'had tipped off our machine-tool manufacturers as to how they should frame their export applications to get round the guidelines for trade with Iraq? "Yes," replied Clark flatly, "and I did it for two reasons. First I was Minister for Trade, so it was my job to maximise exports, despite guidelines which I regarded as tiresome and intrusive. Second, Iran was the enemy and still is. And it was clear to me that the interests of the West were well served by Iran and Iraq fighting each other, the longer the better."' They are comments attributed to you. I ask you firstly about the second comment, the second reason you give. Was that your view?

Yes.

That it was clear that the interests of the West were best served by Iran and Iraq fighting each other, and the longer the better?

Yes.

And then the first reason that you give – 'I was Minister for Trade, so it was my job to maximise exports, despite guidelines which I regarded as tiresome and intrusive'?

Yes.

Is that correct?

It is correct.

To quote your view of their tiresomeness and intrusiveness?

Yes.

And then, was it true that you 'had tipped off our machine-tool manufacturers as to how they should frame their export applications to get round the guidelines'? You are quoted as saying, 'Yes'?

I am not responsible for what Mr Turner says, but I imagine that he was using – it was almost lifted verbatim from the original accusation in the *Sunday Times* – and that, my recollection is that he used this as an opening gambit for this subject. As I say, I do not for one moment deny the validity of the two paragraphs that he was quoted, although they may seem a little intemperate. But the idea that I could 'tip off' anybody is perfectly ludicrous. It is so far removed from the reality of how Whitehall and the machinery of government works, that I am surprised that he even deployed it. I met these people once. It was at a meeting which we have, of course, heard about at some length. There were three very senior civil servants at it. Any, even *suggestion* of 'tipping' or helping them would have been immediately pounced on. It would have been highly improper – and I am an experienced Minister, and would never have done it. It would have immediately been followed by a correction note, and a report to the Permanent Secretary and the whole machinery would have operated to rectify any indiscretion. I mean it just doesn't work like that. This is pure journalistic slang.

If we changed it to, 'Was it true that you had advised our machine-tool manufacturers as to how they should frame their export applications' and put a full stop there, it would be correct, wouldn't it?

It would.

The advice you are giving was to say that these follow-up orders were for 'general engineering purposes' and 'emphasise their peaceful use', 'give a lot of detail'. When they would be going to munitions factories to make munitions?

Yes, but as you say, I said 'Emphasise their peaceful use' and I also said 'Give a lot of detail'. And so to some extent the two militate against each other. And the point of asking them to give a lot of detail is to make sure that the scrutiny to which they are subjected has everything that it needs, or at any rate is put on guard if it needs to ask for more, bearing always in mind of course that there were thresholds beyond which, guidelines or no guidelines, we didn't want to let anything out.

You didn't want to let anyone know that, at this stage, these machines *and* their follow-up orders were going to munitions factories to make munitions?

No.

And the emphasis on 'peaceful purposes' and 'general engineering' and so on would help keep the matter confidential?

I do not think it was principally a matter for public awareness. I think it was probably a matter for Whitehall cosmetics.

A matter for Whitehall cosmetics, to keep the records ambiguous?

Yes, yes.

And simply if the technical boffins picked up something extra-sophisticated, or something related to nuclear or ballistic procurement, that would be there from the details?

Yes. And it would be disqualified at once.

Yes. So the signal you are sending to these people is: 'I am the Minister. I will help you get these orders, and the follow-up orders, through the rather loose guidelines and the rather Byzantine ways of Whitehall. Help me by keeping your mouth firmly shut about military use'?

I think that is too imaginative an interpretation. I think it was more at arm's length than that.

But in any event it was how they would help you, by

not making the Whitehall cosmetics run, but rather by keeping quiet; stating 'nothing military'?

Yes. I do not think they needed that advice from me but –

But they got it?

Not quite in so many words, I do not think I said 'nothing military'.

They got it by implication?

Yes. By implication is different. By implication they got it.

Robertson sat down. The trial was over. Clark had, in these last few extraordinary minutes, given away the prosecution case – and much more besides. Forced down an intellectual route by the contents of his Ministry's own files, he conceded that the message he had sent to Henderson was exactly what the defendants were charged with acting upon: 'nothing military to be stated'. That was the instruction they had received in respect of future licence applications for Nassr: it was an instruction given to them by the Minister who would ultimately be considering their applications. The prosecution had built its case on sand which had shifted dramatically in the course of this cross-examination, and which would soon threaten to engulf the government. Judge Smedley called an adjournment. He asked his clerk, as they left the court: 'Can you believe what you have just heard?' He sent a mesage to the court shorthand writer: he wanted an urgent transcript of the most recent questions and answers.

The court adjourned for the day. At the end of Clark's testimony, Lord Trefgarne – next Ministerial witness due – cooled his heels in the Old Bailey corridors. Alan Moses QC asked for an adjournment. He wanted, he said, to take stock of the position. But there was very little need for him to reflect: he had no choice. Six weeks earlier, Moses had promised the judge: 'If there be any truth in what he [Alan Clark] was reported to have said in the *Telegraph* . . . then, of course, the prosecution could not go ahead.' Customs had obtained a comment from Alan Clark describing the *Telegraph* account as 'balls'. If the portrait in that newspaper profile had truly reflected the Minister's attitude at the time when the munitions machines had been shipped to Iraq, said Moses, 'I say to your Lordship and to everybody else, the prosecution would not go ahead.'

Six weeks and an estimated £3 million in costs later, all the Crown would do was to stop the case as rapidly as possible. Robertson had established by his cross-examination what had become increasingly obvious throughout the trial – the charge that Paul Henderson and his colleagues had deceived the government ought never to have been laid at all.

12

GUILTY MEN

The judicial inquiry is announced, December 1992

> We had no objections to departments taking whatever
> actions they might think fit.
>
> *MI6 letter to Cabinet Office, 24 July 1990*

The collapse of the case caused political uproar. Paul Henderson
and his colleagues were formally acquitted. Now the government was placed on trial. The Prime Minister announced
the setting-up of an inquiry under Lord Justice Scott. He also
announced that serving Ministers would be told to appear.
The question of whether past Ministers, like Alan Clark,
Nicholas Ridley and Margaret Thatcher would testify was
left more vague. So was the question – a key one – of
whether Scott would sit in public. Left to his own judicial
inclinations, it might seem unlikely. Any judge would be
attracted by the promise of fuller answers from intelligence
agencies and officials if they were allowed to speak in private.
This is Whitehall's normal tactic on such occasions.

When Labour MPs demanded the inquiry be broadened to
consider the Supergun scandal, the Prime Minister agreed.
When a censure debate was initiated by the Labour Party,

Trade Secretary Michael Heseltine promised that the inquiry would cover all exports between 1984 and 1990.

One was left with the impression that the government, if asked, would have happily broadened the inquiry's terms of reference to include, say, the incidence of Dutch elm disease in the trees outside the Foreign Office windows in St James's Park: anything to prolong the result of the inquiry as long as possible. By now, ex-Ministers who had spent two years refusing to talk about arms for Iraq, on the grounds of *sub judice*, were looking forward to spending another two years refusing to do so on the grounds of the 'pending inquiry'.

The Scott inquiry, if it is to have any credibility, must address disturbing questions quickly, and seek to answer them in public, rather than slowly smother them in private. The issues of political responsibility go much wider than the matter of whether a maverick Minister, Alan Clark, spoke out of turn in a courtroom.

A new British government policy towards Iraq (and its opponent Iran), was officially stated by the then Foreign Secretary, Geoffrey Howe, on 29 October 1985, in a written parliamentary answer to David Steel. Evidence had emerged that Iraq was using poison gas in a bloody war, which by then had continued uninterrupted for four years. British policy since 1982 had been to sell non-lethal 'defence equipment' to each side, 'on a case by case basis' – the kind of policy which tried to get the best of both worlds, and chimed with the open views of Thatcherite Ministers such as Alan Clark, that these unsavoury foreigners should be egged on to kill each other while Britain made a profit out of it.

Howe's new 'reinforced' policy guidelines were later to be described within the Foreign Office as a claim to the 'moral high ground'. It was a policy, Howe told Parliament, 'of doing everything possible to see this tragic conflict brought to the earliest possible end'. Not only would sales of obviously lethal equipment continue to be banned: 'We should not, in future, approve orders for any defence equipment which, in our view, would *significantly enhance the capability* of either side to prolong or exacerbate the conflict [author's emphasis].'

When Mrs Thatcher was Prime Minister, her Ministerial favourites appear to have been responsible on four occasions for secret 'internal re-interpretations' of these published restrictions on arms sales to Iraq, about which Ministers gave false statements to Parliament. The documents show that these secret manoeuvres were not in fact carried out for intelligence reasons, although the intelligence services were often involved in the decisions.

1 At the beginning of 1988, the Foreign Secretary's guidelines were breached to allow Matrix Churchill and others to equip two Iraqi munitions factories.

2 After the Iran–Iraq ceasefire in 1988, the guidelines were weakened.

3 After the Rushdie affair, they were covertly tightened up again, for Iran only.

4 Margaret Thatcher was party to the secret 1990 decision, only a fortnight before Iraq invaded Kuwait, to scrap the guidelines.

As a result, a long list of military equipment was sold to Iraq with government connivance, behind Parliament's back. Not only were parts for a Supergun successfully exported, assembled and test-fired in Iraq: an unpublished military intelligence survey concluded that, while the embargoes were ostensibly in force, many British companies had provided Iraq with a 'significant enhancement' of its domestic arms production capacity. The Thatcher government therefore was shown to have helped arm Iraq, while claiming that its policy was the opposite.

The list of charges is long and grave – that the Conservative administration practised deception on Parliament and public;

that a Tory faction subverted the government's own professed policies; that Saddam Hussein was both armed and encouraged to build up a war machine which was soon aimed at British troops; and that this happened because the Government's two imperatives were slavishly to follow US Republican policy, and to do short-sighted favours for British businessmen. The upshot was the Gulf War, and British trade credits of more than £900 million on which Saddam defaulted. If stupidity were a crime, and had Thatcher been brought into the dock at the Old Bailey instead of Paul Henderson of Matrix Churchill, the charge sheet would no doubt have included it.

Few in the Conservative government – except in some corners of the Foreign Office – appear ever to have talked about morality. This is perhaps unsurprising. It was a tenet of Thatcherite philosophy that liberal handwringing was an undesirable component of government. But what is truly surprising is that no one seems to have talked common sense, either. Confronted with a murderous and dangerous tyrant, it seems foolish to behave like a grovelling shopkeeper. No wonder Saddam Hussein got the wrong signals.

The present government are the heirs of Thatcher (some, like John Major and Douglas Hurd, irretrievably implicated in the conduct of her administrations). The second indictment in the Matrix Churchill case lies directly against the Major government. John Major's regime charged, prosecuted and tried to withhold important evidence from Paul Henderson of Matrix Churchill and his two colleagues. Had it not been for the defendants' stubbornness and their lawyers' originality – and, indeed, recent reforms in legal practice following the exposure of decades of miscarriages of justice – they could have been convicted and jailed for up to seven years.

Of all the parties involved in this affair, curiously, it is only the investigators of HM Customs who emerge relatively blamelessly. They were given evidence of deceit; they found nothing to contradict it; and once the Gulf War occurred, it must have seemed to them that intelligence agencies,

Whitehall departments and Ministers of the Crown were perfectly willing to paint the accused men in the blackest of colours. It is possible to accuse Customs of unimaginative rigidity: it is hard to see what alternative to prosecution they were given. Indeed, the early attempts to block a Customs investigation by Nicholas Ridley do not look like common sense or common decency: they look like an attempted cover-up.

Where the present government seems to be culpable is in its efforts to conceal relevant – in fact, vital – evidence from the defence, by claiming Public Interest Immunity. Here, the facts are perfectly clear. Geoffrey Robertson QC and the Henderson defence team did their own 'trawl' through available material to see what relevant documents the authorities might possess – and demanded sight of them. Alan Moses QC and the Customs team reacted by asking Whitehall departments to identify relevant documents – they did not engage in a cover-up at that stage, but this scarcely ought to be a matter for astonished congratulation. The recent findings in the Judith Ward miscarriage of justice case had clearly stated what the duties of the prosecution were henceforth to be. Instead, Customs relied on PII to parry the defence. It was a trump card that Cedric Andrew, Customs lawyer, was accustomed to playing, or threatening to play.

Four Ministers of the Crown were prevailed on to sign certificates, attempting to conceal from the defence relevant documents. These revealed that machine-tool shipments had gone to Iraq with government knowledge that they were definitely, or probably, destined to make munitions. There is no clear law that Ministers have any 'duty' to sign such certificates. There is certainly no requirement that they should be written in the bullying language used. Prosecuting counsel, acting, he said, not for Customs but for the Ministers concerned, then told the court that the documents he alone had read 'did not assist the defence'. Acceptance of this claim by the judge, as Judge Smedley himself said with unexpected defiance at the time, 'may well result in a miscarriage of justice'. The claim that the documents would be of no assistance should never have been made; and Ministers should never have signed such certificates. If Ministers genuinely thought that disclosure of government hypocrisy and double-dealing would interfere with successful administration of the country, they could have asked the Attorney-General to stop the trial. They did not – or dared not – attempt such a move, which, had it come to light, would have undoubtedly been seen by the opposition as an attempt to pervert the course of justice.

The indictment, then, is a double one. The administration headed by Margaret Thatcher carried out secret policies towards Iraq which now look, in the light of day, both repulsive and stupid. The administration headed by John Major then sought by its actions to cover them up.

The Government itself is now on trial. There are a number of excuses which the parties concerned will certainly try to place before the Scott inquiry, to explain away the Matrix Churchill events as a saga of accident and incompetence. These should certainly be considered carefully. There were puzzling failures which meant intelligence reached Whitehall too late, only to be further delayed and ignored. There was a curious incapacity within the DTI to see what was staring them in the face, which might partly be explained by ineptitude or overwork rather than by relentless political pressure. And there was, of course, the fact that other European countries – the Germans, the French, the Swiss, the Italians, the Austrians – were behaving just as badly, if not worse, than Britain.

An analysis like this of exactly what happened makes it seem that the participants in the Matrix Churchill affair thought of little else for five years. In reality, many people's minds were genuinely elsewhere for much of the time. The secret service case officers who handled Mark Gutteridge and Paul

Henderson had other figures in their landscape. 'Ford' from MI5 testified that his branch's real fixation was on communism and counter-espionage – he filed the material he got from Gutteridge on Iraq to his sister foreign intelligence agency as something of a dutiful sideline. 'Balsam' from MI6 said that he was only tasked to gather intelligence on nuclear proliferation – and did so by scurrying full-time around a whole stable of informants, of whom Henderson was only one, and not the most significant.

Matrix Churchill itself was not the only machine-tool company selling to Iraq. Most of the British machine-tool industry were. Others were charged, besides Matrix Churchill, with illegal sales. (One company, Wickman Bennett Ltd, 'compounded' by paying a penalty. Another, BSA, had the charges dropped as a result of the Matrix Churchill debacle). Neither was Matrix Churchill exclusively preoccupied with sales to Iraq. Despite Iraqi control, Iraq never took up more than about 40 per cent of its business. Henderson was genuinely selling machines to Iraq for tractor parts and plastics factories, as well as for making artillery shells. He was glad of the Iraqi backing for his management buy-out – and he hoped to use the Iraqis temporarily to inject capital and restore profitability, before regaining personal control when they lost interest. The military contracts were seen as a lucrative expedient, not a permanent feature of the business.

At the 'Department for Enterprise', the sixty-strong Export Licensing Unit thought mainly about ways of getting through the workload, much of which was not about Iraq and Iran at all. The main preoccupation was the Cold War. The DTI enforced the COCOM regulations which restricted high-tech exports to communist countries. The Trade Committee's Commons report elicited accounts of DTI licence unit understaffing, managerial weakness and under-funding. One of the Thatcher government's repeated themes was that the taxpayers' money could be better spent than on encouraging the gentlemen from Whitehall to harass British entrepreneurs.

The DTI in its new incarnation was supposed to help business-men to export, not to strangle them with red tape.

And Ministers, of course, had other issues to think about. John Major, as Chancellor, was so preoccupied with his own thoughts that he said he gave no mind to Matrix Churchill at all, although copy documents passed through his office. Alan Clark, as the minutes of his meeting with the Machine-Tool Manufacturers showed, saw the situation as a chance for lucrative British trade in the margins of the foreign policy of the United States. If US policy changed, as he said, everyone would be towed off in another direction.

When the Thatcherite Nicholas Ridley, as Trade Secretary, fired off a complaint in June 1990 to the Prime Minister about Customs investigations at Matrix Churchill, he was probably only partly thinking about trade with Iraq. His mind was also on a completely different topic: his dislike and distrust for the Germans in the European Community – an attitude which was soon to force his own resignation. Douglas Hurd and William Waldegrave had other battles to fight, on behalf of what was seen as a spineless, foreigner-loving Foreign Office, in those final days of the undoubtedly tyrannical and unreasonable Margaret Thatcher.

Iraq was not an issue to many Conservative politicians in Britain, except as a way of making some money and perhaps assisting US policy – thwarting the Iranians, by propping up the regime that would fight them. Those who did think Iraq important were themselves unimportant people: Iranian teenage soldiers, mown down in human waves; Kurdish children, frozen in posture by cyanide gas like the inhabitants of Pompeii; or the young *Observer* journalist Farzad Bazoft, out for a scoop, seen on an Iraqi TV screen bruised and confessing to 'espionage' – and then not seen any more, his hanged body returned contemptuously to London in a crate. The scandal of arms for Iraq which the Scott inquiry now faces is about justice for those people, as well as for Paul Henderson of Matrix Churchill.

GUILTY MEN

The Government's Ministers and servants will use as many side-issues and mitigating factors as they can drum up in their defence. But the issue for the jury is exactly the same as that posed by Alan Moses QC in the trial of the Matrix Churchill three. What makes members of the Government guilty is if they knowingly practised deceit.

Justice would be done by Lord Justice Scott if he pushed aside the excuses and concentrated on the real 'British disease' which allowed the Matrix Churchill affair to occur. No one knows how many other Matrix Churchill cases there are, locked in Whitehall files.

The government said one thing and did another throughout the Matrix Churchill affair. The constant theme of the secret Whitehall policy documents is how to construct a 'presentation' which will mislead – whether it is a deceptive answer to an MP; an equivocal form of words which will bamboozle the public; a subtle rewriting of history in a minute for a new Minister; or a piece of 'Whitehall cosmetics' to throw another government department off the scent. This ingrained culture of secrecy and deceit makes it impossible in Britain to have open political debate about important questions. There was no reason why the ethical dilemma about Iraq – jobs or morality – should not have been openly debated on television and in pubs in the West Midlands, where the machine-tool engineers lived – both workers and voters. And when the Iran–Iraq ceasefire, or the Rushdie affair changed the position somewhat, there was no reason why the Howe guidelines should not have been newly discussed, out in the open.

As it was, civil servants and Ministers were safe in the knowledge that what they did would not be released to the Public Record Office for thirty years, or if 'sensitive', for a hundred years, or if relating to intelligence, quite possibly never at all. Those who handled the files in Whitehall would be relied upon to treat their contents as 'official secrets' on pain of prosecution or the sack.

The succession of Conservative administrations that have been in power since 1979 have repeatedly refused to bring the UK into line with countries like the United States, Australia and Canada, and introduce Freedom of Information legislation. The existence of a culture of secrecy in Britain has not led to good government. The Matrix Churchill case shows that it merely promotes – as a preferred method of political problem-solving – the habit of deceit.

Lord Justice Scott could achieve a reputation as a genuine reformer if, rather than merely shuffling the 'dirty washing' of Matrix Churchill about, he deals with the original source of the bad smells. He should recommend the immediate introduction of a Freedom of Information Act, and reform of the Public Records Act. A statutory framework in which there was a presumption of disclosure of all Whitehall documents – subject to exemption, appeal and regular review of all security classifications – would, if US experience is anything by which to judge – start bringing routine policy material to light four or five years after the event, not a whole generation later, or only after sensational court cases. Such a development would be a genuine incentive for Ministers and civil servants in Britain to attempt to govern honestly, rather than – as at present – to try to hide away their political 'dirty washing' until the stink finally becomes overpowering.

A NOTE ON THE AUTHOR

David Leigh, the journalist, broadcaster and author, was previously Granada's 'Investigative Journalist of the Year'. His most recent TV film, *The Spies Left Out in the Cold*, contained exclusive interviews with Paul Henderson, managing director of Matrix Churchill. Leigh had access to an extraordinary range of documents to write this book revealing the work of the secret services as never before. He obtained extensive co-operation from the chief participants.

Index

INDEX

INDEX